French revision and practice

D.D. Christie

Oxford University Press 1979

Oxford University Press, Walton Street, Oxford OX2 6DP

OXFORD LONDON GLASGOW NEW YORK TORONTO MELBOURNE
WELLINGTON KUALA LUMPUR SINGAPORE JAKARTA HONG KONG
TOKYO DELHI BOMBAY CALCUTTA MADRAS KARACHI
NAIROBI DAR ES SALAAM CAPE TOWN

Set by Illustration Services, Oxford.
Printed in Great Britain by The Camelot Press Ltd., Southampton.

The publishers would like to thank the following:

Illustrations:
Gay Gallsworthy

Photographs:
Dailloux, Rapho—Part 1 opening
Philippe Francastel—Parts 2 and 3 openings

Preface

This book is intended for students preparing for the French O-level examination, who wish to revise the essential rules of French grammar and syntax necessary for success at O level, and to practise them thoroughly.

The three parts focus on specific problems met in: (i) writing French; (ii) comprehension of and translation from French; and (iii) the aural and oral tests. Within these parts, the various rules and difficulties are explained clearly, and for each section several exercises are provided, ranging from the very simple to the more demanding. Practice in even the most basic of structures is considered necessary to give the student confidence and ensure accuracy.

The book can be used in the classroom or by students working on their own. With the latter in mind, answers to the exercises have been included. It is hoped that the book will have a variety of uses; it can be worked through as a revision course, or sections can be used in any order, according to the needs of the student. Part 1 also serves as a reference grammar. Vocabulary lists relating to the exercises, verb tables and a comprehensive grammar index are included.

Contents

PART ONE: WRITING FRENCH

PART TWO: COMPREHENSION AND TRANSLATION

PART THREE: AURAL AND ORAL

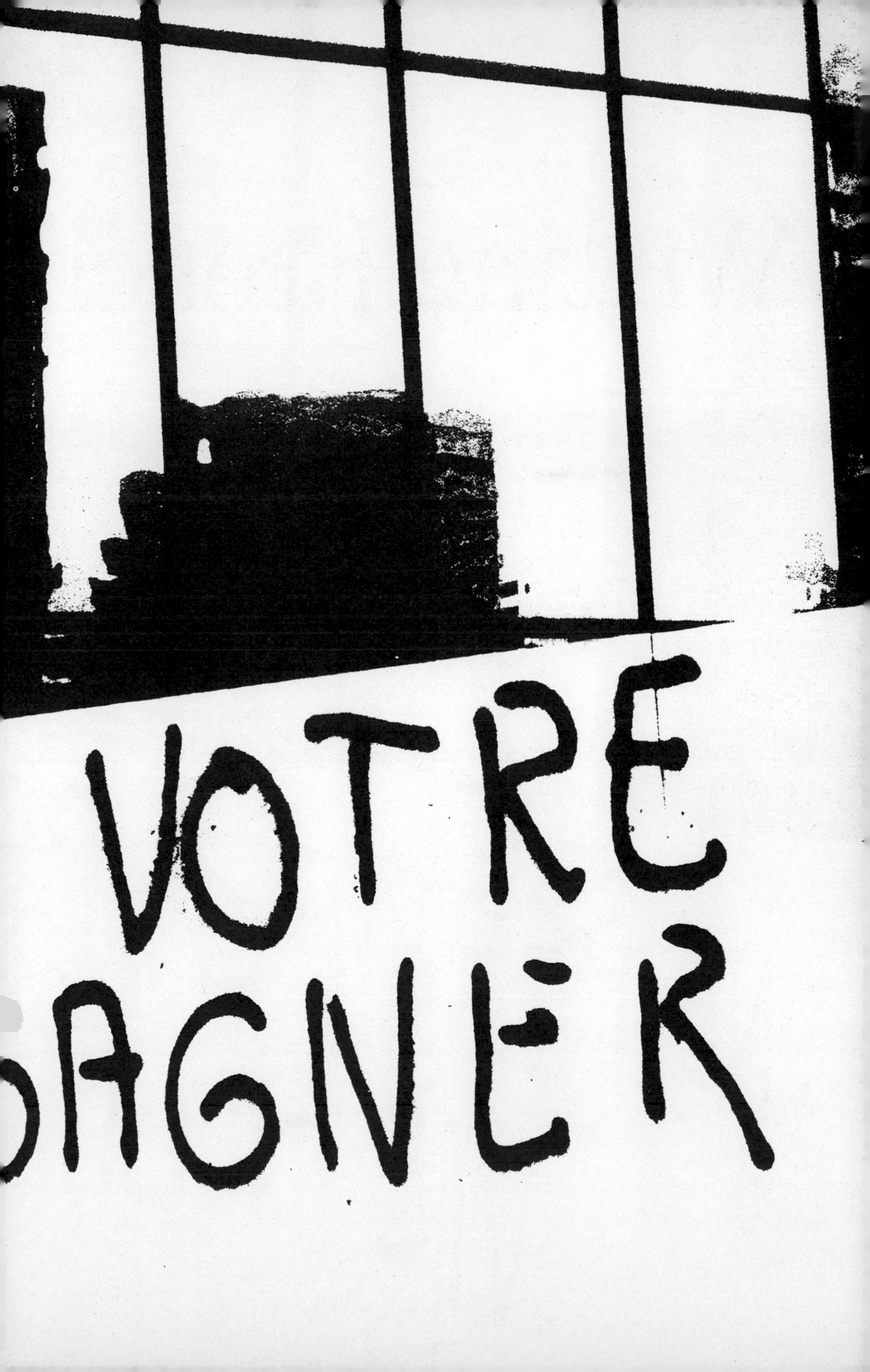
VOTRE
AGNER

1
Writing French

Constructing sentences

Useful words and phrases

When writing French keep to simple sentences. Think out what you are going to say in French before writing it down. You can add interest to what you write, without making things too complicated, by using simple descriptive words and phrases, as suggested in the following lists.

A   **aussitôt**, at once
      bientôt, soon
      d'abord, at first
      un moment plus tard, a moment later
      au bout d'une heure (de dix minutes, etc.), after an hour (ten minutes, etc.)
      le lendemain, the next day
      le lendemain matin (après-midi, soir), the next morning (afternoon, evening)
      la nuit suivante, the following night
      un jour au mois de décembre (etc.), one day in December (etc.)
      pendant les grandes vacances (les vacances de Pâques/Noël), during the summer (Easter/Christmas) holidays

Using the above list, complete the following sentences:
1. . . . je suis allé chez mon oncle.
2. . . . j'ai perdu ma montre sur la plage.
3. . . . il a éteint la lampe.
4. . . . je ne pouvais rien voir.
5. . . . il n'était pas encore arrivé.
6. . . . j'ai fait un rêve extraordinaire.
7. . . . il faisait plus chaud.
8. . . . nous sommes allés souvent à la plage.
9. . . . j'ai vu arriver le facteur.
10. . . . il est revenu.

B   **soudain**, suddenly
      tout à coup, suddenly; all of a sudden
      immédiatement, immediately
      tout de suite, immediately
      puis, then, after that
      enfin, at last
      encore une fois, once more

Using the above list, complete the following sentences:
1. . . . il s'est assis de nouveau.
2. . . . il a quitté la salle.
3. . . . j'ai entendu un bruit à la porte.
4. . . . j'ai essayé, mais sans résultat.

    5. . . . le téléphone a sonné
    6. . . . il s'est mis à s'excuser.
    7. . . . je peux finir cette lettre.

C   **vite**, quickly
    lentement, slowly
    sans perdre de temps, without losing any time
    très doucement, very softly, very quietly
    avec grand soin, with great care
    sans penser, without thinking
    très content(e), very pleased
    trop tôt, too soon
    tôt ou tard, sooner or later

Using the above list, complete the following sentences:
    1. . . . le médecin a examiné le malade.
    2. . . . elle a essayé sa nouvelle robe.
    3. . . . il a caché les allumettes dans sa poche.
    4. . . . l'enfant s'est lancé dans la rue.
    5. . . . il a serré le cou à son ennemi.
    6. . . . nous nous reverrons.
    7. . . . la fin des vacances est arrivée.
    8. . . . ils se sont mis en route.
    9. . . . l'infirmière a pansé sa blessure.

D   **après avoir (parlé, mangé**, etc.), after having (spoken, eaten, etc.)
    après être (arrivé(e), parti(e), etc. — for all verbs with **être** as auxiliary,
       see p. 20), after having (arrived, left, etc.)
    après s'être (lavé(e), couché(e), etc. — for all reflexive verbs, see p. 27),
       after having (washed, gone to bed, etc.)
    étant, being
    tout en, whilst
    chemin faisant, on the way (whilst on the way)
    par un froid matin d'hiver, on a cold winter morning
    pendant une nuit d'automne, during an autumn night; one autumn
       night (similarly: **une journée**, a day, etc.)
    agenouillé(e), kneeling; **assis(e)**, sitting; **couché(e)**, lying
    . . . à la main, . . . in his/her hand
    malgré, in spite of
    tout étonné(e), very surprised
    or, well, well now, now then (used when telling a story, starting a new
       paragraph, etc.)
    une fois monté(e), couché(e), etc., once upstairs, in bed etc.
    ceci fait/cela fait, this/that done

Using the above list, complete the following sentences:
    1. . . . médecin il savait quoi faire.
    2. . . . sur le rocher je pouvais voir le fond de la flaque.
    3. . . . il allait à pied à l'école quand un loup est sorti du bois.
    4. . . . il ne descend plus.
    5. . . . remis le papier il ferma la boîte à clef.

6. . . . elle est sortie de la salle de bains.
7. . . . elle quitte la cuisine.
8. . . . à la gare il est allé au guichet pour acheter son billet.
9. . . . il m'a raconté comment il s'est échappé.
10. . . . une chose curieuse m'est arrivée.
11. . . . le mauvais temps j'irai voir le match.
12. Il déjeune à huit heures . . . lisant le journal.
13. . . . elle s'est retournée vers son mari.
14. Une serviette . . . le directeur s'est dirigé vers le métro.
15. . . . quelques jours plus tard je me trouvais de nouveau près du château.

Useful conjunctions

Added interest can be given to your French, without the dangers of complicated constructions, by linking simple sentences with one or another of these useful conjunctions:

et, and
mais, but
ou, or
parce que, because
comme, as
si, if (with this meaning, never followed by the future or conditional tense; and note: s'il, s'ils — but: si elle, si elles, si on or si l'on)
si, whether (in this sense can be followed by the future and the conditional)
donc, so, therefore (usually follows the verb)
ainsi, so, therefore
aussitôt que, as soon as
pendant que, while
ne . . . ni . . . ni, neither . . . nor (the first verb must have **ne** before it)

A Insert suitable conjunctions in the following sentences. Do not use the same conjunction twice.
1. Il quitte la salle . . . il est prêt.
2. La cloche a sonné; vous pouvez . . . sortir.
3. Elle a mangé le gâteau . . . elle n'a pas bu le thé.
4. Je vais à Londres . . . je veux aller au théâtre.
5. Il n'a . . . livre . . . cahier.
6. Je ne sais pas . . . on parle français ici.
7. Le soldats tireront . . . l'officier donnera l'ordre.
8. Il ne dit rien . . . le professeur lit son devoir.
9. Voulez-vous du jus d'orange . . . de la bière?
10. Je ne sais pas . . . elle viendra demain ou jeudi.

B Rewrite the following description using conjunctions to link sentences together:

Ma chambre n'est pas très grande. Elle est claire. Elle a deux grandes fenêtres. Chaque matin mon réveil sonne à sept heures. Je reste au lit jusqu'à sept heures et demie. Je n'aime pas me lever le matin. J'écoute la radio. Je me lève. Je m'habille. Ensuite je bois du café. Je ne mange pas de pain. Je ne mange pas d'œufs. Je n'ai jamais faim à cette heure du matin. J'arrive au bureau. Je commence à avoir faim.

Using que as a link

Que, meaning *that*, is often used as a link between phrases and sentences. It must be used with great care, because after certain verbs, and also when forming part of certain phrases, it must be followed by the subjunctive (see p. 125).

You may safely use the following phrases with **que**:

il est certain que, it is certain that . . .
il est clair que, it is clear/obvious that . . .
il est évident que, it is evident that . . .
il est probable que, it is probable that . . .
il est vrai que, it is true that . . .
il semble que, it seems/appears that . . .
All these are impersonal expressions. The subject is always **il**. They can be used in any tense.

je dis que, I say that
je réponds que, I reply that
Any subject and tense can be used.

aussitôt que, as soon as
après que, after
dès que, as soon as
aussi bien que, as well as
If linking a sentence in the future or conditional, the second sentence will be in the same tense as the first.

A   Complete the following sentences, using suitable phrases from the list above:
1. . . . qu'il est encore malade.
2. Son français est mauvais . . . que ses maths.
3. Je vous le dirai . . . que j'aurai de ses nouvelles.
4. . . . qu'il acceptera.
5. Je lui ai . . . que ce n'était pas de ma faute.
6. Elle est sortie . . . qu'elle avait fait la vaisselle.
7. Je vous . . . que je ne peux pas le faire.
8. . . . qu'il n'a jamais assez d'argent.
9. . . . qu'il ne viendra pas aujourd'hui.
10. . . . qu'il va pleuvoir.
11. . . . que j'aurai réparé mon vélo, j'irai lui rendre visite.
12. . . . qu'il a tort.

Verbs

Agreement

Every verb must agree in person and number with its subject. **Je** and **nous** are the only first person subjects; **tu** and **vous** are the only second person subjects. All other subjects, whether nouns or pronouns, are third person singular or plural.

La famille, the family, **la foule**, the crowd, **tout le monde**, everybody, and other words denoting a single collection of persons or things are followed by the verb in the third person singular.

La plupart, when it means *the majority* or *the largest number*, is followed by the verb in the plural; but when it means *the largest single portion* the verb must be singular.

You and I becomes: **Vous et moi, nous . . .** with the verb agreeing with **nous**; the same applies to **Jean et moi, nous . . .** or **Jean et toi, vous . . .** etc.

Present tense

The present tense is very important. Not only is it frequently used in speech and writing, but it acts as a guide to the formation of other tenses.

The present tense endings depend on the group to which the verb belongs, as indicated by its infinitive:

-er verbs	-ir verbs	-re verbs	-evoir verbs
e	is	s	ois
es	is	s	ois
e	it	— *	oit
ons	issons	ons	evons
ez	issez	ez	evez
ent	issent	ent	oivent
only exception: **aller**, to go; **-e, -es** and **-ent** are mute (unsounded) endings	only regular **-ir** verbs have **-ss-**	*3rd sing. takes **-t** if stem does not end in **-d**	all **-evoir** verbs follow this pattern; all other **-oir** verbs are irregular

Spelling rules for -er verbs

Although **aller** is the only irregular -**er** verb (see p. 7), the stem of a number of others has to be modified in accordance with normal spelling rules. Applied to -**er** verbs, these are:

(a) Stems ending in -**c** or -**g** become -**çons** and -**geons** in the **nous** line.

(b) Stems ending in e + consonant (e.g. **acheter**), é + consonant (e.g. **posséder**) or é + **ch** (e.g. **sécher**) change this to è before e-mute endings: **j'achète, ils sèchent**, etc.

(c) **Appeler** and **jeter** and their compounds double the final consonant instead: **j'appelle, tu jettes**, etc.
(verbs with ê do not change: **pêcher, je pêche**, etc.)

(d) Verbs ending in -**oyer** and -**uyer** change y to i before e-mute endings, e.g. **employer, j'emploie; essuyer, ils essuient**. Verbs in -**ayer** can either take the i or keep the y.

Examples of these verbs will be found set out in full at the end of the book, p. 152.

A Give the appropriate form of the following verbs in the present tense:

1. ils (aboyer)
2. je m'(appeler)
3. tu (jeter)
4. nous (préférer)
5. ils (amener)
6. il (dégeler)
7. vous (réussir)
8. j'(acheter)
9. elle (envoyer)
10. nous (manger)
11. il (rompre)
12. nous (saisir)
13. elles (choisir)
14. je (pêcher)
15. il (recevoir)
16. nous (apercevoir)
17. tu (payer)
18. ils (employer)
19. tu (rappeler)
20. nous (placer)

N.B. Be very careful with verbs like **saisir, choisir, réussir**, with -s or -ss in the stem: they are easy to spell wrong!

B Give the appropriate form of the following verbs in the present tense:

1. L'agent (arrêter) le voleur et l'(empêcher) de faire mal.
2. Les enfants (finir) leurs devoirs.
3. La mère (amener) ses deux filles à l'école.
4. Est-ce que ça vous (gêner) si la bonne (balayer) le plancher?
5. Jean et moi, nous (manger) les poires.
6. Les garçons (jeter) des boules de neige; nous en (jeter) aussi.
7. Les bons médecins (guérir) leurs malades.
8. Vous et moi, nous (placer) les livres sur les rayons.
9. Je (mélanger) la viande avec les légumes; je les (préférer) ainsi.
10. Les chiens (aboyer) quand ils (apercevoir) le chat.
11. Les vêtements (sécher) dans le jardin.
12. La famille se (promener) le long de la rue.
13. Le marchand (vendre) ses fruits au marché.
14. On (marcher) sur le trottoir; on (traverser) la rue au passage clouté.
15. Charles (prêter) son livre à son ami.
16. L'ami (rendre) le livre à Charles.
17. Nous (ranger) tous les souliers dans l'armoire.

18. Est-ce que vous (réussir) toujours?
19. Le général (apercevoir) l'ennemi de loin.
20. Est-ce que tu t'(appeler) Louise?

The most important irregular present tenses

The following are very common (see pp. 154 ff. for tenses set out fully):
avoir: ai, as, a; avons, avez, ont
être: suis, es, est; sommes, êtes, sont
aller: vais, vas, va; allons, allez, vont
faire: fais, fais, fait; faisons, faites, font
dire: dis, dis, dit; disons, dites, disent
écrire: écris, écris, écrit; écrivons, écrivez, écrivent
prendre: prends, prends, prend; prenons, prenez, prennent
savoir: sais, sais, sait; savons, savez, savent
voir: vois, vois, voit; voyons, voyez, voient
vouloir: veux, veux, veut; voulons, voulez, veulent
pouvoir: peux, peux, peut; pouvons, pouvez, peuvent
N.B. je peux, but puis-je?

Note that in the present tense:
the **tu** line of all verbs (as in all tenses) always ends in **-s**, except for
    pouvoir and **vouloir**;
the **nous** line always ends in **-ons** except **nous sommes**;
the **vous** line always ends in **-ez** except **vous êtes, vous faites** and **vous
    dites**;
the **ils/elles** line always ends in **-ent** except **ils/elles ont, sont, vont** and
    font.

Verb groups

The verbs in each of the following groups form their tenses in the same
way. An example of each group will be found set out in full on pp. 154 f

-ir groups

tenir, venir and their compounds;
dormir, mentir, partir, sentir, servir and **sortir**;
ouvrir, couvrir, offrir and **souffrir**

-re groups

prendre and compounds such as **comprendre, reprendre**;
connaître and similar **-aître** verbs;
craindre, peindre, joindre and compounds

A   Give the appropriate form of the following verbs in the present tense:

1. je (avoir)	7. vous (être)
2. tu (être)	8. ils (faire)
3. il (aller)	9. elles (écrire)
4. elle (avoir)	10. je (pouvoir)
5. on (dire)	11. tu (vouloir)
6. nous (faire)	12. il (savoir)

13. elle (voir)	32. elles (avoir)
14. on (devoir)	33. je (voir)
15. nous (recevoir)	34. tu (pouvoir)
16. vous (tenir)	35. il (couvrir)
17. ils (offrir)	36. elle (reconnaître)
18. elles (retenir)	37. on (interrompre)
19. je (prendre)	38. nous (être)
20. tu (dormir)	39. vous (craindre)
21. il (mentir)	40. ils (apercevoir)
22. elle (ouvrir)	41. elles (prendre)
23. on (servir)	42. je (recevoir)
24. nous (sortir)	43. tu (devoir)
25. vous (connaître)	44. il (souffrir)
26. ils (reconnaître)	45. elle (prendre)
27. elle (craindre)	46. on (savoir)
28. il (peindre)	47. nous (écrire)
29. nous (joindre)	48. vous (savoir)
30. vous (faire)	49. ils (être)
31. ils (aller)	50. elles (vouloir)

B   Give the appropriate form of the following verbs in the present tense:
1. Tout le monde (être) d'accord.
2. Toute la famille (aller) au cinéma.
3. Est-ce que Pierre (venir) chez nous aujourd'hui?
4. Est-ce que vous (vouloir) les vendre?
5. Ils ne (comprendre) pas ce que je (dire).
6. Sa famille (dormir) à l'hôtel.
7. La foule (faire) beaucoup de bruit.
8. Mon père ne (connaître) pas le directeur.
9. Vous et moi, nous (craindre) le chien.
10. Marie et sa sœur (offrir) de l'argent au contrôleur.

C   Give the appropriate form of the following verbs in the present tense:
1. Tout le monde (savoir) comme je (souffrir).
2. (Savoir)-vous ce que ce mot (vouloir) dire?
3. Tu (devoir) le faire si tu (vouloir) aller jouer.
4. Je (peindre) le salon et les autres (peindre) la cuisine.
5. Ils (réussir) toujours; moi, je ne (réussir) jamais.
6. Est-ce que tu (pouvoir) voir ce que je (voir)?
7. Je (devoir) aller travailler; (pouvoir)-je sortir?
8. Je (savoir) qu'il ne me (connaître) pas.
9. (Connaître)-vous bien Paris? Je (savoir) que vous y (aller) souvent.
10. Les enfants qui (jouer) dans la rue (faire) beaucoup de bruit. Ils (être) agaçants.

Other irregular verbs

The following irregular verbs should be known. They are included in the table of irregular verbs on pp. 154 ff.

-ir verbs
mourir; courir; fuir

-re verbs
(se) battre; mettre;
convaincre;
suivre; vivre;
conduire and other verbs in **-uire**;
lire;
plaire;
rire; sourire;
boire; croire

-oir verbs
s'asseoir
Remember that **s'asseoir** means *to sit down* — the action of sitting. *To be seated* is **être assis(e)(s)**, **assis** being treated as an adjective: **Elle est assise sur la chaise.** She is sitting on the chair. *But:* **Elle s'assied.** She sits down.

A Give the appropriate form of the following verbs in the present tense:
1. je (pouvoir); (pouvoir)-je?
2. tu (reconnaître)
3. il (être)
4. nous (voir)
5. vous (vivre)
6. ils (paraître)
7. je m'(asseoir)
8. tu (mentir)
9. elle s'(appeler)
10. nous (rire)
11. vous (suivre)
12. elles (fuir)
13. je m'(endormir)
14. tu (mettre)
15. on (mourir)
16. nous (céder)
17. vous (découvrir)
18. ils (réussir)
19. je (suivre)
20. tu (sentir)
21. il me (plaire)
22. nous (écrire)
23. vous (boire)
24. ils (sourire)
25. elles (pouvoir)
26. Tout le monde (mourir).
27. La famille s'(enfuir).
28. Chaque enfant (courir) après lui.
29. Un groupe d'élèves (suivre) le guide.
30. Beaucoup de gens (venir) ici.
31. Ce pain (être) frais.
32. Mon frère et moi, nous (lire) le journal.
33. Votre sœur et vous, vous (rire) souvent.
34. Mon père et ma mère (courir) après moi.

35. Ma sœur et moi, nous ne (souffrir) pas.
36. La plupart des gens (savoir) lire.
37. Ses cheveux (devenir) blancs.
38. La vieille dame (boire) le café.
39. La salle de bains se (trouver) en haut.
40. Le chat (craindre) le chien.
41. (Écrire) cette page de nouveau!
42. Toute la classe (paraître) contente.
43. Le professeur ne (sourire) pas.
44. Le chauffeur (conduire) la voiture.
45. Le groupe de soldats (joindre) le regiment.
46. Il (mentir); je ne le (croire) pas.
47. (Asseoir)-vous dans le fauteuil.
48. Les visiteurs (boire) du thé.
49. Elles (lire) des romans.
50. Ce vieil arbre (vivre) toujours.

B The verbs in the following sentences are all in the present tense. In each sentence *one* letter has been put in the wrong place, or one accent or cedilla moved to the wrong place, making two incorrectly spelt words in each sentence. These words are all verbs. Rewrite correctly the two words which are wrong.

1. Nous mangons le gâteau que tu vendes.
2. J'apercois où vous plaçez les livres.
3. Je lui envoye les timbres que vous m'envoiez.
4. Nous peinons très mal, je craigns.
5. Ils finisent le livre que je lui prêtes.
6. Il connait le restaurant où vous faîtes la cuisine.
7. Nous jettons notre balle, mais le méchant garçon jete des cailloux.
8. Je m'appele Jean. Comment vous appellez-vous?
9. Je prèfère la voiture que tu achétes.
10. Il êtait là, où vous étes maintenant.

How to use the present tense

In English we have three forms for the present:
I write, I am writing, I do write. The 'do' form is mainly used in the negative (*I do not write*) or interrogative (*Do you write?*).
The French have one form only, which translates any of the English present tense forms.

j'écris $\begin{cases} \text{I write} \\ \text{I am writing} \end{cases}$ **je n'écris pas** $\begin{cases} \text{I do not write} \\ \text{I am not writing} \end{cases}$

Do be careful!

Remember not to translate *do* in *do not* or in *do you?*, etc. If *do* means *make*, *perform* (some action), etc., then it must be translated by the appropriate form of **faire**.
What are you doing? **Que faites-vous?**
Do you? does he? etc. at the end of a sentence, as in *You don't speak Spanish, do you?* is translated by **n'est-ce pas?**

A   Translate:
1. He is reading a book.
2. I am going to Paris.
3. Do you speak English?
4. How do you do?
5. How do you do this?
6. The tree is dying.
7. They are painting the kitchen.
8. I do not like coffee, but I do like tea.
9. Do you like sport?
10. Anne and Marie make a lot of mistakes.

B   Translate:
1. You don't do it, do you?
2. I don't want to drink what you are drinking.
3. Can you drive? I drive very well.
4. I know someone who knows the poem by heart.
5. 'Pierre, Charles, Jean — are you laughing?'
   'No sir, we're reading.'
6. I can't do what you want.
7. We do the cooking for the others.
8. I cannot do it, and I do not want to try.
9. 'You can do this for me.'
   'No, I can't.'
10. 'What are you doing this evening?'
   'We want to go to the cinema.'

Present participle

The French present participle always ends in **-ant**. It corresponds to the English verb-form ending in *-ing*. It is formed from the **nous** line of the present tense, with the **-ons** ending changed to **-ant**:

aller: nous allons → **allant**, going
finir: nous finissons → **finissant**, finishing
boire: nous buvons → **buvant**, drinking

The only exceptions are:

être: nous sommes → **étant**, being
avoir: nous avons → **ayant**, having
savoir: nous savons → **sachant**, knowing

The French present participle is used much less frequently than the corresponding English form. Great care must therefore be taken whenever translating the English *-ing* form into French.

When *not* to use the French present participle:
(a) The French present participle cannot be used to help form a tense:
   I am writing can only be **j'écris.**
   I was writing can only be **j'écrivais.**

(b) The French present participle cannot be used after a preposition (with the sole exception of **en**). The infinitive is used instead: without speaking, **sans parler** (see p. 32).

(c) The English present participle is similarly translated by the infinitive when it closely follows another verb (which is said to 'govern' it):

I like eating. **J'aime manger.**

(d) After verbs of perception (by the senses — hearing, seeing, feeling, etc.) the English present participle is again translated by the infinitive:

I hear the children singing. **J'entends chanter les enfants.**

Note that in such cases the infinitive usually directly follows the verb which governs it.

(e) When an English present participle is governed by a verb other than those in (d) above, it may be translated by a relative clause:

There is someone singing in the street.

Il y a quelqu'un qui chante dans la rue.

The policeman arrests the man stealing his car.

L'agent arrête l'homme qui vole sa voiture.

When you *can* use the present participle:

You can translate the English *-ing* form of the verb by the French **-ant** form in the following cases:

(f) When the English present participle refers to the subject of the sentence, and the action is describes is simultaneous with that of the main verb. In such cases, the French present participle usually follows the preposition **en**, which means *while, at the same time as, by, by means of, in, on* (doing something):

The soldiers sing while marching.

Les soldats chantent en marchant.

(g) To emphasize the fact that the two actions (that of the main verb and that of the present participle) are taking place at one and the same time, **tout en** may be used:

My father reads his paper while eating his breakfast.

Mon père lit son journal tout en mangeant son petit déjeuner.

(h) If the action of the main verb takes place as the result of, or following upon, that of the present participle, **en** is often omitted:

Opening the door, he goes out.

Ouvrant la porte, il sort.

(i) To translate *having* done something, **ayant** is normally used, but with verbs which take **être** as their auxiliary (see below, p. 20), **étant** must be used:

having spoken, **ayant parlé**

having arrived, **étant arrivé** ⎫ The past participles agree as
having washed, **s'étant lavé** ⎭ explained below, p. 24.

When following the preposition **après**, however, the infinitive of the auxiliary must be used (see p. 32):

after having spoken, **après avoir parlé**

after having arrived, **après être arrivé**

after having washed, **après s'être lavé**

(j) The present participle can often be used as an adjective, in which case it will agree with its noun like any other adjective:
This lesson is annoying. **Cette leçon est agaçante.**
interesting books, **des livres intéressants**

But if the English present participle describes an attitude of the body, in French the past participle is used (as an adjective):
He is sitting. **Il est assis.**
She was lying down. **Elle était couchée.**

A   Rewrite the following, putting the verb into its correct form and inserting **en** where necessary. (The letters in brackets refer to the relevant rules given above.)
  1. Le menuisier (is working) dans son atelier. (a)
  2. La vache (is eating) l'herbe. (a)
  3. Jean (is looking at) le tableau noir. (a)
  4. Quand (are you going) à Marseille? (a)
  5. Est-ce qu'il (is coming) cet après-midi? (a)
  6. J'apprends le français (by listening to) la radio française. (f)
  7. Le fermier, (on seeing) les moutons, appelle son chien. (h)
  8. C'est (through studying) que l'on apprend. (f)
  9. (On returning home) il monte à sa chambre. (f)
  10. Les voleurs se sauvent (by running). (f)
  11. Il répond (smiling), et puis il part (whistling) doucement. (f)
  12. Il explique son plan (while driving) vers la ville. (g)
  13. (Having alighted) de l'autobus, il est entré dans la gare. (i)
  14. (After having bought) un billet au guichet, il s'est dirigé vers le quai. (i)
  15. (Having gone to bed) très tard, il s'est endormi aussitôt. (i)

B   Translate (the letters in brackets refer to the relevant rules given above):
  1. She goes out, carrying her umbrella in her hand. (f)
  2. He starts eating without waiting. (c, b)
  3. Lying on my bed, I can hear the cars passing. (j, d)
  4. Knowing the truth, I cannot answer without laughing. (h, b)
  5. He listens carefully to the guide explaining the history of the chateau. (e)
  6. Look! Here's the postman coming now! (e)
  7. I write my letters while watching television. (g)
  8. Having travelled a lot he tells amusing stories. (i, j)
  9. From here she can see the children playing. (d)
  10. When I am working I do not like being disturbed by people asking annoying questions. (a, c, e, j)

C   Translate the following. Which is the 'odd one out'?
  1. a loving mother
  2. a dying tree
  3. a living language
  4. a bathing costume
  5. a moving staircase
  6. interesting letters

D Here are a number of words ending in **-ant**. Arrange them in two columns: in column (a) put those which are present participles, and give their infinitive; in (b) put those which are not present participles and give their English meaning. Some will go in both columns:

suffisant, pourtant, pouvant, différant, différent, enfant, aimant, cependant, instant, suivant, savant, avant, diamant, sachant, ayant

Imperfect

Formation

The stem of the imperfect is always the same as the **nous**-line of the present tense, minus the **-ons** ending.
The imperfect endings are:
-ais, -ais, -ait; -ions, -iez, -aient.
e.g. **recevoir**: nous recevons → je recevais, etc.
   connaître: nous connaissons → je connaissais, etc.
The only exception is **être**: j'étais, tu étais, etc.

The following need special care:
(a) In **-cer** and **-ger** verbs remember to change **c** to **ç** and **g** to **ge** before
   a: je plaçais, je mangeais — but placions, mangiez.
(b) Verbs with stems ending in -s or -ss are easy to spell wrong:
   choisir: choisissais
   réussir: réussissais, etc.
(c) Note the **-ii-** in **rire**: nous riions, vous riiez.

Use

The imperfect is used to describe:
(a) some action or state of affairs which existed indefinitely in the past:
   Avant la guerre je travaillais chez un horloger.
   Before the war I used to work at a watchmaker's.
(b) some action habitually repeated in the past:
   J'allais chaque jour à Paris par le train omnibus qui arrivait souvent en retard.
   I used to go to Paris every day by the slow train, which would often arrive late.
(c) circumstances which existed or an activity which was taking place when some action occurred:
   Un jour je réparais une montre quand j'ai vu entrer un homme très curieux.
   One day I was repairing a watch when I saw a most odd man enter.
(d) The imperfect is also used after **si** (if) in conditional sentences (see p. 18) and for the auxiliary verb in the pluperfect (p. 23).

A Give the appropriate form of the following verbs in the imperfect tense:

1. je (mener)
2. tu (danser)
3. elle (rougir)
4. nous (nager)
5. vous (boire)
6. ils (vivre)
7. je (vouloir)
8. tu (pouvoir)
9. elle (voir)
10. nous (placer)

11. vous (rire)
12. ils (dire)
13. je (comprendre)
14. tu (ouvrir)
15. il (partir)

16. nous (tenir)
17. vous (réussir)
18. ils (choisir)
19. elles (plonger)
20. tu (lancer)

B   Put the verbs in the following passage into the imperfect where appropriate:

Je dois toujours me coucher après le dîner. Je suis obligé de quitter maman, qui reste à causer avec ses amies, au jardin s'il fait beau, dans le salon s'il fait mauvais.

Une fois couché, j'ai l'habitude de lire un des livres que je reçois chaque année à Noël. Je ne comprends pas toujours tout ce que je lis, mais souvent, après avoir posé le livre sur ma table de nuit, je ferme les yeux, je réfléchis sur ce que je viens de lire — et les phrases commencent à me devenir intelligibles.

C   Translate:
1. Mathieu always used to visit me when he was in Paris.
2. During the winter we went to the cinema every Saturday.
3. Were you in Greece at the same time as I was?
4. I always used to drink tea, but now I prefer coffee.
5. We knew that his house was somewhere in the wood, but we couldn't find it.
6. They were eating an enormous meal, and we had nothing to eat.
7. Were you blushing because of what he was saying?
8. Did you already know Alain?
9. Marie said that she wanted to come with us, but she couldn't.
10. I was in the kitchen and I was doing the washing-up, when a man put his hand on my shoulder.

Future

The stem of the future is normally based on the infinitive. There are many irregularities, but the future stem always ends in **-r-**, and the endings are always: **-ai, -as, -a; -ons, -ez, -ont** (present of **avoir** without **av-**).

-er verbs
regular: **parler** → je parlerai
irregular: **aller** → j'irai
            envoyer → j'enverrai
There are no other irregular **-er** future stems; but where the stem is modified in the present before **e**-mute endings, the same occurs throughout the future:
    mener: je mène → je mènerai
    jeter: je jette → je jetterai
    essuyer: j'essuie → j'essuierai
But verbs with **é** in the infinitive do *not* change this to **è**:
    céder: je cède → je céderai
    préférer: je préfère → je préférerai

-ir verbs
regular: **finir** → je finirai
irregular: verbs like **tenir, venir, devenir**: je tiendrai, je viendrai, je
      deviendrai
        verbs ending in **-quérir** like **conquérir**: je conquerrai
        courir and **mourir** both drop the **-i-**: je courrai, je mourrai
        cueillir and compounds: je cueillerai
Other -ir verbs, even if irregular in other tenses, have regular futures.

-re verbs
regular: **vendre** → je vendrai
irregular: **être** → je serai
        faire → je ferai
Other -re verbs, even if irregular elsewhere, have regular futures.

-oir verbs
All **-evoir** verbs, including **devoir**, and also **mouvoir**, drop **-oi-** from the
infinitive: **recevoir** → je recevrai; **devoir** → je devrai
Other **-oir** verbs have irregular future stems (see the list of irregular verbs
on pp. 154 ff.). The most common are:
avoir → j'aurai
savoir → je saurai
asseoir → j'assiérai (or j'assoirai)
pouvoir → je pourrai
falloir → il faudra (always impersonal)
valoir → je vaudrai (usually impersonal: il vaudra)
voir → je verrai
vouloir → je voudrai

The future translates our *shall* or *will* when these indicate the future,
but not when *shall* means *must*, or *will* means *wants to, wishes to*. As
in English, especially when speaking of a near future, or of a future
already determined upon, **aller**, to go, + the infinitive can be used instead of the future tense:
Je vais lui écrire cet après-midi. I am going to write to him this afternoon.
Nous allons passer les vacances en France.
We are going to spend our holidays in France.

The one important difference in the way we and the French use the
future is:
after **quand, lorsque** (both = *when*), **aussitôt que, dès que** (both = *as
soon as*), **après que** (*after*), and other similar conjunctions of time, if
the main verb is in the future, the verb after **quand** etc. will also be in
the future:
He will answer the letter when it arrives (English present).
Il répondra à la lettre quand elle arrivera (French future).
This is known as the *logical future*.
When using si to mean *if* the tenses are as in English:
Je vous dirai s'il vient. I shall tell you if he comes.
The future is never used after si = *if*. But we sometimes use *if* when we
mean *whether*, and the French use si in the same way. When so used si
can be followed by the future:
Je ne sais pas s'il viendra. I do not know whether (*if*) he will come.

A   In the following sentences, substitute **demain** for **aujourd'hui**, and make the necessary changes to the tense of the verbs:
1. Aujourd'hui je mange chez vous.
2. Aujourd'hui le fruitier vend les pommes à 3 francs la livre.
3. Aujourd'hui vous donnez les ordres.
4. Aujourd'hui tu portes la lettre.
5. Aujourd'hui nous ne craignons plus leurs menaces.
6. Aujourd'hui vous essuyez les assiettes.
7. Aujourd'hui j'essaye de vous l'apporter.
8. Aujourd'hui elle amène son enfant chez le médecin.
9. Aujourd'hui elles choisissent leurs nouvelles robes.
10. Aujourd'hui nous voulons aller au cinéma.

B   Rewrite the following, putting the verb in brackets into the appropriate tense and form:
1. Ce que j'apprends cette année mon petit frère (apprendre) plus tard.
2. S'il neige avant midi sur les montagnes, il (neiger) l'après-midi dans la plaine.
3. Ce qu'elle achète aujourd'hui son amie (acheter) demain.
4. Ce que vendent les grands magasins à Noël les petits magasins (vendre) à Pâques.
5. Nous (cueillir) en automne les légumes que nous plantons au printemps.
6. Les enfants (manger) ce soir les gâteaux que la mère a faits ce matin.
7. En ce moment je ne peux pas, mais dans deux heures je (pouvoir) le faire.
8. Il est midi; dans quatre-vingt-dix minutes il (être) une heure et demie.
9. Hier je ne le savais pas; demain je le (savoir).
10. Je le reconnais maintenant; est-ce que je le (reconnaître) l'année prochaine?

C   Translate, using the future tense, **aller**, or the present, as appropriate:
1. He will drink wine if you drink too.
2. When he arrives I shall leave the house.
3. Are you going to the cinema this afternoon?
4. We are going to spend the summer holidays at my aunt's.
5. I shall buy two tickets.
6. If he comes home early we shall be able to leave before dinner.
7. We shall open the door only if he brings the priest.
8. I shall open the door when he brings the parcel.
9. Will you sit down, please?
10. When are you going to the baker's?

Conditional

The conditional is **always** formed from the stem of the future plus the endings of the imperfect: -ais, -ais, -ait; -ions, -iez, -aient.
e.g. **parler**, je parlerais; **être**, je serais; **devoir**, je devrais

The conditional implies that something would happen if something else did. It translates the English *should* and *would* when these are used in a conditional sense, but *not* in the following cases:

(a) when *should* means *ought to* (see below);
(b) when *would* means *used to*, which is translated by the imperfect;
(c) when *would* means *wanted to*, which is translated by the imperfect of **vouloir**.

One of the main uses of the conditional is in indirect speech. A present tense in direct speech becomes imperfect in indirect speech; a future tense similarly becomes conditional.
e.g. Jean m'a dit: « Je reviens tout de suite. »
    Jean m'a dit qu'il revenait tout de suite.
    Jean m'a dit: « Je reviendrai demain. »
    Jean m'a dit qu'il reviendrait demain.

The conditional, like the future, is never used after si = *if*. In a conditional sentence the conditional verb will therefore be found in the other clause and the verb in the si-clause will normally be imperfect.
Il jouerait au football, s'il avait le temps.
He would play football if he had the time.

Si = *whether* can be followed by the conditional.
Je ne savais pas s'il viendrait.
I did not know whether he would come.

Should meaning *ought to* is translated by the conditional of **devoir**.
Il devrait travailler plus souvent.
He should/ought to work more often.
Should have/ought to have is translated by the conditional of **avoir** plus the past participle of **devoir**:
Il aurait dû travailler.
He should have/ought to have worked.

Note also the following common uses of the conditional:
Je voudrais/j'aimerais (faire quelque chose).
I should like to (do something).
J'aimerais mieux . . .
I should prefer . . .
Il vaudrait mieux + infinitive
It would be better . . .
Pourriez-vous? + infinitive
Could you . . . ?
J'aurais pu + infinitive
I could have . . .

Take care not to confuse the spelling of the imperfect and the conditional of verbs with stems ending in **-r**:

	Imperfect	*Conditional*
déchirer, to tear	déchirais	déchirerais
entrer, to enter	entrais	entrerais
montrer, to show	montrais	montrerais

A Put the verb into the conditional:
   1. Il a dit qu'il (venir) à deux heures.
   2. Elle a répondu qu'elle (vouloir) bien le faire.
   3. Mon ami m'a demandé quand je (pouvoir) le voir.
   4. Ils ont répondu qu'ils ne le leur (rendre) jamais.
   5. Le médecin m'a assuré qu'il (espérer) toujours.
   6. Nous leur avons expliqué que nous ne (manger) rien.
   7. J'ai pensé que vous (avoir) l'argent.
   8. Le gamin cria qu'il ne le (lâcher) pas.
   9. Est-ce que tu as cru qu'il t'(aider)?
   10. Le général s'est écrié qu'il ne se (rendre) jamais.

B Rewrite the following, replacing the direct speech by indirect speech:
   1. Le contrôleur m'a dit: « Vous devez payer.»
   2. L'agent nous a répondu: « Il faudra attendre.»
   3. Elles nous ont demandé: « Quand votre père reviendra-t-il?»
   4. Le directeur m'a demandé: « Quand pouvez-vous commencer?»
   5. Je lui ai répondu: «Je pourrai commencer demain, monsieur.»
   6. Jean m'a dit: «Nous devrons partir à six heures.»
   7. «Combien de temps passerez-vous en Grèce?»,nous a-t-elle demandé.
   8. «Je ne viendrai pas samedi», lui ai-je dit.
   9. «On ne t'attendra pas ce jour-là», m'a-t-il assuré.
   10. «Je ferai mieux la prochaine fois», lui ai-je promis.

C Translate:
   1. Paul said he would play for the team if he had time.
   2. Anne told us that we should have seen the film.
   3. You could have come with us if you had finished at five o'clock.
   4. We didn't know whether you would be able to come.
   5. It would be better to go to Greece later.
   6. Could you tell us the time, please, Sir?
   7. They would prefer to go and get an ice-cream in the café.
   8. If I could hear I should answer.
   9. 'You ought to go and do your homework.'
      'Oh, no! I'd much rather watch television.'
   10. Every day the guide showed them wonderful sights, and they knew
       that the next day he would show them yet more spectacular sights.

Perfect

The perfect is formed by combining the present tense of either **avoir** or
être (called, when so used, the *auxiliary verbs*) with the past participle
of the verb in use. Hence the French name **passé composé.** The French
perfect translates the English perfect:

   J'ai parlé. I have spoken.
   Il a fini. He has finished.

In everyday speech and in letters, the French use the perfect where we
would use our simple past:

   J'ai parlé. I spoke.

(The French tense corresponding to our simple past, usually called the past historic, is never used in speech, and need not be used in writing simple French in the past. It is dealt with later, in Part II.)

To form the perfect tense in French you need to know:
(a) which of the two auxiliaries to use — **avoir** or **être** (in English we always use *to have*);
(b) the past participle of the verb you are using. (Sometimes the past participle has to agree with the subject or object of the verb. This important rule is dealt with below, p. 24.)

Which auxiliary?

1. All reflexive verbs use **être** as their auxiliary:
Il s'est lavé. He (has) washed (himself).
Reflexive verbs will be dealt with more fully later. See p. 27.

2. A number of verbs of change of position and condition (also called 'verbs of motion'), if used intransitively (without a direct object) are conjugated with **être** as their auxiliary:
Il est venu. He has come.
These verbs are:
aller, venir, arriver, partir,
naître, mourir, entrer, sortir,
monter, descendre, rester, retourner,
tomber.
To these must be added their compounds, e.g. **devenir, s'en aller, remonter, revenir, rentrer,** etc.
Passer in the sense of **passer chez quelqu'un** is also conjugated with **être.**
Il est passé voir son oncle. He called to see his uncle.
Some of these verbs can also be used transitively (with a direct object), in which case they are conjugated with **avoir**:
Il est monté. He has gone up.
Il a monté l'escalier. He has gone up the stairs.

3. All other verbs — the vast majority — are conjugated with **avoir**, including both **avoir** and **être**:
Il a eu. Il a été.

In the negative **ne** precedes the auxiliary and **pas** (**jamais**, etc.) follows the auxiliary and precedes the past participle.
Il n'a pas parlé.
Il n'est jamais venu.

Past participle

The primary use of the past participle is in the formation of compound tenses, of which the perfect is the most important.
Regular past participles are formed thus:
-er verbs: replace **-er** by **-é**, as in parler, **parlé** (no exceptions)
-ir verbs: replace **-ir** by **-i**, as in finir, **fini**
-re verbs: replace **-re** by **-u**, as in vendre, **vendu**
-evoir verbs: replace **-evoir** by **-u**, as in recevoir, **reçu**

The past participles of irregular verbs are given in the verb tables on
pp. 154 ff. The following irregular past participles are important and
should be learnt:

être, **été**

naître, **né, née**

(These are the *only* two verbs, other than -er verbs, with past participles
in -é.)

tenir, venir and compounds: **tenu, venu**

ouvrir, couvrir, souffrir, offrir: **ouvert, souffert**

-uire verbs like conduire: **conduit**

-aître verbs like connaître: **connu** (exception: naître, **né**)

-aindre, -eindre, -oindre verbs like craindre, joindre: **craint, joint**

Note also: **-ir verbs:** courir, **couru**
                      mourir, **mort**

       -re verbs: écrire, **écrit**
                      faire, **fait**
                      rire, **ri**
                      sourire, **souri**
                      suivre, **suivi**
                      croire, **cru**
                      plaire, **plu**
                      vivre, **vécu**
                      mettre, **mis**
                      prendre, **pris**

-oir verbs (all irregular except those ending in **-evoir**):
                      falloir, **fallu**
                      vouloir, **voulu**
                      pleuvoir, **plu**
                      pouvoir, **pu**
                      voir, **vu**
                      devoir, **dû, due**

A Put the following into the perfect:
1. Il mange la pomme.
2. Je finis mon travail.
3. Nous vendons la maison.
4. Vous manquez le train.
5. Ils mentent.
6. Tu rends l'argent.
7. Je conduis la voiture.
8. Ils aperçoivent la faute.
9. Elle ne sourit jamais.
10. Il ne plaît plus.

B Translate:
1. I have kept my promise.
2. They did not paint the wall.
3. The film did not please the visitor.
4. They have drunk the tea.
5. I did not offer any beer to the workman.

6. Haven't you written the letter?
7. We have taken the room for ten days.
8. He has not read the newspaper.
9. They have read the book, but they did not believe every word.
10. We opened the door.

C   Put the following into the perfect:
1. J'arrive.
2. Il entre dans la chambre.
3. Meurt-il?
4. Il passe me voir.
5. Je retourne à six heures.
6. Il devient très riche.
7. Je tombe en sortant.
8. Il part de bonne heure.
9. Pierre monte à sa chambre.
10. Jean reste en bas.

D   Translate:
1. Hasn't he arrived yet?
2. He came down in the lift.
3. I have returned because I went out without any money.
4. The child became very difficult — that's why I went out.
5. I have remained here because my dog has died.
6. He arrived at the Eiffel Tower; he went up to the first floor.
7. He came down very quickly.
8. He was born in Paris.
9. I looked in at the hospital.
10. It has rained all day.

E   Translate, using the perfect tense throughout:

He was born in Dijon. He went to Paris, where he studied English. He became Professor of Foreign Languages at the Sorbonne — the University of Paris. He wrote many books and bought a very modern flat in the centre of the town, where his son was born. He died in London where he went to visit the family of his English wife.

The perfect participle

The perfect participle is formed by the present participle of the auxiliary + the past participle of the verb:
having spoken, **ayant parlé**
having gone out, **étant sorti**
having washed, **s'étant lavé**

A   Translate:
1. Having spoken thus, he went out.
2. Having arrived late, he started to work without delay.
3. Having gone to bed early, he went to sleep at once.
4. Having got up too late he did not wash.
5. Having taken his pen he started to write.

Pluperfect

The English pluperfect is usually translated by the French pluperfect, formed by combining the imperfect of the auxiliary with the past participle:

J'avais parlé. I had spoken.
J'étais arrivé. I had arrived.

(Another tense is sometimes used to translate the English pluperfect — the past anterior, formed by combining the past historic of the auxiliary with the past participle. Like the past historic, it is a literary tense, not used in speech or in letters, nor is it used in conjunction with the perfect.)

A   Rewrite the following in the pluperfect:
1. Il tombe en descendant l'escalier.
2. Nous ouvrons la porte d'entrée.
3. Vous mettez le linge dans l'armoire.
4. Ils courent vers la gare.
5. Il meurt de faim.
6. Il saute la haie.
7. Vous buvez trop vite.
8. Ils rompent le silence.
9. Ils sont très gentils.
10. Ils ont trop chaud.
11. Vous voyez les montagnes.
12. Elles aperçoivent la mer entre les rochers.
13. Je crains le taureau dans ce champ.
14. Tu ne crois jamais les journaux.
15. Il lui faut faire ses courses.
16. Lisons-nous les mêmes livres?
17. Quand écrivez-vous la lettre?
18. Je pars avant vous.
19. Ceci me plaît beaucoup.
20. Il pleut toute la semaine.

B   Rewrite the following, putting one verb in each sentence into the pluperfect, and any others into whichever past tense (imperfect or perfect) is appropriate:

1. Je (manger) tous les sandwichs bien avant midi.
2. Tu (sortir) depuis longtemps quand je (arriver).
3. Je ne (pouvoir) pas étudier parce qu'il (vendre) mes livres.
4. Les ouvriers (protester) contre l'ordre que l'on leur (donner).
5. Je (savoir) bien comment conduire le camion: je l'(conduire) l'année dernière.
6. Il (venir) me dire qu'ils (découvrir) le trésor dans une caverne.
7. Il (naître) six mois avant leur arrivée.
8. Mon frère (ouvrir) la boîte quand je (entrer) dans la salle.
9. Nous (trouver) qu'il n'(sortir) pas, comme nous (croire).
10. Je lui (demander) ce qu'il (dire).

Agreement of the past participle

1. The past participle can be used as an adjective, to describe a noun, as in English. It will then agree like any other adjective:
   une page déchirée, a torn page
   La page est déchirée. The page is torn.
   This use of the past participle is especially common when describing bodily attitudes:
   Marie, couchée sur le canapé, Marie, lying on the sofa
   le conducteur, courbé sur le volant de sa voiture, the driver, bent over the steering-wheel of his car

2. In the perfect, pluperfect, and all other compound tenses, the past participle frequently has to add **-e, -s,** or **-es** to agree with the noun or pronoun it refers to.
   The rules governing the agreement of the past participle are:

(a) In all verbs which use **être** as their auxiliary *except reflexive verbs* the past participle agrees with the subject of the verb, as if it were an ordinary adjective:
Compare: **Elle est grande.** (adjective)
with: **Elle est arrivée.** (past participle)
Note that **je, tu, nous** and vous can be either masculine or feminine (a woman must write **je suis arrivée**); and that **vous** can show either singular or plural agreement as its use requires.
When **nous** and **vous** refer to mixed genders, masculine always takes precedence.
The impersonal pronoun **on** (for *one, they, someone*) is always singular though we may translate it by *they* (**on est parti,** they have left). **On** is also usually masculine (unless the context makes it clear that it must be feminine).

(b) In reflexive verbs, and all verbs which have **avoir** as their auxiliary, the past participle agrees with a direct object before the verb if there is one.
Vous voyez cette maison? Je l'ai achetée.
The direct object **l'** precedes the verb, and **achetée** agrees with **l'** which stands for **la maison.**
Voici la maison que j'ai achetée.
The direct object **que** precedes the verb, and **achetée** agrees with **que** which stands for **la maison.**
Similarly for reflexive verbs:
Elle s'est lavée. She has washed (herself).
Direct object: **s' (se)** = herself, **lavée** agrees with **s'** (fem. sing.).
But: **Elle s'est lavé les mains.** She has washed her hands.
The direct object here is **les mains,** which follows the verb. **S'** (= to herself) is an indirect object. There is no direct object preceding the verb, therefore there is no agreement. Similarly:
Elle s'est dit. She said to herself. **S'** (= to herself) is an indirect object, therefore there is no agreement.
Some reflexive verbs can be used in a reciprocal sense:
Elles se sont dit au revoir. They said goodbye to each other.
Again the preceding object is indirect and there is no agreement.

A   Rewrite the following, making the past participles agree where neces-
     sary:
     1. Elle est (arrivé) hier.
     2. Nous sommes (sorti) de bonne heure.
     3. Les livres sont (tombé) à terre.
     4. Elle s'est (couché) après minuit.
     5. Mon père m'a (appelé) Marie.
     6. Elle s'est (dit) qu'il fallait le faire.
     7. Il a (raconté) les mêmes histoires qu'il avait (raconté) pendant sa
         dernière visite.
     8. Elle s'est (lavé) dans la salle de bains.
     9. Nous sommes (resté) au lit toute la matinée.
     10. Elle a (sorti) son portefeuille de sa poche.

B   Translate, paying special attention to the agreement of the past par-
     ticiples:
     1. John and Mary arrived here this afternoon.
     2. A troop of soldiers had left by air.
     3. He has spoken to her.
     4. They had travelled from land to land.
     5. I didn't break the plate — you broke it!
     6. I did not believe the things he told me.
     7. All the books have disappeared.
     8. I thought that I had lost my ruler, but I found it under the table.
     9. The flowers which she had put in the vase had fallen on the floor.
     10. The water which she brought is not very hot.
     11. The leaves, fallen from the trees, covered the ground.
     12. They often fought each other, but I don't know who used to win.
     13. The old car which my father has painted now sparkles.
     14. I did not post the letter which you gave me because I forgot it.
     15. He has wiped up the ink which he had spilt.

C   Translate, paying special attention to verb tenses:

Helen got up late on Thursday morning. She did not have time to drink
her coffee, because she had arrived at the office late the day before, and
her boss had scolded her. She ran to the bus stop, but the bus had
already left. She could not make up her mind whether it would be
better to wait for the next bus or to go to the office on foot. At that
moment a Peugeot stopped near to her and she saw her boss who waved
to her, but who did not take her with him in his car. Helen was furious
and she decided to go home.

Passive

A verb is said to be *passive* when the action it describes is done to its
subject, e.g. 'The thief was arrested by the policeman.' The object of
the verb in the *active* — 'The policeman arrested the thief' — becomes
the subject of the verb in the passive.
The French passive is formed with the appropriate tense of être + the

past participle. The past participle agrees with the passive subject, e.g.:

La fête a été organisée par les enfants.

The fête was organized by the children.

The passive is less frequently used in French than it is in English. It can be avoided in various ways:

(a) Where the agent or instrument is mentioned, the sentence can be made active:

Les enfants ont organisé la fête.

The children organized the fête.

(b) Where the agent or instrument is not mentioned, **on** can often be used with an active verb:

On a organisé la fête.

The fête has been organized.

On dit qu'il est très riche.

He is said to be very rich.

(c) A reflexive verb can sometimes be used:

Un bruit s'est fait entendre. A noise was heard.

La porte s'ouvre. The door is opened.

In certain cases the French passive cannot be used. A verb can be turned into the passive if, in the active, it takes a direct object, but not if it takes an indirect object.

In an English sentence such as 'The tourist was shown the museum', 'tourist' is an indirect object. Possible translations are:

On a montré le musée au touriste.

Le musée a été montré au touriste.

Where there is no direct object, **on** must be used:

I was told that he was on holiday.

On m'a dit qu'il était en vacances.

A   Translate the following, using the passive in French:
1. The meal will be prepared by the cook.
2. The window was repaired by his neighbour.
3. The cakes have been eaten by the donkey.
4. The new school will be opened by the mayor.
5. The ground has been warmed by the sun.

B   Translate the following English passive sentences, but avoid using the passive in French:
1. A passer-by had been wounded by the explosion.
2. French is spoken here.[1]
3. She is said to be very intelligent.
4. The bell is being rung.[2]
5. The bell has been rung.[2]
   [1] Ici . . . [2] Don't translate 'bell'.

C   Translate:
1. The winner was given a prize.
2. The prisoner was asked many questions.
3. The beggars were offered some bread and cheese.
4. The guest was shown the room.
5. The actor was taught his part.

6. The tourists were sold a map of the town.
7. Waiter! I have been given a bad egg.
8. The Prince was offered the hand of the Princess.
9. The invalid was brought bunches of grapes.
10. I was asked the name of my dentist.

Reflexive verbs

A reflexive verb is one where the direct or indirect object is the same as the subject.

e.g. **Je me lave.** I wash (myself).
    Je me dis. I say to myself.

Reflexive verbs in French may:

(a) express a true reflexive action as in English, e.g. **se défendre**, to defend oneself; **se blesser**, to hurt oneself;

(b) express an action which is really reflexive, but where the reflexive idea is often omitted in English, e.g. **s'habiller**, to dress (oneself); **s'arrêter**, to stop;

(c) express an action thought of as reflexive in French, but not in the English equivalent, e.g. **se demander**, to wonder; **se promener**, to (go for a) walk;

(d) express a reciprocal action, e.g.
    Les deux hommes se regardaient avec curiosité.
    The two men looked at each other with curiosity.

Word order

(a) The reflexive verb is always accompanied by the reflexive pronoun, which is the same whether the object is direct or indirect.

(b) In a simple tense (present, future, conditional or imperfect), the reflexive pronoun normally comes between the subject and the verb:

je **me** lave	nous **nous** lavons
tu **te** laves	vous **vous** lavez
il/elle **se** lave	ils/elles **se** lavent

(c) In a compound tense, the reflexive pronoun comes between the subject and the auxiliary verb. All reflexive verbs are conjugated with **être**:
Elle s'est lavée. She washed herself.
The rules for the agreement of the past participle in reflexive verbs are given above (p. 24).

(d) The reflexive pronoun precedes the infinitive and the present participle:
se laver, to wash oneself
me lavant, washing myself

(e) The reflexive pronoun precedes all other pronoun objects:
Je me le demande. I wonder about it.

(f) In the imperative, the reflexive pronoun follows the verb (see below, p. 28):
lave-toi! lavez-vous!

(g) In questions involving inversion (see p. 35), the reflexive pronoun remains before the verb, although the pronoun subject follows it:
se lave-t-il?

(h) In the negative, the reflexive pronoun always directly follows **ne**:
je ne me suis pas lavé; ne te lave pas! ne se lave-t-il pas?

A   Translate, choosing the appropriate reflexive verb from the following:

s'amuser, se coucher, se blesser, se moquer de, se marier, se promener,
se déshabiller, s'excuser, se baisser, se dépêcher, s'asseoir, se baigner,
s'appeler, s'en aller, se réveiller, se battre.

1. He goes for a walk in the park.
2. My name is Leroy. What's your name?
3. Goodbye! Have a good time!
4. She excused herself and went away.
5. Hurry up and go to bed.
6. I shall undress, and then I shall have a bath.
7. Excuse me sir, I woke up too late.
8. The soldiers fought and wounded each other.
9. In order to sit on this chair you must bend down.
10. He got married and all his friends made fun of him.

Imperative

The imperative is the verb form used to express a command or wish. It
exists only in the 2nd person singular and the 1st and 2nd persons
plural. In most cases these are the same as the corresponding persons in
the present tense, but without the pronoun subject. In all verbs which
have a 2nd person singular ending in **-es**, and also in **aller (vas)** the **-s** is
dropped (unless followed by **-y** or **-en**).

Present tense	Imperative	
tu parles	**parle!**	speak!
nous parlons	**parlons!**	let's speak!
vous parlez	**parlez!**	speak!
tu finis	**finis!**	finish!
nous vendons	**vendons!**	let's sell!
vous buvez	**buvez!**	drink!

In the case of reflexive verbs, as described above (p. 27), the reflexive
pronoun follows the imperative. The pronoun **te**, yourself (sing.)
becomes **toi** when used on its own:
   Lave-toi! Wash yourself!
Any pronoun objects will be attached to the verb by hyphens:
   Donnez-le-lui. Give it to him.
— except in the negative, when all pronoun objects, including reflexive
pronouns, remain in their normal position between the **ne** and the verb:
   Ne le lui donnez pas! Don't give it to him!
   Ne vous levez pas! Don't get up!
There are four verbs which have irregular imperatives:
avoir: aie, ayons, ayez
être: sois, soyons, soyez
savoir: sache, sachons, sachez
vouloir: veuille, veuillons, veuillez

Veuillez vous asseoir is commonly used for *please sit down*. (The **vous** is the reflexive pronoun belonging to **asseoir** — so no hyphen!)

If you wish to say *Let him* or *Let them* do something (3rd persons singular and plural), use the imperative of **laisser**, to let, to permit:

    Laissez-le faire. Let him do it.

A Give the imperative formed from the following present tenses:

  1. Tu donnes.
  2. Vous saisissez.
  3. Nous vendons.
  4. Tu reçois.
  5. Nous mettons.
  6. Vous dites.
  7. Vous faites.
  8. Tu viens.
  9. Nous allons.
10. Nous y allons.
11. Tu t'en vas.
12. Vous vous asseyez.
13. Vous vous taisez.
14. Tu le sais.
15. Vous vous lavez.
16. Tu le manges.
17. Tu en manges.
18. Tu y vas.
19. Vous me le donnez.
20. Nous l'achetons.
21. Vous voulez me suivre.
22. Vous êtes sage.
23. Tu ne me le rends pas.
24. Vous n'avez pas peur.
25. Tu n'es pas si bête.

B. Translate, using singular forms where indicated:

  1. Please sit down.
  2. Give me your cup, please.
  3. Behave yourself!(s)
  4. Look out!
  5. Come in! Don't wait on the landing.
  6. Let her come with us!
  7. Speak more slowly please. Don't speak so fast.
  8. Give me two.[1]
  9. Push. Pull.
10. Shut up and pay attention.(s)
11. Telephone the police.
12. Bring it here.
13. Go away!
14. Go and[2] get the doctor.(s)
15. Come and see this beautiful view.

[1] Don't forget 'en'.
[2] Translate: Go to get . . .

Negation

Non is used for 'no'. **Non**, or **non pas**, can also be used to make elements other than verbs negative:

  Moi, j'étais là, mais non mon frère.
  I was there, but not my brother.

In more familiar language, **pas** is used:
  Moi, j'étais là, mais pas mon frère.

To make a verb negative, **ne** plus a second element is used. The main negative expressions are:

> **ne . . . pas**, not
> **ne . . . point**, not, not at all (less common than **ne . . . pas**)
> **ne . . . jamais**, never
> **ne . . . rien**, nothing, not anything
> **ne . . . guère**, hardly, scarcely
> **ne . . . plus**, no more, no longer
> **ne . . . personne**, no-one, not anyone
> **ne . . . aucun(e)**, no (followed by a noun)
> **ne . . . pas un(e)**, not one
> **ne . . . nulle part**, not anywhere
> **ne . . . nullement**, in no way
> **ne . . . ni . . . ni**, neither . . . nor
> **ne . . . que**, only

With a verb, **ne** must always be used; the second element cannot stand alone. But it may keep its negative force when used without a verb:

> « Qu'est-ce que tu fais?» «Rien.»
> 'What are you doing?' 'Nothing.'
> «Elle est grande, la maison?» «Pas très grande.»
> 'Is the house big?' 'Not very big.'

In a simple tense **ne** and **pas**, etc., are separated by the verb and any pronoun objects:

> **Jean ne le lui donne pas.**
> Jean does not give it to him.

In compound tenses, **ne** plus **pas/point/jamais/rien/guère/plus** or **nulle-ment** are separated by the auxiliary and any pronoun objects:

> **Jean ne le lui a pas donné.**
> Jean has not given it to him.

Personne normally follows the past participle:

> **Je n'y ai vu personne.**
> I saw no-one there.

Aucun, when used as an adjective, precedes the noun it qualifies:

> **Il paraît que je n'ai aucun ami ici.**
> It seems that I have no friend here.

Que precedes the word to which the idea of *only* applies:

> **Il ne m'a donné que dix francs.**
> He gave me only ten francs.

Jamais, rien, personne, aucun, pas un, and **ni** may all begin the sentence, but **ne** must still be used before the verb:

> **Personne n'est arrivé.**
> No-one has arrived.
> **Ni Paul ni son frère ne voulaient la voir.**
> Neither Paul nor his brother wanted to see her.

Where the sense requires, double negatives may be used, e.g. **jamais rien, plus personne.**

> **Il ne fait jamais rien.**
> He never does anything.

A Translate:
1. I have not finished.
2. He is no longer working.
3. We have never eaten snails.
4. They have hardly begun.
5. I saw no one in the street.
6. You will find nothing there.[1]
7. They only ate two.[2]
8. She has no more paper.
9. I have not seen any of the films.
10. Give him neither wine[3] nor beer.

[1] See p. 38 for position of pronouns.   [2] Don't forget en before verb.
[3] No need for de or du after ni.

B Here is a statement made by you to the police. (You were, of course, innocent of any crime!) Unfortunately the typist left out all the negatives. Before you could sign your statement you had to put them in by hand. Here is your statement with blanks: write it out with the blanks suitably filled in with negatives:

Quand je suis entré dans la maison, la lampe . . . était . . . allumée et je . . . pouvais . . . voir. J'étais certain que . . . . . . était arrivé avant moi, et je . . . ai . . . entendu. Soudain, quelqu'un s'est approché de moi; je . . . ai entendu . . . bruit, mais cette personne m'a frappé sur la tête. Dès ce moment-là je . . . savais . . . rien.

C Answer the following questions in French, in the negative. Use pronouns instead of nouns where possible, and use as many different negative forms as possible:
1. Qui est dans le jardin?
2. Avez-vous acheté quelque chose dans la ville?
3. Avez-vous mangé les poires?
4. Est-ce que vous avez jamais visité la Chine?
5. Est-ce que vous parlez le japonais ou l'indonésien?
6. Est-ce que tu vas toujours à l'école?
7. Où est-ce qu'on voit des igloos en Angleterre?
8. Est-ce que l'année est presque finie à la fin de janvier?
9. Qu'est-ce qu'il y a dans une boîte vide?
10. Qui se trouve dans une maison qui n'a pas d'occupant?

Infinitive usage

In English the infinitive is denoted by the word *to*: to speak, to finish, etc. In French the infinitive is denoted by one of the four endings: **-er, -ir, -re** or **-oir**.
(a) The French infinitive is used to translate the English infinitive:
Voyager, c'est apprendre. To travel is to learn.
Note: When, as in this example, the subject and the complement of the verb **être** are both infinitives, **c' (ce)** must be placed before the verb.

(b) The French infinitive is used to translate the English present participle (*-ing*) after all prepositions and prepositional phrases, except **en** (see p. 12):
sans parler, without speaking
au lieu d'écrire, instead of writing
avant de partir, before leaving

(c) **Pour** + infinitive is used to translate *to* meaning *in order to*:
Il se lève de bonne heure pour arriver le premier. He gets up early (in order) to arrive first.

(d) After the preposition **après**, the perfect infinitive, i.e. the infinitive of the auxiliary + the present participle, is used:
après avoir parlé, after speaking, after having spoken
après être parti, after leaving, after having left

(e) The French infinitive is used to translate an English present participle following the main verb of a sentence:
Ils aiment jouer au football. They like playing football.

(f) The French infinitive is used as a verbal noun:
Travailler peut être dangereux. Working can be dangerous.
Some infinitives have become ordinary nouns: **le devoir, le dîner, le pouvoir, le vouloir**, etc. These are always masculine.

Verbs followed by an infinitive

(a) Some verbs are followed by a direct infinitive. These are the modal verbs **devoir, falloir, pouvoir, savoir** and **vouloir**, and a number of verbs expressing the ideas of motion, saying, thinking and wishing, including:

aimer, to like, love (may also take à)	**oser**, to dare
aimer mieux, to prefer	**pouvoir**, to be able, can
aller, to go	**préférer**, to prefer
désirer, to desire, want	**savoir**, to know, to know how to
devoir, to have to, must, owe	**sembler**, to seem
écouter, to listen to	**valoir**, to be worth
entendre, to hear	**(il vaut mieux**, it is better to)
espérer, to hope	**venir**, to come
faire, to do, make	**voir**, to see
falloir, to be necessary	**vouloir**, to wish, want
laisser, to let, permit	

e.g. **Je sais nager.** I can swim.
Ils aiment mieux jouer au tennis. They prefer to play tennis.
Vous devez travailler. You must work.
Je veux chanter. I want to sing.
But note that when there is a change of subject, this construction is not possible:
Je veux qu'il chante. I want him to sing.

(b) Verbs which require **à** before a governed infinitive usually express the idea of intention, purpose, or 'in' or 'by' doing something. The following are important:

apprendre à, to learn (to)

commencer à, to begin (to)
continuer à, to continue (doing)
s'intéresser à, to take an interest (in doing)
se mettre à, to start (to)
s'occuper à, to be busy (at, in, doing something)
servir à, to serve (as, for); to be used as

e.g. **Il s'intéresse à collectioner les timbres.** He is interested in collecting stamps.
Une clef sert à ouvrir et à fermer les portes. A key is used for opening and shutting doors.

Note: **par**, and not **à**, is used after **commencer** when it means to begin *by* doing something:
Il commence la journée par manger le petit déjeuner.
He begins the day by eating breakfast.
Par is similarly used after **finir**:
Il finit la journée par s'endormir.
He finishes the day by going to sleep.

(c) The majority of verbs require **de** before a governed infinitive. This includes most verbs expressing the ideas of ordering, asking and telling; of emotion, fear, regret, joy; of ceasing and refusing; also most impersonal verbs and verbs whose English equivalent is followed by the word *of* or *from*.
Some important examples are:

avoir peur de, to be afraid (of)
s'arrêter de, to stop (doing)
cesser de, to stop (doing)
commander de, to command (to)
décider de, to decide (to)
demander de, to ask (to)
empêcher de, to prevent (from)
essayer de, to try (to)
faire semblant de, to pretend (to)
oublier de, to forget (to)
permettre de, to allow (to)
promettre de, to promise (to)
refuser de, to refuse (to)
remercier de, to thank (for)
tâcher de, to try (to)
il s'agit de, it is a question/matter (of doing)
il est temps de, it is time (to)
il importe de, it is important (to)

Note also the special meaning of **venir** followed by **de** + infinitive:
venir de, to have just (done something).

e.g. **Il décide de partir demain.** He decides to leave tomorrow.
Il s'agit de payer la note. It is a matter of paying the bill.
Je vais tâcher de répondre immédiatement. I am going to try to answer at once.
Nous venons de voir la pièce. We have just seen the play.

A   Complete the following sentences with **à** or **de** where necessary:
1. Ils ont refusé . . . nous aider.
2. Michel veut . . . venir avec nous.
3. Elle fait semblant . . . être malade.
4. Il commence . . . pleuvoir; nous devrons . . . rester à la maison.
5. Il vaut mieux . . . essayer . . . le faire.
6. Avez-vous décidé . . . accepter son offre?
7. Pendant les vacances ils ont appris . . . faire du ski.
8. Venez . . . voir le jardin.
9. J'ai demandé à Marie . . . faire mes courses.
10. Permettez-moi . . . vous aider . . . porter vos valises.

B   Translate:
1. I learnt to swim last year.
2. We are going to visit the museum this afternoon.
3. He's afraid of losing.
4. I'm interested in collecting old bottles.
5. The teacher has forgotten to bring his glasses.
6. I prefer not to help them.
7. It is better to say nothing.
8. They will come tomorrow to mend the lift.
9. Start by reading this file, then you will meet the client.
10. I don't dare let him use my motor-bike.

Verb + object + infinitive

When a verb is followed by a direct object plus an infinitive, **à** usually precedes the infinitive:

> He helps his sister (to) find her pen. **Il aide sa sœur à trouver son stylo.** (Note: in English the *to* may be omitted — in French the **à** cannot.)

If, however, a verb is followed by an indirect object preceded by **à**, the infinitive is normally preceded by **de**:

> He asks his wife to shut the door. **Il demande à sa femme de fermer la porte.**

A   Using the information above, translate:
1. He asks his father to give him a bike.
2. His father forbids him to ride his motor-bike.
3. I have my homework to finish.
4. She has promised her daughter to give her a new dress.
5. You are invited to dine at our house.

B   Translate:

Paul was learning to play the trumpet. He played very badly. As soon as he started to play, his family tried to prevent him from continuing. His mother pretended to have a headache, his father asked him to go and run some errand, and his sister told him that she could not endure the noise. But Paul refused to listen to them; he hoped to become a great musician one day.

Interrogative

To interrogate is to ask questions. In French, questions can be asked in three ways:

(a) In everyday speech a question can be asked simply by using the same words as in a normal statement, but with a rising intonation: **Vous vous en allez déjà?** Are you going already?

(b) Also common in speech is the use of **est-ce que** before a statement to change it into a question, e.g.:
Tu viens avec nous → **Est-ce que tu viens avec nous?** Are you coming with us?
Je dois partir → **Est-ce que je dois partir?** Must I leave?

(c) A question can be formed by putting the subject pronoun after the verb, to which it is then joined by a hyphen. This is known as *inversion*. Inversion in the 1st person singular is rare, except for the special form from **pouvoir: puis-je?** It can, however, be used in all other persons.
Venez-vous? Are you coming?
A-t-il de l'argent? Has he any money?
Note that -t- is inserted after a verb ending in a vowel, when it is followed by **il, elle,** or **on.**
When the subject of the verb is a noun and inversion is used, the noun remains before the verb and the appropriate pronoun is inserted after it:
Jean travaille-t-il? Is Jean working?
Where inversion is used in a negative question, the **ne** remains before the verb, and the **pas,** or other element of the negative, follows the attached pronoun:
N'avez-vous pas mangé? Haven't you eaten?
Jean n'a-t-il rien mangé? Hasn't Jean eaten anything?
(Other ways of asking questions are dealt with later: p. 88.)

A Translate each of the following sentences twice, using different interrogative forms:
1. Are you coming?
2. Have you any change?
3. Do you know the time?
4. Can I leave the room, please?
5. Does John know how to drive?
6. Do you speak English, Madam?
7. Haven't you finished your homework?
8. Would you mind[1] opening the door?
9. Did you find my pen?
10. Could you[2] do this for me?

[1] polite form: conditional of **vouloir**   [2] polite form: conditional of **pouvoir**

B Write in French questions to which the following could be the answers:
1. Oui, je viens.
2. Non, il ne peut pas le faire.
3. Oui, mais dépêche-toi!

4. Pas beaucoup — un tout petit peu, Monsieur.
5. Pas encore: je vais apprendre pendant les grandes vacances.
6. Si, j'ai mangé à midi.
7. Mais oui, je vous reconnais très bien.
8. J'espère le finir dans une heure.
9. Oui, ils travaillent dans le jardin.
10. Non, pas les pommes; mais j'aime bien les poires.

Inversion after speech

When spoken words are quoted, inversion is required in French for phrases such as *he says*, *John asked*, etc., when these follow any of the words spoken:
« Venez avec moi », dit-il.
« Oui », répond Jean, « c'est bien ça. »
« Qu'est-ce que c'est? » demande-t-elle.
Remember that -t- must be inserted between a verb ending in a vowel and a pronoun beginning with a vowel.
In the perfect tense, a pronoun will follow the auxiliary verb:
« Je viens tout de suite », a-t-elle répondu.
« Il faut le faire », s'est-il dit.
A person's name or other noun, however, will follow the past participle:
« Je viens tout de suite », a répondu la jeune fille.
« Il faut le faire », s'est dit Pierre.

A   Translate, paying attention to necessary inversion. In the past use the perfect.
1. 'Good', he says.
2. 'Never!' he answered.
3. 'And you?' he asks.
4. 'Are you coming?' she asked.
5. 'Quietly!' she whispered.
6. 'I must try', he said to himself.
7. 'Not yet!' they cried.
8. 'It's too dangerous', I thought.
9. 'Come here!' the door-keeper ordered.
10. 'And you too!' Pierre replied.

B   Translate, paying attention to necessary inversion. In the past use the perfect.
1. 'When are you coming?' Marie asked.
2. 'Eat it!' my mother ordered me.
3. 'Kill him!' ordered the general.
4. 'I don't want to do it!' she exclaimed.
5. 'I don't know yet', Georges confessed to me.
6. 'May I go out?' Pierre asked the master.
7. 'It's still much too dangerous', I told myself once more.
8. 'Quietly! Don't make a noise', I told them in a low voice.
9. 'Oh yes, I do — I understand very well', I contradicted.
10. 'Who is it? What's the matter?' Charles asked himself.

Look for the hidden catch

There is a hidden catch in many verbs, both in French and in English. Some French verbs need to be followed by a preposition (**dans, à**, etc.) where we have none; and equally, some English verbs are followed by a preposition (usually *for*) where the French verbs have none.

Among the latter are:
to look for, **chercher** (quelque chose)
to wait for, **attendre** (quelque chose)
to pay for, **payer** (quelque chose)
to look at, **regarder** (quelque chose)
to listen to, **écouter** (quelqu'un; quelque chose)
to ask for, **demander** (quelque chose)
When using **demander** the thing asked for is the direct object, with no preposition; the person of whom the thing is asked is preceded by **à**:
Il demande une pomme à la dame. He asks the lady for an apple.

Important verbs which take a direct object in English but need a preposition in French include:
to enter, **entrer dans** (a building, room, etc.), **chez** (someone)
          entrer à (become a member of, e.g. entrer au collège)
to obey, **obéir à** (quelqu'un; similarly désobéir à . . .)
to allow, **permettre à** (quelqu'un . . . de faire quelque chose)
to answer, **répondre à** (quelqu'un; à une lettre, à une question etc.)
to telephone, **téléphoner à** (quelqu'un)
to need, **avoir besoin de** (quelque chose; faire quelque chose)
to approach, **s'approcher de** (quelqu'un, quelque chose)

A   Translate:

I was approaching a hotel in Paris when a man who was looking at a map stopped me and said:
   'Excuse me, sir. I am looking for a chemist's.'
   'Take the first street on the right and the second on the left.'
   He thanked me and he left. A moment later I entered the hotel and asked the receptionist for a room.
   'Yes sir,' said the receptionist, 'but you must pay for it now.'
   'Why?' I asked him.
   'Because there are so many people who leave without paying.'
   I told him I would take the room, and I asked him for the key. Before going upstairs, I phoned my office, and then I had to wait for the lift. I could hear the radio in the big sitting-room. I wanted to listen to the music, but first I needed to rest.

Pronouns

Conjunctive pronouns

Pronouns replace nouns. Their use avoids unnecessary repetition and makes what we say much shorter. Pronouns used with a verb are called conjunctive pronouns. They normally precede the verb (or the auxiliary in a compound tense) in the order shown below:

1	2*	3	4	5	6	7	8	9*	10
je		me							
tu		te							
il		se	le	lui					
elle		se	la	lui				pas,	
(on)	ne	se			y	en	verb (or	rien,	(past
nous		nous					auxiliary)	jamais,	participle)
vous		vous						etc.	
ils		se	les	leur					
elles		se	les	leur					

*Columns 2 and 9 apply if the sentence is in the negative.

Notes

Only one word from any one column can be used at one time.

Column 1: These are the *subject* pronouns, and they may be replaced by a noun. The verb must agree with its subject.

Column 2: In a negative sentence, **ne** directly follows the subject. When there is no subject, as in an imperative, or when the subject pronoun follows the verb, as in a question, **ne** comes first.

Column 3: These pronouns are used for both direct and indirect objects. They can all be used as reflexive pronouns to mean *myself, to myself*, etc., as well as *me, to me*, etc., but **se** is always reflexive (himself, themselves, to himself, to themselves etc.). After a verb in the imperative, **me, te** and **se** become **-moi, -toi** and **-soi**.

Column 4: These are direct objects: **le** = him or it, m; **la** = her or it, f; **les** = them, m. or f. They do not combine with **de**: **Il vient de le faire.** He has just done it.

Column 5: These are indirect objects: **lui** = to him, to her, to it; **leur** = to them. They are used mainly of persons, and replace à plus a noun object, e.g. **Il parle à mon père**, He speaks to my father, becomes **Il lui parle**, He speaks to him.

Column 6: Y = there, in that place, to that place, etc. **Il va à Paris**, He goes to Paris, becomes **Il y va**, He goes there. Y is also used after **penser** to express *to think about* (a thing): **Je pense à**

mon voyage, I am thinking about my journey, becomes **J'y pense**, I think about it.

Column 7:   **En** is used to replace **de** plus a noun when **de** includes the idea '*of*'. **Il mange des pommes**, He eats some apples, becomes **Il en mange**, He eats some (of them). Like **y, en** is used only of things, not persons.

Column 8:   Wherever the verb comes in a simple tense, the auxiliary will come in a compound tense.

Column 9:   When the second element of a negative follows the verb, then in a compound tense this will normally follow the auxiliary: for exceptions see p. 30.

Column 10: In a compound tense, the past participle comes last. The past participle must agree with a preceding direct object (**la** or **les**) but it does not agree with the indirect objects **lui** and **leur**, or with **y** and **en**.

For the position of pronouns in the imperative, see p. 28. For inversion in questions see p. 35, and after speech, p. 36.

A   Rewrite the following in French, replacing the nouns or nouns + adjectives in italics by pronouns and making the past participle agree where necessary:

Monsieur Dubois voulait laver sa voiture. *Monsieur Dubois* avait décrotté *sa voiture*. Il a appelé son fils Pierre, et il a demandé *à Pierre* de chercher de l'eau chaude. Pierre est allé à la maison. *Pierre* a trouvé *dans la maison de l'eau chaude*. *Pierre* a rapporté *l'eau chaude* à son père.

    A ce moment Madame Dubois a appelé *Monsieur Dubois et Pierre*.

    — Venez vite, a dit *Madame Dubois*; la soupe est chaude. *La soupe* est sur la table. Il faut vite venir manger *de la soupe*. *La soupe* est si bonne.

B   Answer the following questions using pronouns wherever possible. Remember to make past participles agree where necessary.
1. Où est-ce qu'on achète de la viande?
2. Est-ce que vous avez vu la lune?
3. Est-ce qu'on donne de l'argent au marchand quand on achète quelque chose?
4. Est-ce qu'on peut acheter des choux chez le fruitier?
5. Combien de jours y a-t-il dans une semaine?
6. Avez-vous compté les étoiles?
7. Parlez-vous souvent à votre meilleur ami?
8. Est-ce qu'on peut entendre le silence?
9. Avez-vous jamais goûté la bière?
10. Est-ce que votre famille a visité la France pendant l'été dernier?

C   Translate:
1. Give it (f) back to me: I bought it.
2. Did you find them (f) in the drawer?
3. We have got six of them. How many did you buy?
4. The two ladies walked there with their dogs.

5. Give it (m) to me: I want to eat some of it.
6. Why did Georges put them (f) there?
7. I'm not going to give it to them.
8. No one lives there any longer.
9. Go away! Don't touch them!
10. I asked him what he thought of it.

D   Translate:

'Can you take me into town this afternoon, Michèle?'

'Yes, I'm going anyway. What do you want to do there?'

'I've got to go to Jean-Luc's to pick up my books. I left them there last week. Jean-Luc wanted to borrow them and he promised to give them back to me, but now I need them, and I haven't seen him and I can't phone him.'

'Hasn't he got a phone?'

'No, he hasn't got one and he doesn't want one. He says that a phone would disturb him when he's trying to work.'

'Right, let's go.'

Disjunctive pronouns

Disjunctive or *emphatic* pronouns are those used apart from the verb. Their forms are as follows:

Subject pronoun	Disjunctive pronoun
je	moi
tu	toi
il	lui
elle	elle
nous	nous
vous	vous
ils	eux
elles	elles

The reflexive form is soi.

Disjunctive pronouns are used:
(a) after a preposition or after comme:
   sans moi, without me
   comme lui, like him
   chez eux, at their house
   pour soi, for oneself
(b) for emphasis, in addition to or instead of the normal pronoun:
   Moi, je ne le fais jamais.
   I never do it.
(c) alone or as the complement of the verb être:
   Qui l'a dit? Moi.
   Who said it? I did.

C'est lui qui a voulu venir.
He's the one who wanted to come.
(d) in comparisons:
   Je suis plus fort que lui.
   I am stronger than he is.
(e) as the double subject of a verb:
   Vous et moi, nous allons réussir.
   You and I are going to succeed.
(f) with the addition of **-même(s)** to mean *self*(*selves*):
   Je le ferai moi-même.
   I shall do it myself.

A   Translate:
   1. After you, gentlemen.
   2. They work for us.
   3. Go without me.
   4. We want to come with you (s).
   5. We sing like them (f).
   6. They work for him.
   7. Think of me.
   8. You are as stupid as they (m) are.
   9. As for me, I shall not come back.
  10. *We* are rich.

B   Translate:
   1. 'Is it you?' 'Yes, it's me.'
   2. Why me? Why not her?
   3. He and I can do it together.
   4. You and I will mend it ourselves.
   5. One cannot do it oneself.
   6. The mothers teach their children themselves.
   7. He thinks about her but she doesn't think about him.
   8. Behind you, ladies, you will see a portrait of the King himself.
   9. 'Who has broken the window — you?' 'No, Daddy, not me.'
  10. He himself would not dare to say it.

C   Translate this conversation between friends:
'You're going to pay.'
'Who? Me?'
'Yes, you!'
'Why not him?'
'Because he's going to pay for her.'
'For her? She never pays. It's always us, isn't it?'
'Not us, this time — just you!'

Articles

Unless clearly defined by a demonstrative adjective (**ce, cet, cette, ces**) or by a possessive adjective (**mon, ton, son**, etc.), a noun in French must normally be preceded by an article, either definite, indefinite or partitive, as explained below.

No article is used:
(a) when speaking of someone's profession or state in life:
Il est étudiant. He is a student.
Son frère est devenu médecin. His brother became a doctor.
(b) in many set phrases and adverbial expressions:
sans peine, without difficulty
en hiver, in winter
(c) before nouns in apposition:
Monsieur Dufrais, directeur de la société.
Monsieur Dufrais, manager of the company.
(d) in exclamations:
Quelle idée! What an idea!

1. The *definite article* has the forms **le, la, les**. Preceded by the prepositions **à** or **de**, these become **au, à la, aux** or **du, de la, des**.

The definite article is used:
(a) as the equivalent of the English *the*, showing that the noun refers to a particular object or objects:
Les deux garçons ont pris le cheval.
The two boys took the horse.
(b) when speaking of the noun in a general sense, i.e. as a class:
Les chiens poursuivent les chats. Dogs chase cats.
Le pouvoir corrompt. Power corrupts.
(c) before the names of countries, continents, provinces, mountains, rivers and seas:
la France, le Japon, les États-Unis, la Bretagne, les Alpes, la Seine
(d) before the names of languages:
le français, l'anglais, le japonais
(but the article is usually omitted after **parler: Je parle français.**)
(e) before proper names preceded by a title or an adjective:
le président de Gaulle, le pauvre petit Pierre
(f) before parts of the body, where English uses the possessive adjective (see p. 64):
Elle a ouvert les yeux. She opened her eyes.
(g) to form the superlative (see p. 62).

2. The *indefinite article* has the forms **un** and **une** for singular nouns. These correspond to the English *a*, meaning that the noun represents one of its particular species or type. The plural form is **des**, corresponding to the English *some* or *any*.
J'ai acheté un melon et des pommes.
I bought a melon and some apples.

3. The *partitive article* has the forms **du, de la, des**. It corresponds to the English *some* or *any* as in 'I have some wine; have you any beer?', indicating that what the noun describes is present in an indefinite quantity. The words *some* and *any* are sometimes omitted in English, but the partitive article must not be omitted in French:

Il y a des pommes dans le placard.
There are apples in the cupboard.

In certain cases **de** must be used on its own. These are:

(a) after a negative:
Il n'a pas de pain.
He hasn't any bread.
(b) after an adverb of quantity such as **beaucoup, assez, tant, peu:**
Il a beaucoup de livres.
He has many books.
(c) in careful French, when an adjective precedes the noun:
Il y a de belles fleurs dans le parc.
There are some beautiful flowers in the park.

Du, de la and **des** are however also found in this construction, especially where the adjective and noun are frequently used together, e.g.:

des petits pois, peas
des jeunes filles, girls
de la bonne soupe, good soup

A Rewrite the following, putting the correct form of the article, with **à** or **de** if necessary, in place of the dots. If nothing is needed, put nothing:
1. . . . pluie tombe rarement sur . . . désert.
2. J'aime bien . . . thé, mais je préfère . . . café.
3. Son père est . . . marin, et sa mère est . . . infirmière . . . hôpital.
4. Quand . . . voiture roule, . . . roues tournent.
5. Elle s'assied sur une . . . chaises . . . premier rang.
6. . . . photographe a . . . appareil très moderne.
7. Il y a beaucoup . . . jolies maisons dans . . . village.
8. . . . tour . . . église se voit de loin.
9. D'habitude . . . gens boivent . . . lait . . . vaches.
10. Manger . . . ongles est . . . mauvaise habitude.

B Translate:
1. The brother and sister can both drive, but the family has no car.
2. Some children were playing football in the playground.
3. The cook makes cakes with flour, eggs and sugar.
4. There is snow on the top of the mountain, but there is no snow in the valley.
5. He speaks English and he is learning French.
6. King Henri II reigned from 1547–1559.
7. Poor little Marie-Louise: she doesn't like school!
8. Paris is the capital of France; it is a very beautiful town.
9. He goes to the restaurant at the corner of the street.
10. Modern aeroplanes can carry many passengers.

C   Translate:
Yesterday evening, while I was watching the TV news, the door bell
rang. I opened the door and saw an old woman with a big basket. I
asked her what she wanted. She told me she had some fruit to sell —
some apples, some good pears and a lot of the best cherries.
I bought the apples and a few pears, but I did not buy any cherries. I do
not like cherries.

Nouns

Gender Problems

In French all nouns, including those which refer to inanimate objects, are either masculine or feminine in gender. There is no neuter 'it' as far as nouns are concerned.

Since it is impossible to write or speak French correctly if wrong genders are used, it is essential to know whether a noun is masculine or feminine.

There is only one completely safe way to learn genders: always learn a noun together with its article, **le** or **la**, or if the noun starts with a vowel or h-mute, **un** or **une**.

There are a number of rules which can be used as guides. Unfortunately none of them are without exceptions, and in learning the rules the most common exceptions must also be learnt.

Persons

Nouns which refer to persons cause little difficulty. A noun which normally refers to a male person is nearly always masculine; a noun which normally refers to a female person is nearly always feminine:

le garçon, the boy
le soldat, the soldier
la fille, the girl
la bonne, the maid-servant
Among the few exceptions note: **la sentinelle**, the sentry.

Many nouns referring to persons have both a masculine and a feminine form. Sometimes the feminine is the masculine form with a feminine ending; sometimes the two words are completely different. The most important are:

un acteur, actor	**une actrice**, actress
un ami, friend, boy-friend	**une amie**, friend, girl-friend
un compagnon, companion	**une compagne**, (female) companion
un duc, duke	**une duchesse**, duchess
un étudiant, student	**une étudiante**, (female) student
un fils, son	**une fille**, daughter
un garçon, boy	**une jeune fille**, girl
un garçon, waiter	**une serveuse**, waitress
un grand-père, grandfather	**une grand-mère**, grandmother
un héros (le héros), hero	**une héroïne (l'héroïne)**, heroine
un homme, man	**une femme**, woman
un maître, (school) master	**une maîtresse**, (school) mistress
un mari, husband	**une femme**, wife
Monsieur, sir	**Madame**, madam
un monsieur, gentleman	**une dame**, lady
un muet, dumb person (m)	**une muette**, dumb person (f)

un **neveu**, nephew	une **nièce**, niece
un **oncle**, uncle	une **tante**, aunt
un **paysan**, peasant	une **paysanne**, peasant woman
un **pêcheur**, fisherman	une **pêcheuse**, fisherwoman, fisherman's wife
un **père**, father	une **mère**, mother
un **prince**, prince	une **princesse**, princess
un **roi**, king	une **reine**, queen
un **serviteur**, servant	une **servante, une bonne**, female servant
un **vieillard**, old man	une **vieille**, old woman

Words ending in **-er** change this to **-ère**, as in:

un **boulanger**, baker	une **boulangère**, baker woman
un **fermier**, farmer	une **fermière**, farmer's wife

and many words ending in **-eur** change this to **-euse**:

un **danseur**, dancer	une **danseuse**, female dancer
un **voyageur**, traveller	une **voyageuse**, female traveller

If the noun ends in **-e**, only the article changes:

un **touriste**, tourist   une **touriste**, a female tourist

The ending also remains the same for **enfant**:

un **enfant**, child   une **enfant**, female child

Words which formerly referred only to men, but which nowadays may refer to women, frequently have only a masculine form:

un **auteur**, author

un **médecin**, physician, medical doctor

un **professeur**, teacher

Un bébé, a baby, is also always masculine in grammar whatever it may be in reality; and **une personne**, a person, is always feminine.

Animals

A few common and domestic animals have feminine forms in everyday use; but often the male word is used for both as in:

un **chat**, cat	une **chatte**
un **cheval**, horse	une **jument**, mare
un **chien**, dog	une **chienne**

In common use are:

un **bœuf**, bullock, ox	une **vache**, cow
(un **taureau** = bull for breeding, bull-fights)	
un **coq**, cock	une **poule**, hen
un **lion**, lion	une **lionne**, lioness
un **tigre**, tiger	une **tigresse**, tigress

The majority of animals have only one gender, regardless of sex:

une **souris**, mouse

un **rat**, rat

Genders from endings

If you have to guess the gender of a noun, the ending may often act as a guide. The following are the most helpful:

(a) Masculine — words ending in:
   -age: le village, le voyage, le courage
       exceptions: la plage, la nage, la page (of book), une image, la
           cage, la rage
   -eau and most other words ending in a pronounced vowel: le bateau,
       un oiseau, le café, le pneu
       exceptions: l'eau (f), la peau, la radio, and abbreviations of
           feminine nouns: une auto, la moto, etc.
   -ment: le commencement, le serment
       exception: la jument

(b) Feminine — words ending in:
   -sion, -tion, -xion, -çon, -son: la mission, la nation, la façon,
       la chanson
       exceptions: le poison, le poisson
   -ée: la journée, la fée
       exceptions: le lycée, le musée
   -ance, -anse, -ence: la chance, la danse, la patience
       exception: le silence
   and words ending in a double consonant + e: une assiette, la bouteille
       exceptions: le beurre, le télégramme, le verre, le tonnerre, le mille

The exceptions given are a selection only: make a note of any others
you come across.

A   The gender of the following words is often mistaken. Write them out
   with **un** or **une** before them:
   honneur, peur, personne, malheur, bonheur, prix, paix, beurre, groupe,
   verre, terre, sentence, silence, étage, encre, village, plage, rage, couleur,
   problème, reste, légume, pouce, tour=*tower*, tour=*turn*, radio=*radio
   receiver*, livre=*book*, livre=*pound (weight or money)*, poste=*position*,
   (radio)set, poste=*mail*.

B   Translate:
   The King sent a servant to fetch the Duke's daughter. The young girl
   arrived accompanied by her mother.
       'Your daughter must marry my son, the Prince', the King said to the
   Duchess. 'Then she will become Queen one day.'
       The Duchess knew that her daughter did not like the Prince, who
   was ugly and very fat. So she went to see her friend, the Queen.
       'My daughter does not want to marry the Prince', the Duchess ex-
   plained. 'She loves an actor, and wants to become an actress. The idea
   of becoming a queen or even a duchess does not please her.'
       'I understand', said the Queen. 'But the King is an old man, and he
   does not understand young people. He has forgotten that I was the
   daughter of a peasant, and that my niece is a farmer's wife. I was a
   dancer: it was only after I married my husband that I was given the title
   of princess.'
       'It seems to me, Madam,' the Duchess said, 'that life is easier for the
   man-servant who loves a maid-servant, or for a peasant who loves a
   peasant woman, than it is for the ladies and gentlemen of the Court.'
       'That's true,' said the Queen, 'but there will always be girls who

would love to become the wife of a prince — as if every prince was handsome and charming and very, very rich!'

Compound nouns

The English often join together two nouns to make a compound word or use a noun as an adjective, as in 'exercise book'. The French prefer to link the descriptive noun to the main word by means of a preposition: **un cahier de devoirs**. But they do sometimes link a verb or an adjective to a noun with a hyphen to make a 'double-barrelled' noun, as in **un porte-crayons**, a pencil case.

When a preposition is used, it is very often **à**, which may mean *with*, *for*, *worked by*, *in*, *at* etc., or **de** which usually means *made of* or *of*, but can also mean *for*:

e.g. **une locomotive à vapeur**, a steam engine
     une carte à jouer, a playing card
     un chemin de fer, a railway
     une carte d'identité, an identity card

Words linked by hyphens are normally masculine, whatever the gender of the second part when used alone; words linked by **à** or **de** have the gender of the first noun.

A   Here is a French 'word kit'. It gives all the necessary components to make up the equivalents of the English words listed below. Words are repeated the exact number of times you will need them. Genders are shown by the indefinite article, and hyphens have been attached to the appropriate elements:

Your 'kit' consists of the following:
à, à, à, à, à, aux, de, de, de, de, de, de, -de-, d', d', -en-, un porte-, un porte-, un porte, une salle, une salle, une salle, une salle, une arme, un bateau, un bateau, une boîte, un agent, un bureau, une agence, une chambre, un bain, une montre, un arc, un rouge-, au rez, attente, bains, change, chaussée, ciel, classe, coucher, feuille, gorge, lettres, manger, monnaie, or, feu, plume, police, soleil, vapeur, voiles, voyages

The words to put into French are:

1. a wallet	11. a sailing-ship
2. a letter-box	12. a penholder
3. a purse	13. a robin (redbreast)
4. a steamship	14. a waiting-room
5. a rainbow	15. a gold watch
6. a firearm	16. a policeman
7. a classroom	17. a sun bath
8. a dining-room	18. a bedroom
9. on the ground floor	19. a travel agent's
(at street level)	20. an exchange office (for
10. a bathroom	changing money)

Plurals

Nouns and adjectives form their plurals in the same way. Adjectives must be plural when the noun they qualify is plural.

(a) The plural is normally formed by adding -s, as in English.
le grand arbre, big tree: **les grands arbres**

(b) Words ending in -s, -x, -z do not change:
un nez, nose: **des nez**
un prix bas, low price: **des prix bas**

(c) Words ending in -au and -eu add -x:
l'eau, water: **les eaux**
le feu, fire: **les feux**
exceptions: le pneu, tyre: **les pneus**
bleu, blue: **bleus**

(d) Words ending in -ou normally add -s:
fou, fool, foolish: **fous**
exceptions: le genou, knee: **les genoux**
le chou, cabbage: **les choux**
le bijou, jewel: **les bijoux**

(e) Words ending in -al change this to -aux:
le cheval, horse: **les chevaux**
le mal, ill, pain: **les maux**
exceptions: le bal, ball (dance): **les bals**
fatal, fatal: **fatals**

(f) Words ending in -ail normally add -s:
le détail, detail: **les détails**
exception: le travail, work: **les travaux**

(g) Note the following irregular plurals:
un œil, eye: **les yeux**
le ciel, sky: **les cieux**
monsieur, **messieurs**; madame, **mesdames**; mademoiselle, **mesdemoiselles**; un grand-père, des **grands-pères**
NB: une grand-mère, **des grand-mères**

(h) When speaking of a family by their surname, the plural is shown by the article **les**; no -s is added to the name itself:
Monsieur Duroy est . . . Mr Duroy is . . .
Les Duroy sont . . . The Duroys are . . .

(i) For compound nouns the meaning must be taken as a guide:
rainbows, **des arcs-en-ciel** (several 'bows' but still only one sky);
farmyards, **des basses-cours** (both plural because the first half is an adjective agreeing with a plural noun).
In compound nouns, only such parts as are themselves nouns or adjectives can be turned into the plural where the sense allows: any element which is a verb, preposition or adverb will not vary.

(j) In the singular of œuf, egg, bœuf, bull, and os, bone, the final consonant is sounded: in the plural the final -fs of œufs and bœufs, and the -s of les os, are not sounded.

(k) When a number of persons each have only one of something, or when only one part of the body for each person is referred to, the French use the singular where the English use the plural:

Tous les spectateurs ont jeté leur chapeau en l'air.
All the spectators threw their hats into the air.
Plusieurs des enfants ont levé la main.
Several of the children put up their hands (i.e. one hand each).

A   Put the following into the plural, as far as the sense allows:

Quand je voulais aller du côté de Lyon pour rendre visite à Lebrun, j'y suis toujours allé à cheval, même si le cheval gris était fatigué. Il me fallait prendre avec moi un vêtement chaud, peut-être un vieil anorak bleu, pour le fils de Lebrun, ou bien un blue-jean, car Lebrun était très pauvre, et il souffrait toujours du froid pendant l'hiver interminable. Je me rappelle très bien le nez rouge de l'enfant qui guettait mon arrivée derrière la vitre de la fenêtre de la chaumière.

B   Translate:
1. The two old men were reading French newspapers.
2. The actress was wearing magnificent jewels: rings, bracelets and a diamond necklace.
3. The horses were racing through the fields and over the streams.
4. My nephews are twins and have black hair.
5. I cannot remember all the details of the plan.
6. Two of the children had red faces.
7. Both my grandmothers were very beautiful.
8. In the market I bought two cauliflowers and three cabbages.
9. Please put the wine-glasses on the table, and look for the corkscrews.
10. I met the Lecomtes at a party last week.

Adjectives

Adjectives describe nouns or pronouns. They must agree with the noun or pronoun they qualify in gender and number.

Feminine of adjectives

(a) When an adjective ends in -e it remains the same whatever the gender of the noun, e.g.:
drôle, comic, funny
tranquille, quiet
triste, sad
Otherwise, to make an adjective feminine, the basic rule is to add -e:
grand, big: grande

(b) Adjectives ending in -x change this to -se:
furieux, furious: furieuse
exceptions: doux, soft, sweet, quiet: douce
faux, false: fausse

(c) Adjectives ending in -er change this to -ère:
dernier, last: dernière; cher, dear: chère

(d) Adjectives ending in -el or -il change this to -elle or -ille:
cruel, cruel: cruelle; gentil, kind: gentille

(e) Adjectives ending in -f change this to -ve:
neuf, new (i.e. brand new): neuve

(f) The following have not only irregular feminine forms but also a special masculine singular form which is used before a vowel or an h-mute:
beau, handsome, beautiful: bel, belle
fou, mad, foolish: fol, folle
mou, soft: mol, molle
nouveau, new (another): nouvel, nouvelle
vieux, old: vieil, vieille

(g) the following irregular feminine forms should be known:
ancien, old, ancient: ancienne
bas, low: basse
blanc, white: blanche
bon, good: bonne
frais, fresh: fraîche
gras, fatty: grasse
gros, fat: grosse
long, long: longue
muet, dumb: muette
public, public: publique
sec, dry: sèche
secret, secret: secrète
un tel, such a: une telle.

For the plural of adjectives, see p. 49.

Position of adjectives

(a) Certain common adjectives normally precede the noun. These are: beau, bon, court, grand, gros, haut, jeune, joli, long, mauvais, méchant, meilleur, moindre, petit, pauvre, vaste, vieux, vilain.

(b) Adjectives of nationality, shape, colour and taste follow the noun: **un homme anglais, une table ronde, une poire verte**

Adjectives of nationality include:

allemand	German	gallois	Welsh
anglais	English	grec, greque	Greek
américain	American	indien, -nne	Indian
australien	Australian	irlandais	Irish
belge	Belgian	japonais	Japanese
britannique	British	norvégien, -nne	Norwegian
canadien, -nne	Canadian	polonais	Polish
chinois	Chinese	portugais	Portuguese
danois	Danish	russe	Russian
écossais	Scotch, Scottish	suédois	Swedish
espagnol	Spanish	suisse	Swiss
français	French	turc, turque	Turkish

Note: **un homme danois**, a Danish man
but **un Danois** (with capital letter), a Dane
The feminine form of the above remains the same for words ending in **-e**; other words add **-e** unless otherwise shown.

(c) Some adjectives change their meaning with their position:

mon **ancienne** maison	my former house
une maison **ancienne**	an old house
un **certain** homme	a certain man (some man or other)
un homme **certain**	a certain man (sure of himself)
un **cher** ami	a dear (beloved) friend
un livre **cher**	a dear (expensive) book
la **dernière** année	the last year (of a series/of the war etc.)
l'année **dernière**	last year (the one before this one)
un **grand** homme	a great man
un homme **grand**	a tall man
un **méchant** garçon	a naughty boy
un chien **méchant**	a savage (ill-tempered, evil) dog
un **nouveau** stylo	a new (= newly bought) pen
un stylo **nouveau**	a new kind of pen
un **pauvre** homme	a poor (to be pitied, wretched) man
un homme **pauvre**	a poor (without money) man
mes **propres** mains	my own hands
mes mains **propres**	my clean hands
un **simple** soldat	a simple soldier (nothing more in rank)
un soldat **simple**	a simple-minded soldier
une **triste** personne	a wretched (despicable) person
une personne **triste**	a sad (unhappy) person.

The position of an adjective may also be changed for emphasis, euphony or effect.

(d) When more than one adjective qualifies the same noun, the normal position before or after the noun is usually retained and their order is that which best suits the meaning:
un bon petit livre français
If style or emphasis requires it, all the adjectives may follow the noun, using **et** where necessary:
une femme suédoise, grande et élégante

(e) When one adjective is used to qualify more than one singular noun it is used in the plural. If both these nouns are masculine it will be masculine plural:
un père et un fils cruels, a cruel father and son
If both nouns are feminine the adjective will be feminine plural. When there is a noun of each gender, however, the masculine noun is normally placed next to the adjective, which is then masculine plural:
Il s'est cassé la jambe et le bras droits. He broke his right leg and arm.

A Rewrite the following sentences, putting the adjectives before or after the nouns and making them agree, as required:

1. Je crois qu'il est acteur: c'est un (homme/beau) en tout cas.
2. Les (enfants/méchant) étaient poursuivis par le (chien/méchant).
3. C'est un (homme/brave); il fait ce qu'il peut pour aider les (gens/pauvre).
4. Le (chat/pauvre) allait se noyer, mais la (fille/jeune/allemand) l'a sauvé.
5. La (dame/vieux/danois) habite une (maison/ancien) à la campagne.
6. Elle portait une (robe/joli/bleu) quand elle est allée voir une (amie/cher).
7. J'ai passé la (année/dernier) de mes études en France.
8. La (semaine/dernier) je suis allé voir un (film/nouveau/français).
9. Cette (table/vieux/carré) est probablement (italien).
10. Dans ce (jardin/grand/magnifique) il y a beaucoup de (arbres/beau/étranger), et de (fleurs/petit/rouge/bleu/jaune).

B Fill in the gaps in the following using suitable adjectives. Choose adjectives which normally precede or follow their noun according to the position of the gaps and check the endings for agreement.

Un . . . homme . . . que j'ai rencontré pendant les . . . vacances, l'année . . . , est venu me rendre visite hier. Il m'a donné un . . . livre, un livre très . . . , qu'il avait trouvé chez le . . . bouquiniste qui vend les livres d'occasion dans la . . . maison au coin de la rue. Ce livre contient des histoires . . . et beaucoup de . . . photos de la côte. . . .

C Translate:

1. Napoleon was a great soldier, but he was not a tall man.
2. He has bought a new house — a pretty, very old, house.
3. The new house they are building is very ugly.
4. The men seem very cruel, but the women are kind.
5. She was furious when she saw that the chairs were so expensive.
6. This story is false, but it is very funny.

7. The ground was covered with fresh white snow.
8. At the end of the long street there is a little public square.
9. She was sitting on the fresh green grass under the old tree.
10. She was not very happy when she found that the wooden box was empty.

Beware of these!

Hot, *cold*, *afraid* and *fine* are all English adjectives, but they are not always translated by adjectives in French.

When speaking of things there is no difficulty:

La soupe est froide. The soup is cold.
L'eau est chaude. The water is hot.

Here **froide** and **chaude** are adjectives agreeing normally with their nouns. However, when speaking of living beings with sensations, particularly of humans and the higher animals, **être** with an adjective is replaced by **avoir** with a noun, which does not (and cannot) agree:

Il a peur. He is afraid.
Ils ont peur. They are afraid.

This form is used for the following:

avoir froid, to be cold
avoir chaud, to be hot (or warm)
avoir faim, to be hungry
avoir soif, to be thirsty
avoir tort, to be wrong
avoir raison, to be right
avoir sommeil, to be sleepy
avoir honte, to be ashamed

To these can conveniently be added:

avoir l'air, to seem (appear) (+ adjective or **de** + infinitive)
Elle a l'air contente. She seems pleased. (agreement with subject usual)
Elle a l'air de s'amuser. She seems to be enjoying herself.

and **avoir besoin de**, to need

Il a besoin d'un nouveau cahier. He needs a new exercise book.
Il a besoin de se faire couper les cheveux. He needs to have his hair cut.

To describe the weather, the impersonal pronoun **il** is used with the verb **faire**, as in:

il fait beau, it is fine
il fait doux, it is mild
il fait mauvais, it is bad weather
il fait du soleil, it is sunny
il fait du brouillard, it is foggy
il fait chaud, it is hot
il fait froid, it is cold
il fait du vent, it is windy

but: **il pleut**, it is raining
il neige, it is snowing
il gèle, it is freezing

A   Translate:
1. Last summer, when the weather was fine, we went to the beach
    every day.
2. The French say that in England it is always foggy or else it is always
    raining.
3. You must drive slowly because it is freezing.
4. When I am hungry I eat chocolate.
5. I was right and he was wrong, but I was afraid to tell him so.
6. My brother drinks a lot of beer when he is thirsty.
7. I need a lot of money to buy a new motorbike.
8. My friend came to see me yesterday; she seemed to be very happy.
9. This soup is cold, and I am cold: I asked for hot soup.
10. He seemed angry when I asked him if he had been frightened.

Adverbs

Adjectives qualify nouns; adverbs qualify verbs, adjectives or other adverbs. They answer (or ask) the questions:
How? How much? Where? When?

Formation of adverbs

(a) As in English, many French adverbs are formed from adjectives. In English we normally add *-ly* to an adjective (near: *nearly*). In French **-ment** is added to the adjective, either directly, if it ends in a vowel:
poli, polite: **poliment**, politely
or if the adjective does not end in a vowel, **-ment** is added to the feminine form (which always ends in **-e**):
certain, certaine, certain: **certainement,** certainly
Adjectives which have an alternative masculine form, such as **fou, fol,** form their adverbs regularly from the feminine:
fou, folle, foolish, mad: **follement,** foolishly, madly

(b) Some adjectives change the final **e** of the feminine form to **é** and then add **-ment**, whether or not the adjective ends in **-e**:
e.g. **aveugle**, blind: **aveuglément**, blindly
The most important of this group are: **conforme, énorme, obscur, précis, profond** and **profus.** Note also **expressément** from **exprès.**

(c) Adjectives which end in **-ant** or **-ent** change the **-nt** to **-mment**:
constant, constamment; prudent, prudemment;
but **lent,** slow, changes to **lentement,** slowly

(d) Occasionally the adjective and adverb have the same form:
vite = quick and quickly
soudain = sudden and suddenly
fort = strong, loud and strongly, loudly, very

(f) The following adverbs differ considerably from their adjectives:

Adjective	*Adverb*
bon, good	**bien,** well
meilleur, better	**mieux,** better
mauvais, bad	**mal,** badly
petit, little, small	**peu,** little, a little

Très = very has no corresponding adjective.
Both **peu,** little and **mal,** badly, can be used as nouns:
La cuisinière a un peu de farine. The cook has a little flour.
Tout va mal — j'ai mal à la tête et mal aux dents.
Everything is going badly — I have a headache and toothache.

Adverbs of quantity

The following adverbs of quantity are followed by **de** (except when translating 'of the', when **du, de la** or **des** must be used):

 assez, enough, quite, rather
 beaucoup, a lot, much, many
 combien, how much
 trop, too much
 tant, so much, so many
 autant, as much, as many
 peu, little (see **un peu** above).

The following are followed by the partitive article, **du, de la,** or **des**:

 bien, much, many
 la plupart, most

Note: **beaucoup** cannot be qualified by another adverb: you cannot say 'très beaucoup'. Think of **beaucoup** as meaning *a lot* rather than *much* or *many* and you will be less likely to use it incorrectly.

Examples:

 J'ai beaucoup de sucre. I have a lot of sugar.
 Il a mangé trop de pommes. He has eaten too many apples.
 Il parle très peu. He speaks very little.
 Il y a bien des choses que je ne comprends pas. There are many things
  I do not understand.

but: **Il a encore beaucoup des souvenirs qu'il a achetés à Paris.**
  He still has many of the souvenirs which he bought in Paris.

Interrogative adverbs

Some adverbs are used for asking questions. The most important are:
Combien? = how much? how many? Always followed by **de** before the noun:

 combien de sucre? how much sugar?
 combien de pommes? how many apples?

Comment? = what? how? what like? Often used when asking someone to describe what someone or something is like:

 Comment est la maison? What is the house like?

Où = where?

 Où va-t-il? Where is he going? **Où est mon livre?** Where is my book?

Pourquoi? = where?

 Pourquoi pleurez-vous? Why are you crying?

Quand? = when?

 Quand est-ce qu'il vient? When is he coming?

All these words can be used for statements as well as questions:

 Il me dit combien. He tells me how much.
 Il sait comment il faut le faire. He knows how it is to be done.
 Je sais où il demeure. I know where he lives.
 Il m'a expliqué pourquoi il y est allé. He explained to me why he
  went there.

Position of adverbs

(a) Adverbs of place (e.g. **où**, where; **ici**, here; **là**, there) normally follow the verb, or the past participle in compound tenses:
Il est en bas. He is downstairs.
Les feuilles sont tombées partout. The leaves fell everywhere.
(b) Adverbs of precise time (e.g. **hier**, yesterday; **demain,** tomorrow) also usually follow the verb or past participle, but may be placed at the beginning of a sentence, as in English:
Il vient maintenant. He is coming now.
Elle est arrivée avant-hier. She arrived the day before yesterday.
Demain nous le ferons ensemble. Tomorrow we'll do it together.
(c) Other shorter adverbs follow the verb, or the auxiliary in compound tenses:
Il marche vite. He walks quickly.
Il est déjà parti. He has already left.
(d) Longer adverbs normally follow the past participle in compound tenses:
Il s'est approché doucement. He approached quietly.
(e) Most adverbs can be placed elsewhere for emphasis:
Souvent, il travaille dans le jardin. Often, he works in the garden.
Tout à coup il a entendu un cri perçant. Suddenly he heard a piercing cry.

Reference list of adverbs

Adverbs indicating 'how'

à genoux	kneeling
à haute voix	aloud, in a loud voice
à pied	on foot
à toute vitesse	at full speed
à voix basse	in a low voice, in a whisper
ainsi	thus
aussi	also
bien	well, very
certainement	certainly
comme	as, like
debout	standing, upright
de cette façon	in this/that way
doucement	quietly, softly
en courant	running
ensemble	together
facilement	easily
fort	very, very much, loudly, strongly
lentement	slowly
mal	badly
naturellement	naturally
par accident	accidentally, by mistake
si	so
tout	very, quite

tout à coup	suddenly
tout d'un coup	all at once
tout à fait	altogether, quite
très	very
vite	quickly
vraiment	truly, really

Adverbs indicating 'how much/many'

assez	enough
beaucoup	a lot, many, much
combien	how much
peu	little
un peu	a little
trop	too, too much

(When used before nouns these words are followed by **de**.)

Adverbs indicating 'where'

à côté	near by, at the side
à droite	on the right, right
à gauche	on the left, left
à la maison	home (as in: 'I go home')
au-dessous	below (it)
au-dessus	above (it)
autour	around
tout autour	all around
derrière	behind (it)
devant	in front (of it)
en arrière	behind, at the back, backwards
en avant	ahead, forwards
en bas	below, downstairs
en face	opposite (it)
en haut	above, upstairs
en plein air	out of doors, in the open
ici	here
là	there (but often used where English is 'here')
là-bas	down there, over there
là-haut	up there
par terre	on the ground
partout	everywhere
près	near (it), nearby
tout près	quite near, very near, close by

Adverbs indicating 'when'

alors	then, after that
après	after
avant	before (in time)
bientôt	soon
d'abord	at first, first of all

de bonne heure	early
déjà	already
de nouveau	(to do) again/once more
à nouveau	(to start) afresh/anew
encore	again, still = yet
encore une fois	once more
pas encore	not yet
enfin	at last, finally
ensuite	then, next
jamais	never (takes **ne** before verb)
longtemps	for a long time
maintenant	now
puis	then, after that
quelquefois	sometimes
soudain	suddenly
souvent	often
tard	late
tôt	early, soon
toujours	always, still
tout à l'heure	soon, presently
tout de suite	at once, immediately

A   Form adverbs from the following adjectives, translating each one:
bon, mauvais, petit, lent, vite, constant, honnête, aveugle, prudent,
doux, meilleur, pire, heureux, fou, nouveau.

B   Write out the following in French, translating the adverbs which are
given in English:

(Yesterday) j'ai dû me lever (very early) parce que je voulais aller à
Londres. (After) le petit déjeuner j'ai quitté la maison en fermant la
porte (quietly) derrière moi. (Unfortunately) il n'y a pas de bus à cette
heure du matin, et j'ai dû (thus) aller (on foot). Mais (luckily) j'ai vu un
ami qui va (often) à la ville de (very) bonne heure, et il était (very) content de m'accompagner à la gare dans sa voiture. Le train était (already)
(there). Après quelques minutes il est sorti (slowly) de la gare, mais
(then) il s'est mis à rouler (much faster) et je savais que (soon) j'arri-
verais à Londres. J'étais (extremely) content, car (nearly) (always) le
train part (late) et le voyage dure (a long time).

C   Translate:
1. Many people visit this château each summer.
2. Have you enough money?
3. Most of the books are too old.
4. His wife is quite pretty.
5. This room is much too small.
6. The farmer has as many cows as his neighbour.
7. Few people eat here; it is a little too expensive.
8. He makes so many mistakes most of the time.
9. The hall is certainly too dark.
10. This trunk is big enough: I no longer have so many things.

D Translate:
1. The days passed quickly.
2. We shall visit the museum tomorrow.
3. He was really afraid.
4. Here you are at last!
5. First of all give us something to eat, please.
6. Unfortunately they soon left.
7. She died suddenly a few days later.
8. He wanted so much to put it back at once.
9. Suddenly the thief ran away.
10. John slowly took out some money, then replaced his wallet in his pocket.
11. Very well. After all, I often do so, too.
12. Everything is going very well today.
13. I quite simply looked it up in the dictionary.
14. Luckily he was soon caught.
15. 'Since you are here, you can stay', she said coldly.

E Translate:
1. How many people are going to come tomorrow?
2. Will we have enough pears? Why did you buy so many peaches?
3. After reading a little he was rather tired.
4. That's enough for the moment; come and see me tomorrow.
5. You've given me too much sugar and not enough milk.
6. The majority of Parisians take the metro; there are not enough buses, and they go too slowly.
7. I still have some of the apples you gave me yesterday.
8. They sell fruit here: buy some oranges, please.
9. I don't know how he went to the United States, because he had very little money.
10. He has had at least thirty driving lessons, but he drives as badly as at the beginning.

Comparisons

Both adjectives and adverbs can be used in comparisons. In French the comparative is formed by adding **plus** to the positive, and the superlative is formed by adding **le, la** or **les** as required to the comparative.

(a) Adjective:
   grand, big   **plus grand,** bigger   **le plus grand,** biggest

   The adjective and article agree with the noun:
   Ils sont plus grands que nous.
   They are bigger than us.
   Elle est la plus grande.
   She is the biggest.

(b) Adverb:
   vite, quickly   **plus vite,** more quickly   **le plus vite,** quickest

   The adverb and the **le** are invariable:
   Elle a couru le plus vite.
   She ran the fastest.

Plus indicates *more*, and **moins** indicates *less*:
   moins grand, less big
   le moins grand, the least big
   moins vite, less quickly
   le moins vite, the least quickly
If two things are equal, **aussi . . . que** (in the negative, **pas si . . . que**) is used:
   Ma maison est aussi grande que la vôtre.
   My house is as big as yours.
   Ma voiture va aussi vite que la sienne.
   My car goes as fast as his.
   Mon frère n'est pas si laid que le tien.
   My brother is not as ugly as yours.
In all comparisons the word *than* ('is bigger than') or the second *as* ('as big as') is always **que.**

Irregular Comparisons

A few adjectives and adverbs have irregular comparatives and superlatives:

Adjectives:
   bon, good; **meilleur,** better; **le meilleur,** the best
   mauvais, bad; { **plus mauvais,** worse;   { **le plus mauvais,** worst
                     { **pire**[1]   { **le pire**

[1] **Pire** usually has the sense of *morally worse*.

petit, small, little; { plus petit, smaller; { le plus petit, smallest
                      { moindre[2] lesser   { le moindre least

[2]Moindre means less in importance and plus petit, less in size.

Adverbs:
   bien, well; mieux, better; le mieux, the best
   mal, badly; plus mal, worse; le plus mal, the worst
Pis and le pis are also used, mainly in certain set phrases such as:
tant pis! so much the worse!
   peu, little; moins, less; le moins, the least
Note: Adverbs are invariable. Do not confuse the adjective *better* (e.g.
the better man) with the adverb *better* (he works better). Similarly,
do not confuse the adjective *little* (a little child) with the adverb *little*
(he speaks little).

A   Use comparatives or superlatives to make the best possible sense of the
    following, and make all necessary agreements:
    1. Un arbre est (grand) qu'une fleur.
    2. Une fleur est (petit) qu'un arbre.
    3. Une fleur est (grand) qu'un arbre.
    4. 1 kilomètre est (long) que 1,000 mètres.
    5. Un mètre est (court) qu'un centimètre.
    6. Un kilolitre n'est pas (petit) qu'un litre.
    7. Le sol est toujours (froid) que le soleil.
    8. La lune est (grand) que la terre.
    9. Une livre de plumes est (lourd) qu'une livre de plomb.
    10. La tour Eiffel est (haut) que la tour à Blackpool.
    11. L'Australie est l'île la (grand) et le continent le (petit) du monde.
    12. Un mal de tête est mauvais, mais le mal de dents est encore
        (mauvais).
    13. Parce que Georges est le (petit) garçon de la classe cela ne veut pas
        dire qu'il est le (peu) important.
    14. Annette pleure pour la (petit) raison.
    15. Celui qui travaille le (bien) aura les (bon) résultats.

B   Translate:
    1. She is the best singer in Paris.
    2. Of the two brothers the elder became the more famous.
    3. We lived in Germany when I was younger.
    4. Who is the youngest of the children? Marie is the youngest.
    5. This book is better than the other, isn't it?
    6. If you wish to succeed you must work better.
    7. The tower is higher than the church, but the church is the more
       beautiful.
    8. I am as intelligent as Paul, but I have studied less.
    9. Half an hour later he was sleeping more deeply than ever.
    10. He was becoming more and more difficult to understand.

Possession

In French, the preposition **de** must be used to show possession when the possessor is a noun. There is no equivalent of the English *'s. Paul's book* is translated as **le livre de Paul**. After the verb *to be*, possession is indicated by **à**. It is Paul's: **C'est à Paul.**

Possessive adjectives

The possessive adjective precedes and agrees with the thing possessed:

mon livre, my book   **ma maison**, my house
mes livres, my books   **mes maisons**, my houses

It indicates the person but not the gender of the possessor. Thus **son père** could mean *his father* or *her father*. The masculine form **son** is used to agree with **père**. Similarly, **sa mère** could mean *his mother* or *her mother*, **sa** agreeing with **mère**. In the plural, there is only one form for either gender, e.g. **leur père, leur mère.**

The forms of the possessive adjective are:

	singular		*plural*
	m	*f*	*m & f*
my	mon	ma	mes
your (sing.)	ton	ta	tes
his/her/its	son	sa	ses

	m & f	*m & f*
our	notre	nos
your (plural or polite sing.)	votre	vos
their	leur	leurs

If a noun begins with a vowel or h-mute, the masculine forms **mon, ton** and **son** are used whatever the gender of the thing possessed: **mon ami, mon amie, son histoire**
When speaking of parts of the body (other than as the subject of the verb) the definite article is often used instead of the possessive adjective):

Il se gratte la tête. He scratches his head.

Possessive pronouns

The possessive pronoun stands instead of the thing possessed. It indicates the person of the possessor, and the gender and number of the thing possessed:

Ce livre est le mien.
This book is mine.
Ces livres sont les miens.
These books are mine.
Cette maison est la sienne.
This house is his/hers.

The forms of the possessive pronoun are:

| | *singular* | | *plural* | |
	m	f	m	f
mine	le mien	la mienne	les miens	les miennes
your (sing.)	le tien	la tienne	les tiens	les tiennes
his/her/its	le sien	la sienne	les siens	les siennes
ours	le nôtre	la nôtre	les nôtres	
yours (plural)	le vôtre	la vôtre	les vôtres	
theirs	le leur	la leur	les leurs	

The definite article is required before all possessive pronouns. It combines with the prepositions **à** and **de**, giving **au tien, des leurs** etc.

Possession with à + disjunctive pronoun

As the complement of **être**, the possessor can be indicated by a disjunctive pronoun (see p. 40):
    Cette voiture est à moi.
    This car is mine.
    Ils sont à lui.
    They are his.
In this form the gender of the possessor in the third person is indicated
— **lui, elle, eux, elles.**
To ask who owns something, the usual form is **à qui . . . ?**
    À qui est ce manteau?
    Whose coat is this?
    À qui sont ces livres?
    Whose books are these?
Note that the expression **c'est à moi, toi,** etc. can mean *It's my/your turn*, etc.

A   Give the French for:
  1. my book
  2. my pound
  3. my books
  4. my pounds
  5. your (sing.) boy-friend
  6. your (sing.) girl-friend
  7. his mother
  8. her brother
  9. his sisters
 10. his ink
 11. our house
 12. your (pl.) houses
 13. your wife
 14. your husband
 15. your children
 16. their egg
 17. their eggs
 18. their bone
 19. their bones
 20. their girl-friends

B   Give the French for the following, using the two forms: **c'est le mien** and **il est à moi** in each case. The thing possessed is given in brackets, but will not appear in your answer:

1. (voiture) It's mine.
2. (journal) It's yours. (sing.)
3. (chemise) It's his.
4. (robe) It's hers.
5. (chaussures) They are mine.
6. (gants) They are hers.
7. (vélos) They are his.
8. (robes) They are hers.
9. (montres) They are ours.
10. (gâteaux) They are yours.
11. (chats) They are theirs (f).
12. (bouteilles) They are ours.
13. (fleurs) They are theirs (m).
14. (arbres) They are yours.
15. (tableaux) They are theirs (f).
16. (maison) It's ours.

C   Translate:

1. Those books are theirs.
2. My ideas are not the same as yours.
3. Will you exchange my bike for yours?
4. The girls said the cups were not theirs.
5. You scratch my back and I'll scratch yours.
6. He has put all my handkerchiefs in his drawer.
7. Your girl-friend is waiting downstairs with mine.
8. I don't know whether this money is mine or his.
9. It's your turn to read, not mine.
10. He raised his head and asked me if I had seen his father.

D   Translate:

1. He found his seat.
2. To his great surprise his mother was there.
3. He went upstairs, a candle in his hand.
4. He opened the door for his mother and her friend.
5. They came to look for their bikes, but they took ours.
6. Whose is this coat? It's mine.
7. What are you doing in my bedroom?
8. The judge condemns the man for his crimes.
9. 'Whose is this car?' asked the policeman.
10. I have found your socks, but I can't find mine.

Relative pronouns

A relative pronoun refers to a preceding noun or pronoun (the antecedent) and introduces a clause. In English, the relative pronouns are *who*, *whom*, *whose*, *which* and *that*. The relative pronoun is often omitted in English, but it must not be omitted in French.

The forms of the relative pronouns in French are:

	Persons	*Persons and things*
Subject: who, which		qui
Object or complement: whom, which		que
Genitive: whose, of whom, of which	de qui	dont duquel
After prepositions other than **de**: to whom, for which etc.	à qui pour qui etc.	auquel pour lequel etc.

(a) **Qui, que** and **dont** are invariable. **Que** elides before a vowel or h-mute: **Ce qu'il a dit**, but **qui** does not: **Celui à qui il l'a dit.**

(b) **Lequel** agrees in gender and number with its antecedent. It has the forms **lequel, laquelle, lesquels, lesquelles.** It combines with à and **de** to give the forms **auquel, à laquelle, auxquel(le)s** and **duquel, de laquelle, desquel(le)s.**

The following examples show how the relative pronouns are used:

Subject: **L'homme qui est parti est mon père.**
The man who left is my father.
Le livre qui était sur la table a disparu.
The book which was on the table has disappeared.

Object: **La femme que vous avez rencontrée est ma cousine.**
The woman you met is my cousin.
Les fleurs qu'elle a achetées sont fanées.
The flowers she bought are withered.
Note the agreement with the preceding direct object.

Genitive: **L'homme dont il parle est mon ami.**
L'homme de qui il parle est mon ami.
The man of whom he is speaking is my friend.
Un pays dont il n'avait jamais entendu parler.
Un pays duquel il n'avait jamais entendu parler.
A country he had never heard of.

Dont is the more common form for both persons and things. It cannot, however, be used after **de**, nor in a relative clause starting with any other French preposition: **de qui** or **duquel** must be used instead:

> **Mon père, sans l'aide de qui je n'aurais pu réussir. . .**
> My father, without whose help I could not have succeeded. . .

After prepositions:
> **L'homme à qui il parle est français.**
> The man to whom he is speaking is French.
> **La ville dans laquelle je demeure . . .**
> The town in which I live . . .

After a preposition, **qui** is used only of persons. **Lequel** may also be used of persons, and must be after the prepositions **parmi** and **entre**.

Ce qui, ce que and **ce dont** translate the English *what, that which* and *that of/about which*, and are used when the relative pronoun would otherwise have no antecedent:

> **Ce que vous dites est vrai.**
> What you say is true.
> **Ce dont vous parlez est impossible.**
> That of which you are speaking (what you are speaking about) is impossible.

These forms are used when the antecedent is **tout**:
> **tout ce que j'ai vu**
> everything I saw

Quoi is used after a preposition where the antecedent is **ce**, or to refer not to an actual noun previously expressed, but to an idea or event.

> **ce à quoi je pense**
> what I am thinking of
> **Dites-moi de quoi il s'agit.**
> Tell me what it is about.

A   Put **qui, que, dont** or the correct form of **lequel** into the following:
  1. Le stylo (which) il a acheté hier est déjà cassé.
  2. La moto (which) mon père m'a achetée marche très bien.
  3. Les fauteuils dans (which) elles sont assises sont plus confortables que la chaise sur (which) je dois m'asseoir.
  4. Elle porte la même vieille robe (which) elle portait à Noël, et (of which) je parlais hier.
  5. Ce vieux monsieur, (who) est très savant, a écrit le livre (which) se trouve sur ma table de nuit.

B   Using a suitable relative pronoun, link the two sentences in each of the following to form one complex sentence (main clause + relative clause), making any other adjustments necessary:
  1. Ce soldat est un officier. Il porte un revolver.
  2. Voilà la vache. Elle donne tant de lait.
  3. Il est midi à l'horloge. L'horloge se trouve au-dessus de la porte d'entrée.
  4. J'ai trouvé le carnet. Il a écrit ses mémoires dans ce carnet.
  5. Voilà la jeune fille. Je suis allé au cinéma avec cette jeune fille hier.

6. C'était l'hiver de 1921. Pendant cet hiver beaucoup de neige est tombée.
7. L'enfant est malheureux. Il a perdu sa balle.
8. Ils habitent un appartement moderne. L'appartement se trouve près du parc.
9. Je n'ai pas mis de timbre sur la lettre. Vous venez de mettre la lettre à la poste.
10. Voici la clef. Il a ouvert la porte de sa chambre avec cette clef.

C Translate:
1. The car which is in front of the house is an old Renault (f).
2. The boy who is running after the football is my brother.
3. The woman I saw yesterday has come back today.
4. I've lost the ruler you lent me.
5. In which of these streets do you live?
6. For whom did you buy the apples I saw on the kitchen table?
7. I've written to the agency of which I spoke.
8. Anne has lost the parcel in which I had put the necklace.
9. He burned everything there was in the house.
10. What is strange is that he never came back.

Demonstratives

Demonstrative adjectives

The demonstrative adjective has the following forms:

masc. sing.	fem. sing.	m & f plural
ce	cette	ces
cet (before vowel or h-mute)		

There is no distinction between *this* and *that*, *these* and *those*.
> **Donnez-moi ce livre.**
> Give me that book.
> **Ces pommes ne sont pas mûres.**
> These apples are not ripe.

To make the distinction between *this* and *that*, i.e. what is nearer and what is farther away, **-ci** or **-là** can be added to the noun:
> **Cet outil-là est plus utile que ces outils-ci.**
> That tool is more useful than these tools.

Demonstrative pronouns

When *this* and *that* mean *this one* and *that one*, and are used instead of a noun, they are demonstrative pronouns. They take the gender and number of the noun they refer to, and have the following forms:

masc.		fem.	
sing.	plural	sing.	plural
celui	ceux	celle	celles

These pronouns are used:
(a) followed by a relative clause:
> **Voici les billets. J'ai trouvé celui que j'avais perdu.**
> Here are the tickets. I found the one I had lost.

(b) followed by **de**:
> **J'ai trouvé ma serviette, mais je ne peux pas trouver celle de mon frère.**
> I've found my brief-case, but I can't find my brother's.

(c) with the suffix **-ci** (meaning this or these) or the suffix **-là** (meaning that or those):
> **J'ai acheté deux chemises, celle-ci est pour moi, et celle-là est pour toi.**
> I bought two shirts; this one is for me, and that one is for you.

Celui-ci can also be used to mean *the latter*, and **celui-là** to mean *the former*.
> **Monsieur Lacroix s'est assis à côté de son ami. Celui-ci n'a pas levé la tête.**
> Monsieur Lacroix sat down next to his friend. The latter did not look up.

Ceci and cela

The demonstrative pronouns described above refer to nouns of known gender and number. When *this* and *that* are unspecific, referring to some fact or idea, or to something which is unnamed and therefore has no gender, **ceci** and **cela** are used.

> **Ne fais pas cela!**
> Don't do that!
> **Regardez ceci.**
> Look at this.

Cela is often replaced by the shortened form **ça**:

> **Ça ne fait rien.**
> It doesn't matter.

Ça va? in the interrogative means *How are things?*, and as a reply *fine, OK* etc.

A   Give the French for the following, without distinguishing between *this* and *that* or *these* and *those*:

1. this book
2. this flower
3. this tree
4. these houses
5. these enemies
6. that cup
7. those chairs
8. this water
9. those streets
10. these men

B   Give the French for the following, distinguishing between *this* and *that* and *these* and *those*:

1. this table
2. that mountain
3. this clock
4. those shirts
5. these ideas
6. this picture
7. that spider
8. these eggs
9. this bone
10. that tomato

C   Translate:

1. I shall take this book, but not that one.
2. Those who have no money cannot do this.
3. Don't speak like that!
4. Here are two pencils — take this one.
5. I like dogs, but not the farmer's.
6. Take some apples — no not those ones, these ones!
7. These rooms are as big as those in our house.
8. You can go in by this door, but that one is locked.
9. 'How are things?' 'Fine, thanks!'
10. I have read all the books in my room, but not those which are in the sitting room.

D   Translate:

'Come in, ladies and gentlemen. I'm going to show you this beautiful house, which the nation has just bought. You are my first visitors.'

'Thank you', said one of the tourists — the one with a black beard.

'This is the great hall.'

'It's magnificent', exclaimed the tourist with the black beard.

'And this is the dining-room.'

'This?' asked a lady. 'I'd like to have a dining-room as big as this one!'

'What a beautiful table!' exclaimed another tourist. This time it was not the one with the black beard.

'And what is this?' asked a small boy who was with a lady — the one who had admired the dining-room.

'That?' said the guide. 'It's an old gramophone.'

'Does it work?'

'Oh, yes, very well. They collect old things here. Look here: this is an old wireless set.'

'That must be the one I saw on the poster near the entrance', said the boy.

'He's a clever boy, he is', the guide said to the boy's mother. 'And now, let's continue the visit, ladies and gentlemen. First of all the cellar . . . Here we are! — Enter, please.'

'This door is very solid!' said the man with the black beard.

'Naturally. We have over seven hundred bottles of the best wines of France in this cellar.'

'And this key? Does it work?'

'Yes, of course!'

'You go on. I am going to try it. A moment please. There, the door is locked.'

A voice was heard on the other side of the door: 'But sir, we are shut in!'

'Yes, You see, I too collect things. Have a good time — you have over seven hundred bottles of the best French wines — that should be enough for the moment.'

The guide and his visitors shouted — but in vain. As the man with the black beard had said, the door was very thick!

Indefinite pronouns

Not every pronoun stands for a clearly defined person or thing. Those that do not are called indefinite pronouns. The most important are listed below.

On corresponds to the English *one* as used in 'where can one go to play tennis?' but it is much more widely used. It can translate the English *you, we, they*, or *people in general*:

D'ici on peut voir la mer.
From here you can see the sea.
On dit qu'il est allé en Italie.
They say he has gone to Italy.

On can also refer to a specific, but undefined person:

On vient.
Someone is coming.

It often translates the English passive (see p. 26):

On vend la maison.
The house is being sold.

On is found only as the subject of a sentence. For the other cases, **nous** or **vous** is used. Agreements with **on** are normally masculine singular. The corresponding reflexive pronoun is **se**, the disjunctive pronoun is **soi**, and the possessive adjective is **son (sa, ses)**.

Personne, nobody, no one. Whether it is the subject or the object of the verb, the verb must be preceded by **ne**:

Personne n'est ici.
No one is here.
Je n'y ai vu personne.
I saw nobody there.

Quelque chose, something, is always masculine. When followed by an adjective, the adjective must be preceded by **de**:

quelque chose de nouveau
something new

Quelqu'un, as an invariable masculine pronoun, means someone:

Il y a quelqu'un dans la pièce.
There is someone in the room.

The plural pronoun **quelques-un(e)s** means some, a few:

Quelques-unes de ces fleurs sont fanées.
Some of these flowers are faded.

Rien, nothing. Whether it is the subject or the object of the verb, the verb must be preceded by **ne**:

Rien ne me plaît.
Nothing pleases me.
Je ne vois rien.
I see nothing.

When followed by an adjective, the adjective must be preceded by **de**:
Rien d'intéressant ne se passe dans cette ville.
Nothing interesting happens in this town.
Note: **rien du tout**, nothing at all.

Tout, everything:
J'ai tout vu.
I've seen everything.

Tout le monde, everyone. Agreements are masculine singular:
Tout le monde est arrivé.
Everyone hás arrived.

A Write out the following conversation, replacing the English words with French ones. Check your answer by translating back into English.

Pièce Nocturne

Scène: une chambre à coucher
L'heure: entre deux et trois heures du matin
Personnages: un mari et sa femme

Femme: Tu entends (something)?
Mari: Non, (I don't hear anything).
Femme: (Nothing?) Il y a (someone) en bas, j'en suis sûre.
Mari: (I hear no one.)
Femme: (No one?) Tu as fermé les fenêtres?
Mari: J'en ai laissé (some) ouvertes, je crois.
Tout à coup ils entendent un bruit affreux.
Mari: Écoute! Maintenant j'entends (something).
Femme: (You) croirait que (everyone) est là-bas! Qu'est-ce qu'il faut faire?
Mari: (One) peut toujours se cacher sous les draps.
Femme: Bonne idée!
Ils se cachent, tous les deux, sous les draps.
Quel héros!
Quelle héroïne!
(Mais ce n'était qu'un chat, qui est entré par la fenêtre ouverte, et qui a renversé (something).)

B Translate:
1. Someone has locked the door and hidden the key.
2. 'Have you bought anything?' 'No, nothing!'
3. I think there's something in my bed — something horrible!
4. He never does anything practical.
5. Some of my friends are French, some are English.
6. There is someone here who wants to speak to you.
7. Everyone is listening, but no one dares speak.
8. He has something important to tell us.
9. They say you are mad if you talk to yourself.
10. 'Is there someone down there?' 'No, no one.'

Problem words: prepositions etc.

The majority of the smaller words which most frequently give rise to translation problems are prepositions, though others, mainly adverbs related to prepositions, must be included in the list. These words, unless correctly translated, may easily make nonsense of what we write or say, or they may convey a meaning very different from the one we intend. The problem arises from the fact that such words do not have one single corresponding translation, suitable for use in every context. The purpose of the following list is to give a selection of the more common of these problem words, with examples of meanings and idiomatic uses covering a variety of circumstances.

a	The apples cost 2 francs a kilo. **Les pommes coûtent deux francs le kilo.** He writes twice a week. **Il écrit deux fois par semaine.** What a hero! **Quel héros!**
about	He speaks about his work. **Il parle de son travail.** Come about five. **Venez vers cinq heures.** about six kilometres from here, **environ six kilomètres d'ici** He was about to speak. **Il était sur le point de parler.**
above	The lamp hangs above the table. **La lampe est suspendue au-dessus de la table.** He lives in the flat above. **Il habite l'appartement d'en haut.** above all, **surtout**
across	He runs across the yard. **Il court à travers la cour/Il traverse la cour en courant.**
after	They arrived after a long journey. **Ils sont arrivés après un long voyage.** after an hour, **au bout d'une heure** The dog runs after the cat. **Le chien poursuit le chat.**
against	He pushes the chair against the door. **Il pousse la chaise contre la porte.**
along	He was walking along the boulevard. **Il se promenait le long du boulevard.** Come along! **Viens! (Venez!)** Go along this street. **Prenez cette rue.**
as	as he cannot come, **comme il (parce qu'il) ne peut pas venir** He is working badly, as usual. **Il travaille mal, comme d'habitude.** You are as strong as he is. **Tu es aussi fort que lui.**
as far as	I will take you as far as the station. **Je vous accompagnerai jusqu'à la gare.** as far as the eye can reach, **aussi loin qu'on peut voir**
aside	He puts some money aside. **Il met de l'argent de côté.**
at	He arrives at the station. **Il arrive à la gare.** The dog rushes at the intruder. **Le chien se précipite sur l'intrus.**

	at home, **à la maison, chez moi, chez nous** at John's, at my uncle's, at the butcher's etc., **chez Jean,** **chez mon oncle, chez le boucher,** etc. Look at that plane. **Regardez cet avion.** at peace, **en paix**
back	*Back* is included in the following verbs: **revenir**, to come back; **retourner**, to go back; **reculer**, to recoil, fall back; **rendre**, to give back; **ramener**, to bring (a person) back; **rapporter**, to bring (a thing) back; **repayer**, to pay back; **renvoyer**, to send back; **remettre**, to put back.
before	**un an auparavant**, a year before before Tuesday, **avant mardi**
behind	He shuts the door behind him. **Il ferme la porte derrière lui.** to leave behind, **laisser, abandonner**
by	by bike, **à vélo, à bicyclette** by foot, **à pied** by car, **en voiture, en auto** by boat, **en bateau** by plane, **en avion** by air, **par avion** by train, **par (le) train, par chemin de fer** He was frightened by the idea. **Il était effrayé à l'idée.** a book by Dumas, **un livre de Dumas** The burglar was followed by a detective. **Le cambrioleur** **était suivi d'un détective.** He took the child by the hand. **Il a pris l'enfant par la main.** two by two, **deux par deux**
down	Do not translate *down* in the following verbs: **poser**, to put down; **descendre**, to go/come down; **tomber**, to fall down.
for	I have been here for four years. **Je suis ici depuis quatre ans.** the train for Toulouse, **le train pour** (or **de**) **Toulouse** He will be here for two hours. **Il sera ici pour deux heures.** I have been waiting for you for twenty minutes. **Je vous** **attends depuis vingt minutes.** He worked for an hour. **Il a travaillé pendant une heure.** (statement after the event) Thank you for your letter. **Je vous remercie de votre lettre.** For luggage he had only his ruck-sack. **Comme bagage il** **n'avait que son sac à dos.**
from	He came from the house. **Il est sorti de la maison.** From where do you come? **D'où venez-vous?** I saw a car coming from the direction of Dijon. **J'ai vu une** **voiture qui venait de la direction de Dijon.** drink from a glass, **boire dans un verre** from nine o'clock (onwards), **à partir de neuf heures** from time to time, **de temps en temps** from flower to flower, **de fleur en fleur** You can see from the castle to the church. **On peut voir** **depuis le château jusqu'à l'église.** the train from Toulouse, **le train de Toulouse**

in	Usually **dans** when *in* means *enclosed by*: also when followed by a defining word like *the*, *a*, *this*, *my*. Usually **en** in figurative expressions, and when directly preceding the noun. Often also **à**, especially where it means *at*: in my opinion, **à mon avis** in the kitchen, **à la cuisine** I met him in Paris. **Je l'ai rencontré à Paris.** I met her in England. **Je l'ai rencontrée en Angleterre.** (**en** for all feminine countries) I met her in Japan. **Je l'ai rencontrée au Japon.** (**au** for all masculine countries) dressed in, **vêtu(e) de** in the sun, **au soleil** in a word, **en un mot** in that case, **en ce cas** in silence, **en silence** in vain, **en vain** in the interior (inside), **à l'intérieur** with a book in his hand, **avec un livre à la main** in a low voice (quietly), **à voix basse** to pass the time in (studying, etc.), **passer le temps à (étudier, etc.)** in January, etc., **au mois de janvier, en janvier**, etc. in spring, **au printemps** in summer, in autumn, in winter: **en été, en automne, en hiver** I shall be ready in (= at the end of) an hour. **Je serai prêt dans une heure.** I can finish it in (= within) an hour. **Je peux le finir en une heure.** the best in the group, **le meilleur du groupe**
in front of	He stops in front of the door. **Il s'arrête devant la porte.**
instead of	I shall take a shower instead of a bath. **Je prendrai une douche au lieu d'un bain.**
into	He went into the inn. **Il est entré dans l'auberge.** Can I change these English pounds into French money? **Peut-on changer ces livres anglaises contre de l'argent français?**
just	His friend follows just behind. **Son ami suit juste derrière.** He arrived just in time. **Il est arrivé de justesse.** just one, **un seul** He just smiled. **Il n'a fait que sourire.** He has just come out of the house. **Il vient de sortir de la maison.**
like	He speaks like a Frenchman. **Il parle comme un Français.** Do it like him. **Faites comme lui.**
near	The car stops near the hotel. **La voiture s'arrête près de l'hôtel.**
of	Nearly always **de**: the head of the family, **le chef de la famille**

But note: He presses the hands of the two boys. **Il serre la main aux deux garçons.**
a view of the mountains, **une vue sur les montagnes**
a jug made of earth, **une cruche en terre**

off
No French word corresponds to *off*, which is included in various phrases such as:
far off, **loin d'ici**
from far off, **de loin**
and in these and similar verbs:
to cut off, **couper**
to carry off (take away), **emporter**
to run off (escape), **se sauver en courant**
to take off (a garment), **enlever, ôter**
to take off (detach), **détacher**
to turn off (switch off), **fermer, couper**

on
Usually **sur**:
on the platform, **sur le quai**
But note: on the first floor, **au premier étage**
on Wednesday, on Wednesdays, **mercredi, les mercredis**
on the third of April, **le trois avril**
on leaving, **en partant**
on the ground, (describing position) **par terre**; (including movement) **à terre**
to go on (to continue), **continuer**
to go up on, **monter sur**
on the television/radio, **à la télévision/radio**
on foot, **à pied**
on a bike, **à vélo, à bicyclette**
on horseback, **à cheval**
to turn on, switch on, **allumer**

opposite
He found himself opposite a police station. **Il s'est trouvé en face d'un poste de police.**

out
Out is included in the following verbs:
sortir, to go out, to take out (In this sense the auxiliary is **avoir. Il a sorti son portefeuille.** He took out his wallet.)
partir, se mettre en route, to set out (on a journey, etc.)
être épuisé, to have run out, (of stock etc.); **sortir en courant**, to run out.
He takes it out of the drawer. **Il le prend dans un tiroir.**
He drinks out of a cup. **Il boit dans une tasse.**

over
The film is over. **Le film est fini/terminé.**
bent over his work, **courbé sur son travail**
He has over 100 books. **Il a plus de cent livres.**
all the world over, **dans le monde entier**
blue all over, **bleu partout**

since
I've been here since one o'clock. **Je suis ici depuis une heure.**

through
I saw him through the window. **Je l'ai vu par la fenêtre.**
They advance through the forest. **Ils s'avancent à travers/ au travers de la forêt.**

till
See until.

to	Normally à (au, à l', à la, aux), but very often de when translating the *to* of an infinitive following another verb (see pp. 32–33) to + towns, à: à Londres, à Paris, au Havre to + feminine countries, en: il va en France to + masculine countries, à + le (= au, aux): Il va au Japon, aux États Unis. He has a lot to do. Il a beaucoup à faire. from flower to flower, de fleur en fleur He goes to the baker's. Il va chez le boulanger. in order to, pour + infinitive
too	(= too much) He speaks too much. Il parle trop. (= also) He does it too. Il le fait aussi.
towards	He turns towards the wall. Il se tourne vers le mur. He is kind towards his enemies. Il est gentil envers ses ennemis.
under	He found the burglar under the bed. Il a trouvé le cambrioleur sous le lit. He is under 14 years old. Il a moins de quatorze ans.
until	He worked until six o'clock. Il a travaillé jusqu'à six heures. not until three o'clock, pas avant trois heures
up	to get up, se lever to stand up, se lever, se mettre debout, se tenir debout to wake up, se réveiller, réveiller (quelqu'un)
with	Avec, when *with* means *in the company of*, or *by means of*: He comes with his wife. Il vient avec sa femme. He cuts it with a saw. Il le coupe avec une scie. with pleasure, avec plaisir with care, avec soin attentively, avec attention Otherwise *with* is usually translated by de: he trembles with fear, il tremble de peur he fills with, covers with, il remplit de, couvre de For personal attributes *with* is translated by à: a man with red hair, un homme aux cheveux roux
without	without fear, fearlessly, sans peur without doubt, doubtless, sans doute without noise, soundlessly, sans bruit

A   To find the answers to this crossword puzzle, read the clues given and fill in the blanks with the French word which translates the word given in brackets.

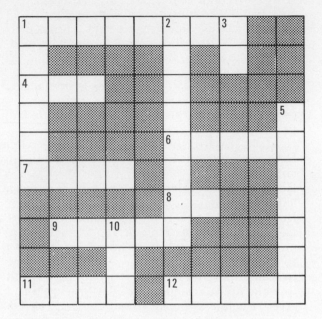

Across:
1. Il se cache (behind) la porte. (8)
4. On voit des arbres (through) la fenêtre. (3)
6. (As) il n'est pas venu, je commencerai. (5)
7. Elle balaye la poussière (under) le tapis. (4)
8. Le train (from) Paris aura vingt minutes de retard. (2)
9. Pierre est (just) derrière les autres. (5)
11. Je suis venu ici (for) une semaine. (4)
12. Il faut finir (before) cinq heures. (5)

Down:
1. J'attends ici (for) quinze minutes. (6)
2. Elle s'est trouvée (opposite) l'école. (2, 4, 2)
3. (In) printemps nous plantons des tomates. (2)
5. Je lui parlerai (during) l'entr'acte. (7)
10. Il met le vase (on) la table. (3)

B   Fill in the blanks in the following with prepositions:
1. Ils se promènent ___ ___ ___ la rue.
2. Tu arrives ___ retard, ___ d'habitude, et ___ excuse, je suppose.
3. En arrivant ___ la frontière ___ voiture, nous nous sommes arrêtés ___ la douane; ___ l'autre côté de la rue un gendarme se tenait, ___ bouger, ___ le poste de police.
4. Voulez-vous mettre cette lettre ___ la poste, s'il vous plaît? Il y a une boîte ___ lettres ___ coin ___ la rue, ___ ___ ___ l'église.

5. Si tu travailles bien tu seras remboursé ___ tous tes efforts, ___ réussissant — devenir riche. Alors, cela vaut la peine — travailler, n'est-ce-pas?

6. Il est arrivé ___ le bateau ce soir, mais ___ bagages. Il n'a même pas une brosse ___ dents, ni une brosse ___ cheveux.

7. Il a emporté son slip ___ bain pour aller ___ la piscine.

8. ___ la poche de son vieux blue-jean il a trouvé une pièce ___ cinq francs, et deux tickets ___ métro qui n'étaient plus valables.

9. La mère est montée ___ bruit ___ ne pas éveiller le bébé, qui dormait ___ son petit lit.

10. ___ hiver la terre est couverte ___ neige; ___ été nous nous allongeons ___ terre ___ soleil.

C Answer the following, in French, with a complete statement:
1. Aimez-vous voyager par chemin de fer, ou préférez-vous voyager en voiture?
2. Préférez-vous travailler au lieu d'aller en vacances?
3. Est-ce qu'il est sage de mettre un peu d'argent de côté?
4. À quelle heure vous couchez-vous d'habitude?
5. Est-ce qu'il y a une bibliothèque publique près de chez vous?
6. Contre qui est-ce que l'on fait la guerre — contre ses amis ou contre l'ennemi?
7. Est-ce que les voitures roulent à droite en Angleterre?
8. On écrit une lettre avec quoi et sur quoi?
9. Lequel vient avant midi: le soir ou le matin?
10. Est-ce que la plupart des gens travaillent le dimanche comme les autres jours?
11. Est-ce que l'on trouve des nuages au-dessous de la mer?
12. Voudriez-vous apprendre l'allemand au lieu du français?
13. Contre quoi faut-il changer les livres anglaises en France?
14. Boit-on d'habitude du thé dans un verre ou dans une tasse, en Angleterre?
15. Est-ce que l'on achète les journaux chez le boucher?
16. Pendant quels mois de l'année fait-il beau en Angleterre?
17. Pendant combien de temps faut-il bouillir un œuf à la coque?
18. Peut-on acheter quelque chose sans argent?
19. Est-ce qu'un autobus roule sur des rails?
20. Préférez-vous aller en vacances en hiver ou en été?

D Translate:
1. From time to time one can see them through the window.
2. The squirrel ran across the road just in front of my bike.
3. He arrived by plane, but he will return by train.
4. There is a little garden in front of the house, and another larger one behind.
5. He walked along the street, his umbrella in his hand.
6. He listened in silence to the man at his side.
7. In my opinion it is better to work in the kitchen than in the shop.
8. In summer I take a shower instead of a bath.
9. One can see the light of the lighthouse from far off when it is fine.
10. I heard him talk about his travels in China on the radio.

11. He will leave after lunch, at about one-thirty.
12. The burglar ran off, leaving his bag behind him.
13. I'll do it for you, but after my own work.
14. I came to Paris for six months but I have been here for two years.
15. I should like to speak French like a Frenchman.

Translating 'it'

It is

1. (a) When *it*, as the subject of **être**, refers to a noun previously men-
tioned, it is translated by **il** or **elle**:
Regardez cette montre; elle est très ancienne.
Look at this watch; it is very old.
   (b) When *it*, as the subject of **être**, refers to a noun which comes later
it is translated by **ce**:
C'est une bonne idée.
It's a good idea.
   (c) When *it is* is followed by an adjective, plus a phrase introduced by
de or **que**, the impersonal **il est** is used:
Il est impossible de le faire aujourd'hui.
It is impossible to do it today.
Il est vrai que nous les avons vus hier.
It is true that we saw them yesterday.
   (d) When *it is* is followed by an adjective which refers to some fact,
statement or idea which has already been mentioned, **c'est** is used:
Il m'a montré comment le faire: c'est très facile.
He showed me how to do it: it's very easy.
   (e) When *it* is the subject of **devoir** or **pouvoir** plus **être**, it is translated
by **ce**:
Ce peut/doit être vrai.
It may/must be true.
   (f) In weather expressions, *it* is always **il**:
Il fait beau. It is fine.
Il fait chaud. It is hot.
   (g) When telling the time, *it* is always **il**:
Il est deux heures. It is two o'clock.
Il est midi. It is noon.
   (h) When stating the day or date, *it* is **ce**:
C'est le deux juin. It is the second of June.
C'est lundi. It is Monday.

Other uses of 'it'

2. (a) When *it* is an object pronoun, it has the forms **le** and **la**:
J'ai gagné de l'argent; je vais le dépenser.
I've won some money; I'm going to spend it.
   (b) With a verb which would normally be followed by **de**, *of it* is trans-
lated by **en**:
Il en mange. He eats some of it.
Il m'a dit ce qu'il en pense. He told me what he thinks of it.
But: **Il y pense.** He thinks about it. (from **penser à quelque chose**)

(c) Note the translation of *it* in:
What is it? meaning 'What's the matter?' or 'What do you want?':
Qu'est-ce qu'il y a?
It is said that . . . **On dit que** . . .
Isn't it? **N'est-ce pas?**

(d) In certain cases, the English *it* has no equivalent in the French translation:
outside (it), **dehors**
inside (it), **dedans**
under (it), **dessous**
in front of (it), **devant**
behind (it), **derrière**
beside (it), next (to it), **à côté**
in the middle (of it), **au milieu**
« **Est-ce que le chat est sur le lit?** » « **Non, il est dessous.** »
'Is the cat on the bed?' 'No, under it.'
Il y a un grand arbre au fond du jardin avec un petit buisson à côté.
There's a big tree at the bottom of the garden, with a little bush next to it.

A Translate:
1. It is pleasant here, isn't it?   *2c)*
2. 'It must be the postman.' 'No, it's a policeman!'   *1e) 1b)*
3. It is said that he's the best photographer in the town.   *2c) 1b)*
4. 'What is it?' 'It's a bike lock, and this is the key for it.'   *2c) 1b) 2d)*
5. 'It's snowing!' 'No, it's not! It's raining.'   *1f)*
6. I'll do it now, while I think of it.   *2a) 2b)*
7. I'd like a little of it, please.   *2b) 2c)*
8. The entrance is this way, isn't it?   *2c)*
9. 'What time is it?' 'It's half past one.'   *1g)*
10. 'It's not freezing any more, is it?' 'Oh yes, it is!'   *1f)*
11. 'What is it?' 'It's nothing serious.'   *2c)*
12. 'Where is my coffee?' 'Here it is. There's no sugar in it.'   *2a) 2d)*
13. 'Is it Thursday today?' 'No, it's already Friday.'   *1h)*
14. 'Drink your tea!' 'It's too hot.'
15. 'It's nice here, in the garden, isn't it?' 'Not when it's cold, like today.'   *2c) 1f)*
16. 'Does it hurt?' 'Yes, it hurts a lot.'
17. It is possible that they have sold it (m).   *1c) 2a)*
18. In the valley there is a wood, and in the middle of it a thatched cottage.   *2d)*
19. His horse? I don't know where it is, but it's not true that it has been sold.   *1c)*
20. Look at my poor bike! Look at it! What has happened to it?   *2a) lui (2b)*

B Translate:

It was Christmas Day. It was also my birthday. Usually it is not very nice to have your birthday on Christmas Day because people give you a present and say: 'Here is something for Christmas — it's for your birthday too', as if that makes the present better. But this time I'd been promised something exceptional, good enough for Christmas and my birthday together.

I had waited for a long time to find out what it was — and at last the moment had arrived. There it was — a big parcel on the table with my name on it.

It was difficult to open it, but at last I managed it. And there it was, just as I had hoped, a stereo tape-recorder! It was, this time, 'just what I wanted!'

Each, every, all, very, enough

each, adjective:	**chaque**, m & f; singular only: **chaque livre**, each book; **chaque maison**, each house
each one, pronoun:	**chacun, chacune**; always singular: **On a donné à chacune des filles une nouvelle poupée et à chacun des garçons un cerf-volant.** Each of the girls was given a new doll, and each of the boys a kite.
every, adjective:	**tout, toute, tous, toutes:** **tout homme**, every man; **toute femme**, every woman; **tous les jours**, every day; **tous les deux jours**, every other day
every, pronouns:	everybody, everyone: **tout le monde** (+ singular verb) everything: **tout**: **Il a tout mangé.** He has eaten everything. every thing: **toute chose; tout** everything that . . . **tout ce que . . .** every one of (each one of), **chacun(e) de . . .**
all, pronoun:	**tous, toutes** (plural only): **Je les ai tous vus.** I have seen them all. (e.g. films, m) **Je les ai toutes vues.** I have seen them all. (e.g. maisons, f) **toutes celles qui sont ici/tous ceux qui sont ici,** all those who are here
all, adjective:	**tout, toute, tous, toutes:** used with **le, la** or **les** or a demonstrative or possessive adjective before the noun: **tous les hommes**, all men **tous les livres**, all the books **toutes les maisons**, all the houses **J'ai fini tout mon travail.** I have finished all my work.
very	Very is normally **très**, which is the safest word to use. **Tout, fort** and **bien** can all be used as alternatives in certain cases. very much: **beaucoup.** You cannot say 'très beaucoup' but you can often translate *very much or very many* by some other phrase, such as **une très grande quantité de** or **un très grand nombre de.** Very well: **très bien; fort bien** Very good in the sense of *all right*, or *well done* is also **très bien.**

enough
enough, sufficient, sufficiently: **assez**:
as pronoun: **J'en ai assez.** I have enough. (**En** must be included before the verb if *of it* or *of them* could be added in English.)
as adverb: **Vous avez assez dit.** You have said enough.
Assez may also mean *rather* or *fairly*: The town is fairly big. **La ville est assez grande.**

A Translate:
1. Each of the soldiers carries a rifle.
2. All my friends were there.
3. He is very rich, and has many possessions.
4. All that he does is well done.
5. I haven't all the money I'd like, but I've enough.
6. You can sell all these books — I've read them all.
7. I like him very much: he has many friends.
8. She found a husband for each of her daughters.
9. 'Everything is ready.' 'Very good, we can all leave now.'
10. The garden is fairly big, but I cannot plant in it everything I'd like to.

Asking and answering

1. Asking

Questions can be asked using:
(a) normal word order with a rising intonation
(b) **est-ce que**
(c) inversion.
These are described on p. 35.

Interrogative pronouns

Besides the above forms, special words are used to introduce questions. Those used alone, without an adjoining noun, are called interrogative pronouns. There are different forms for persons and for things.

(a) Persons
Qui? is used for both *who?* and *whom?*
Qui est à la porte?
Who is at the door?
Qui avez-vous vu?
Whom did you see?
The forms **qui est-ce qui?** for *who?* and **qui est-ce que?** for *whom?* are also used, especially in conversation.
Qui? is also used after a preposition:
A qui pensez-vous?
Of whom are you thinking?

(b) Things
Qu'est-ce qui? is used for *what?* as the subject of the following verb:
Qu'est-ce qui est arrivé?
What has happened?
Qu'est-ce que? is used for *what?* as the object of the following verb:
Qu'est-ce que vous dites?
What are you saying?
Que? can be used on its own, as the object of the following verb:
Que dites-vous?
Quoi? is used for *what?* after a preposition:
De quoi parlez-vous?
What are you speaking about?
A quoi sert ceci?
What is this used for?
Where there is a preposition, it must come first.

Note that normal word order is used after **qui?** = *who?*, **qui est-ce qui?** **qui est-ce que?** **qu'est-ce qui?** and **qu'est-ce que?** but that the noun and verb are inverted after **qui?** = *whom?* and after any interrogative pronoun preceded by a preposition.

Interrogative adjectives

The interrogative adjective has the forms **quel, quelle, quels, quelles.**
It agrees with its noun in gender and number.
Quel homme? which/what man?
Quelle femme? which/what woman?
Quels livres? which/what books?
Quelles maisons? which/what houses?
The interrogative adjective can also be used when separated from its
noun by a tense of **être:**
Quel est son avis?
What is his opinion?
Quel can be used after prepositions:
Dans quelle direction est-il parti?
In which direction did he go?
Quel is also used in exclamations to mean 'What a . . . !'
Quelle surprise! What a surprise!
Quel dommage! What a pity!
Other interrogative words include:
pourquoi? why?
quand? when?
où? where?
comment? how?
And note: **Qu'est-ce que c'est que . . . ?** What is (something)?
as in: **Qu'est-ce que c'est que ça?** What is that?

2. Answering

When answering questions on a French text, whether the answer has to
be written in French or English, remember these rules:
(a) Answer the question without the addition of matter not asked for.
(b) Be brief, using pronouns instead of nouns where possible.
(c) Make sure your answers are complete sentences, and in the appropriate tense.

A Each of the following consists of a statement and a question referring to
that statement. Answer the questions briefly, using pronouns where possible. Each answer must be a complete sentence, and in the appropriate
tense:
  1. Le soleil brille.
     Quel temps fait-il aujourd'hui?
  2. C'était dimanche hier.
     Quel jour sommes-nous aujourd'hui?
  3. Ma montre avance de dix minutes. Elle marque dix heures à ce
     moment.
     Quelle est l'heure exacte à ce moment?
  4. Jean était encore au lit à neuf heures ce matin.
     Où était-il à huit heures ce matin?
  5. Les sœurs de Pierre s'appellent Brigitte, Chantal et Anne; ses frères
     s'appellent Jean et François.
     Combien de sœurs Pierre a-t-il?

6. Le fermier habite une maison à la campagne. Il a un taureau, vingt vaches à lait, dix cochons et deux chevaux.
   Combien de bétail le fermier a-t-il?
7. Marie a dix ans, sa sœur aînée Jeanne a douze ans, et sa cousine Louise a neuf ans.
   Laquelle des sœurs est la plus jeune?
8. La fermière est assise sous un arbre dans le verger de son mari.
   Où se trouve l'arbre sous lequel est assise la femme du fermier?
9. Monsieur Levoyage est monté dans le seul compartiment de première classe, et il a choisi une place au coin, près de la fenêtre, face à la locomotive.
   Décrivez la place que Monsieur Levoyage a choisie.
10. Mon ami, Charles Duretête, ne croyait pas aux revenants, mais une nuit il a vu une dame blanche sans tête au pied de son lit, et tout de suite il a changé d'avis.
    (a) Est-ce que Charles Duretête croit aux revenants?
    (b) Est-ce qu'il a toujours cru aux revenants?

B   Read the following, and then answer the questions in French:

Georges s'est levé à sept heures dix et il est descendu dix minutes plus tard. Il n'a pas pris de bain parce qu'il était en retard, comme d'habitude, mais il s'est lavé le visage et les mains. Il a dû manger très vite son petit déjeuner — une tasse de café noir et un croissant avec un peu de beurre et de la confiture. Heureusement il est arrivé à l'arrêt d'autobus au même moment que le bus lui-même.

1. A quelle heure Georges est-il descendu?
2. Pourquoi n'a-t-il pas pris de bain?
3. S'est-il lavé?
4. A-t-il pris du lait ou de la crème dans son café?
5. Qu'est-ce qu'il a mis sur son croissant?
6. Est-ce que le bus était déjà parti quand il est arrivé à l'arrêt d'autobus?

C   Read the following, translate the questions into French, then answer each in French:

— Regarde, François, dit Jean. Je mets le livre bleu à gauche, le livre rouge à droite, et mon stylo à bille au milieu. Les deux livres représentent les quais de la gare, le stylo est le train. Est-ce que tu comprends mieux maintenant ce que j'ai essayé de t'expliquer?
— Non, pas encore, répond son ami.

1. What is the name of Jean's friend?
2. On which side does Jean put the red book?
3. What is the colour of the other book?
4. What does his ball-pen represent?
5. Does François understand what his friend is trying to explain to him?

D Translate the following questions into French, and answer each in French:

1. Have you a brother or a sister?
2. What did you do yesterday evening?
3. What did you have for breakfast this morning?
4. When is it necessary to send for a doctor?
5. Why do people read newspapers?

E Read the following, then answer the questions as explained below.

Marc et son ami Louis allaient à la ville qui se trouvait pas loin de leur village. Ils allaient à pied parce qu'un des pneus du vélo de Louis était crevé. Il faisait très froid, et il avait neigé pendant la nuit.

Chemin faisant, ils ont trouvé un homme couché sur la neige à côté de la rue. D'abord ils croyaient qu'il était mort, mais puis ils ont vu qu'il était endormi.

« Je crois qu'il est ivre, a dit Marc. Il sent l'alcool.
— Il faut le réveiller, a déclaré Louis. Autrement il va mourir de froid.»
Les deux garçons ont secoué l'homme, mais sans succès.
« On ne peut pas l'abandonner, a dit Marc. Qu'est-ce qu'il faut faire?»
A ce moment ils ont vu un camion qui approchait.
« C'est Monsieur Meunier en route pour la ville, a dit Louis. Arrêtons-le; il pourra nous aider. C'est un homme gentil.»

Et, en effet, Monsieur Meunier les a aidés à hisser l'ivrogne, toujours profondément endormi, dans son camion, et lui et les garçons l'ont déposé au poste de police en arrivant dans la ville.

Answer the following questions as if you were Marc. If you wish to quote what someone said, use indirect speech. Note that **tu** refers to you, Marc, alone, but **vous** to both of you.

1. Qui est Louis?
2. En quelle saison êtes-vous allés à la ville, ce jour-là?
3. Pourquoi êtes-vous allés à pied?
4. Ton vélo n'avait pas de crevaison. Pourquoi n'es-tu pas allé à vélo?
5. Qu'est-ce que vous avez trouvé en route?
6. Qu'est-ce que tu as dit après avoir examiné l'homme?
7. Comment as-tu su qu'il était ivre?
8. Pourquoi n'était-il pas sage de le laisser dormir?
9. Est-ce que vous avez essayé de réveiller l'homme?
10. Avez-vous réussi?
11. Qu'est-ce que vous avez vu approcher de loin?
12. Est-ce que le chauffeur du camion s'est arrêté?
13. Qu'est-ce que M. Meunier vous a aidé à faire?
14. Est-ce que tu es allé, toi, à la ville dans le camion?
    Et ton ami aussi?
15. Qu'est-ce que vous avez fait avec l'ivrogne en arrivant dans la ville?

F   Translate:

Dear Alain,

   How are you? Did you receive my last letter? I sent it three weeks ago, and have not yet had an answer. You aren't ill, I hope? Have you been on holiday?
   I should like to ask you: Can you come here at Easter? And could I visit you later, perhaps in August or at Christmas?
   Do you want to speak English when you are here? You will help me speak French in France, won't you? Write soon.

                    Your friend,

                        Mark

Now write, in French, Alain's answer — answering all Mark's questions in the order they were asked.

Numbers, dimensions, dates, time

Numbers

Cardinal numbers (1, 2, 3 etc.)		Ordinal numbers (1st, 2nd, 3rd etc.)
un, une	1	premier, première
deux	2	deuxième, second(e)
trois	3	troisième
quatre	4	quatrième
cinq	5	cinquième
six	6	sixième
sept	7	septième
huit	8	huitième
neuf	9	neuvième
dix	10	dixième
onze (le onze)	11	onzième (le onzième)
douze	12	douzième
treize	13	treizième
quatorze	14	quatorzième
quinze	15	quinzième
seize	16	seizième
dix-sept	17	dix-septième
dix-huit	18	dix-huitième
dix-neuf	19	dix-neuvième
vingt	20	vingtième
vingt et un (une)	21	vingt et unième
vingt-deux etc.	22	vingt-deuxième etc.
trente	30	trentième
trente et un (une)	31	trente et unième
trente-deux etc.	32	trente-deuxième etc.
quarante	40	quarantième
cinquante	50	cinquantième
soixante	60	soixantième
soixante-dix	70	soixante-dixième
soixante et onze	71	soixante et onzième
soixante-douze etc.	72	soixante-douzième
quatre-vingts	80	quatre-vingtième
quatre-vingt-un	81	quatre-vingt-unième
quatre-vingt-deux etc.	82	quatre-vingt-deuxième
quatre-vingt-dix	90	quatre-vingt-dixième
quatre-vingt-onze	91	quatre-vingt-onzième
quatre-vingt-douze etc.	92	quatre-vingt-douzième

quatre-vingt-dix-neuf	99	quatre-vingt-dix-neuvième
cent	100	centième
cent un	101	cent unième
deux cents	200	deux centième
deux cent un	201	deux cent unième
mille.	1.000	millième
deux mille	2.000	deux millième
un million	1.000.000	millionième
deux millions	2.000.000	deux millionième

Notes:
(a) **Quatre-vingts** ends in -s only when it is not followed by another number. **Cent** in the plural takes -s only when not followed by another number: **trois cents** but **trois cent cinq.**
(b) The word **et** occurs only in 21, 31, 41, 51, 61, and 71.
(c) Hyphens are used to link compounds up to 99, but never before or after **et**; nor before or after **cent** or **mille.**
(d) **Mille** never takes -s. **Deux milles** means two miles.
(e) The only cardinal number that agrees is **un, une.**
(f) The only ordinal numbers that have a feminine form are **premier, première,** and **second, seconde** (alternative form of **deuxième**). All ordinals can take the plural -s if necessary: **les premiers rangs,** the first rows; **trois huitièmes,** three eighths.
(g) Fractions are expressed by combining cardinals with ordinals, e.g. **trois huitièmes,** except:
un quart, a quarter; **trois quarts,** three quarters
un demi, a half; used as an adjective it precedes the noun and does not agree: **une demi-bouteille,** but it does agree in gender in *and a half*: **une bouteille et demie.**
une moitié, a half; used as a noun (**la moitié des soldats,** half the soldiers). Not used in arithmetic.
un tiers, a third; **deux tiers,** two thirds
(h) The ordinals are formed by adding -ième to the cardinal number, dropping the final -e if there is one. **Unième** and not **premier** is used in compounds. **Second** is never used in compounds. Note -v- in **neuvième.**
(i) A point is used in large numbers where we use a comma, and a comma is used where we use the decimal point: 1.250; 1,5.
(j) *Nought* is **zéro** when speaking of numbers, such as telephone numbers. When telephone numbers are spoken they are split up into pairs, e.g. 01–23–47 would be **zéro un, vingt-trois, quarante-sept.**

Round numbers

une douzaine, a dozen
Other similar numbers are used to mean *approximately*:
une centaine, about a hundred; **une dizaine,** about ten

These words take **de** before the following noun: **une vingtaine de voitures**, some twenty cars. They are normally formed by adding **-aine** to the cardinal (dropping the final **-e**), except for **mille: des milliers de gens**, thousands of people.
Une quinzaine is used to mean *a fortnight*.

Dimensions

There are various ways of stating dimensions, such as:
Ce jardin est long de 50 m. ⎫
Ce jardin a 50 m de long. ⎬ This garden is 50 m long.
Cette rue est large de 10 m. ⎫
Cette rue a 10 m de large. ⎬ This street is 10 m wide.
Cette tour a 100 m de haut. This tower is 100 m high.
L'eau est profonde de 10 m. ⎫
L'eau a 10 m de profondeur. ⎬ The water is 10 m deep.
Un jardin de 50 m de long. ⎫
Un jardin long de 50 m. ⎬ A garden 50 m long.
Une tour haute de 100 m. ⎫
Une tour de 100 m de haut. ⎬ A 100 m high tower.

By when stating areas or volumes is **sur**:
Cette pièce a 10 m de long sur 5 m de large.
This room is 10 m long by 5 m wide.

Note: **long, large** and **haut** do not agree when used after **de**.

A   Answer the following in French, writing out figures in full:
  1. Combien fait deux fois quatre-vingt-dix-neuf?
  2. Combien font deux mille trois cent un et trois mille cent quinze?
  3. Lequel est le plus long: six milles ou huit kilomètres?
  4. Alain achète une douzaine de pommes. Il en mange trois. Combien de pommes lui reste-t-il?
  5. Marie a une chambre 2 m de large sur 9 m de long; Jean a une chambre 3 m de large sur 8 m de long.
     Laquelle de ces deux chambres est la plus grande — celle de Marie ou celle de Jean?

B   Translate the following, writing all numbers in full:
  1. My second sister has three sons and a daughter.
  2. The judges gave the first prize to Louise.
  3. If you want to phone you must dial 02–18–97.
  4. There are some twenty apple-trees in the garden.
  5. The river is three metres deep, but the lake is much deeper than the river.
  6. The Great Wall of China is about 3,000 km long.
  7. He is 160 cm tall.
  8. He has been working there for some 10 years.
  9. When I go by train I travel second class.
  10. There are thousands of people in this town, but I only know about ten of them.

Dates

Years   Year is translated by **an**:
after a cardinal number: **Il a quinze ans.** He is fifteen
(years old).
in dates: **en l'an 1066**, in the year 1066
in **le jour de l'an**, New Year's Day, and **le nouvel an**, the New Year
In all other cases, year is translated by **année**:
toute l'année, the whole year; **l'année scolaire**, the school year;
la première année de la guerre, the first year of the war.
The date of the year can be expressed in two ways:
1979 — **dix-neuf cent soixante dix-neuf**
          mil neuf cent soixante dix-neuf
Note the special form **mil**.

Seasons   **au printemps**, in spring
en été, in summer
en automne, in autumn
en hiver, in winter

Months   The months of the year are written with small initial letters:
**janvier, février, mars, avril, mai, juin, juillet, août, septembre,
octobre, novembre, décembre**
au mois de janvier, en janvier, in January
In dates, *on* and *of* are not translated: **le premier mai**, on the
first of May
For all dates other than the first, ordinal numbers are used:
le huit mai, le onze mai, le vingt et un mai, etc.

Days   The days of the week are written with small initial letters. All
are masculine:
dimanche, lundi, mardi, mercredi, jeudi, vendredi, samedi
on Monday, **lundi**
on Mondays, **le lundi**
every Monday, **tous les lundis.**
Day is usually translated by **le jour**:
Ce jour-là il est parti de bonne heure. That day he left early.
La journée is used when the day is considered as a period of
time within which things happen:
Pendant la journée il travaillait au bureau. During the day he
used to work at the office.
There is a similar distinction between:
le matin and **la matinée**, morning
le soir and **la soirée**, evening
L'après-midi (m), the afternoon, and **la nuit**, night, have only
one form.
When speaking of times of the day, *in* is not usually translated:
le matin, in the morning.
To convey the idea of *during*, **dans** or **pendant** can be used:
dans la nuit, in the night.
aujourd'hui, today
demain, tomorrow

le lendemain, the next day
après-demain, the day after tomorrow
hier, yesterday
avant-hier, the day before yesterday
une semaine, a week
une quinzaine, a fortnight
aujourd'hui en huit, a week today

Time

To speak of *time* in a general sense, as in 'I haven't the time' or 'time flies', le temps is used.
Times as in 'how many times must I tell you . . .' is translated by fois: Combien de fois . . . ?; How many times . . . ?
trois fois par an/par semaine/par jour (or trois fois l'an/la semaine/le jour), three times a year/a week/a day
In telling the time, heure is used:
Quelle heure est-il? What time is it?
Il est midi. It is noon.
Il est une heure six. It is 6 minutes past one.
trois heures moins six, 6 minutes to three
cinq heures et quart, a quarter past five
sept heures moins le quart, a quarter to seven
midi et demi, half past twelve (noon)
huit heures et demie, half past eight (-e is added when a feminine noun — heure — precedes demi)
minuit, midnight
un quart d'heure, a quarter of an hour
une demi-heure; half an hour
There is no equivalent to the English a.m. or p.m., but you can say du matin, de l'après midi, du soir, de la nuit.
à huit heures du matin, at 8 a.m.

A   Translate, writing all numbers in full:
1. 10 o'clock in the morning.
2. 3 o'clock in the afternoon.
3. What's the time?
4. It's 9 o'clock.
5. He does not work on Sundays.
6. There is a market in the town every Thursday.
7. The journey took the whole day.
8. Take this medicine three times a day: at eight o'clock, at midday, and at half past six in the evening.
9. I'll come to see you again a week tomorrow at a quarter to five.
10. If you come on Wednesday the 21st of February I shall be there.
11. During the first year he had to take his holidays in the spring or in the autumn.
12. He is seventeen; his birthday is on New Year's Day.
13. On the eleventh of September I shall be sixteen.
14. I cannot do it today, but I'll do it tomorrow or the day after.
15. The day after my arrival I got up early and went to bed late.

B   Translate, writing all numbers out in full, and using the 2nd person singular:

The two young men went to bed a little after midnight. The next day Paul was the first to wake up — after 8 o'clock. Jean was still asleep. 'Get up!' Paul said, shaking him. 'We must leave today, as I told you yesterday evening.'
'I know', Jean said, opening one eye. 'Today is Saturday the 21st of June, isn't it? Ah! I slept well last night! Have you counted the money?'
'Yes', Paul answered. 'We have eight fifty-franc notes — that makes four hundred francs; and we also have thirty-one francs in change.'
'What's the time?' Jean asked. 'I forgot to wind up my watch yesterday.'
'It's already a quarter to eight — no, I mean a quarter past eight. Hurry up! The train leaves in an hour, at nine fifteen.'
'It will be the third time we leave without eating', grumbled Jean.
'Too bad! It will be a long journey.'
'It will be a long day, too. Let's hope there is a dining-car on the train.'

A few minutes later the two young men set off on foot for the Gare de Lyon. Their destination — Florence, in Italy. And why? Yesterday they visited the Louvre, in Paris. But they visited the Louvre a little before midnight.
Today they are leaving by train, with one big parcel, about two metres long by one and a half metres wide. This parcel contains something they hope to sell for a hundred million francs — La Joconde — The Mona Lisa!

Passages for revision

1. I don't know Peter very well; but I do know that he lives in France, in Dijon I think, and that he writes books.

2. The French say that they have the most beautiful country in the world, the most beautiful language, the best cars, the best cooking and the best wines. The English would not agree — except for the wines.

3. In a self-service restaurant there is neither waiter nor waitress, but you can get, for example, good soup, good bread, fresh rolls, and chicken with green peas. They also sell wine and beer.

4. The cruel Queen was furious.
   'Cut off her head,' she exclaimed.
   Poor Alice thought that they were really going to cut off her head; but then she woke with a start — it was only a dream.

5. 'How many stamps have you got in your collection?'
   'I've got more than three hundred, and I'll have still more when my uncle sends me some. He travels quite often, and this time he's going to Sweden, Japan and the U.S.A. I'd really like to go there too.'

6. Every Thursday I have to take the bus to go to the market. I like to buy fresh fruit and vegetables, but there is very little choice in the village shop. After having done my shopping, I often go to see a friend and we go to the cinema together.

7. Yesterday I had an awful headache and I did not want to go out, but I had promised Philip that I would go sailing with him if the weather was fine. As I was putting on my anorak, I heard a thunder clap, and looking out of the window I saw that it was pouring. Two minutes later Philip phoned me to say that it would be better to wait till the next day.

8. Over the main entrance of the Cathedral of St. Mark, in Venice, there are four great gilded horses. The Venetians brought them back from Istanbul, formerly Constantinople, more than seven hundred years ago — in the year 1204.
   Napoleon stole them and placed them on the Arc de Triomphe which he was building in Paris. But during the First World War the French sent them to Italy to preserve them from the Germans.
   Naturally the Italians kept them and put them back over the main entrance of St. Mark's Cathedral.

9. While my uncle was speaking to me I looked, not without emotion, at the little sitting-room which I had not seen for so long.
   Nothing had changed. Still the sofa with its yellow squares, the two red armchairs, the armless Venus on the mantlepiece, the portrait of grandad on the wall, and, in a corner, near the window, the desk, heavily laden with old books and dictionaries.
   In the middle of this desk I noticed a thick open note-book —

doubtless the novel which my uncle had been writing for at least seven years.

10. The widow entered the kitchen where her son was waiting for her. Painfully she placed her basket of stores on the table. After a long silence she said:

'I saw in the street women who have nothing with which to feed their children. Poverty is everywhere.'

'There is no time to lose', answered her son. 'We must guillotine those who steal the food of the people. We must set up a tribunal to judge those who rob us.'

'Let it be', his mother answered him. 'You are young; you have illusions. We must not guillotine people any more — not even the enemies of the Republic.'

'Yes we must!' exclaimed the young man, standing up. 'The Revolution will bring happiness to humanity for centuries to come. Long live the Revolution!'

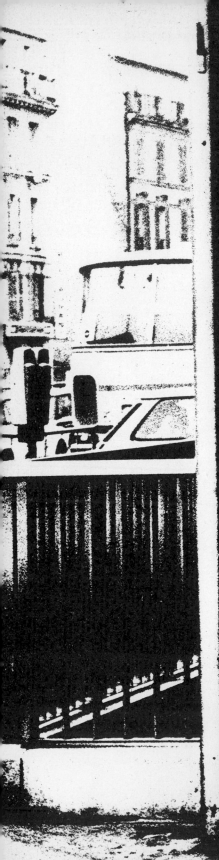

2
Comprehension and translation

Questions on a French text

Questions on a French text requiring answers in English are intended to reveal to what extent the French has been understood. Answers which do not keep to the point, and which contain a mass of irrelevant detail, suggest that the writer is unsure of himself, and that the meaning has not been fully grasped. Answers should therefore always be brief and to the point, without any unnecessary padding.

Read the following, and then answer the questions in English as briefly as possible.

A Mon mari m'avait accompagnée à la gare, mais il ne pouvait pas attendre mon départ à cause de son travail. Ainsi je me trouvais seule sur le quai sauf deux messieurs que je ne connaissais pas. Le plus grand, qui portait un chapeau noir et un vieux pardessus gris, était probablement italien; l'autre, qui fumait un grand cigare avec l'air d'un millionaire, était certainement américain. Le train arriva deux minutes après mon arrivée, et l'Américain, montant dans le même compartiment que moi, prit une place au coin, près de la fenêtre, face à la locomotive. L'autre s'en alla chercher une place ailleurs — mais c'était celui-ci que je devais rencontrer de nouveau, le lendemain.

   1. How do you know that the narrator is a woman?
   2. Which of the two men was the tallest?
   3. What was the colour of the Italian's hat?
   4. How long did the woman have to wait on the platform?
   5. Did the woman know either of the two men?
   6. Why was the husband unable to wait to see his wife off?
   7. Which of the two men seemed the richer? Why?
   8. Which of the two men travelled in the compartment with the narrator?
   9. Describe the seat chosen by her companion.
  10. Which of the two men did she meet the following day?

B Ayant éteint les lumières, fermé les fenêtres et fermé la porte à clef, la veuve s'est couchée comme d'habitude à dix heures et demie. Depuis la mort de son mari il y avait quatre ans elle vivait seule, et elle s'y était accoutumée.

   Vers deux heures du matin la veuve s'est réveillée, croyant qu'elle avait entendu un bruit en bas. Elle n'était pas timide, et après avoir allumée, elle a mis sa robe de chambre et a pris le revolver qu'elle gardait toujours dans le tiroir de sa table de chevet.

   Elle est descendue très doucement. Tout était silencieux. Elle a vérifié la porte et les fenêtres: elles étaient toujours fermées. Rien ne semblait avoir été dérangé, rien ne manquait, et la veuve a décidé de se recoucher, croyant qu'elle avait imaginé le bruit. D'abord elle est allée dans la cuisine, pour se faire une tasse de chocolat chaud.

Soudain elle a remarqué sur le plancher de petites flaques d'eau. D'où venaient-elles? Il pleuvait dehors, mais les fenêtres étaient bien fermées. ... Et puis, sur la table, elle a vu une statuette en jade qui représentait une licorne. La veuve était étonnée. Son mari lui avait donné cette statuette pour le premier anniversaire de leur mariage, il y avait presque quarante ans, mais elle avait été perdue pendant l'année qu'ils avaient passée en Inde, quand son mari y travaillait. Qui avait rapporté la statuette? La veuve ne l'a jamais su.

1. What did the widow do before going to bed?
2. How long had she lived alone?
3. Why did she wake up?
4. What did she do before going downstairs?
5. What did she find on first inspection?
6. What did she decide to do?
7. What did she notice on the kitchen floor?
8. What object was on the kitchen table?
9. On what occasion had it been given to the widow and by whom?
10. When had it been lost?

Misleading appearances

Many words in French look like English words, but have different meanings. For example **un homme sensible** is not a *sensible* man but a *sensitive* man. Such words are often called **faux amis.**

Occasionally the same spelling may be used for two different words, and a number of words have secondary, less obvious meanings in certain idioms or contexts. The apparently 'obvious' translation is not always the correct one. If it does not make sense it must be wrong.

A   Translate:
1. Il fait une promenade en bateau.
2. Il étudie la médecine.
3. Il est en train d'y aller.
4. Elle fait la vaisselle.
5. C'était un orphelin qu'avaient adopté les sœurs.
6. Il a caché le vin dans la cave.
7. Qu'il est bête!
8. Les habits du mendiant sont en lambeaux.
9. Ce moteur ne marche pas bien.
10. Il y a un tapis bien usé dans cette pièce.

B   Translate:
1. Il a mal au cœur.
2. Je suis mon père avec des fils de fer.
3. Les cabinets sont en face.
4. Il dit qu'il vient de passer son examen.
5. Il prétend qu'il a réussi.
6. Garçon! Donnez-moi des chips, s'il vous plaît, et une blonde.
7. Il aime beaucoup la lecture.
8. Ils causent beaucoup.
9. Ils portaient tous une veste bleue.
10. Le malade s'est dressé dans son lit.

C   Translate:
1. Une lampe à pétrole.
2. Il le charge.
3. Il va assister à un match de football.
4. La voiture roule mieux sur ces larges roues.
5. Le photographe est très habile.
6. Il cherche à tâtons l'interrupteur.
7. Elle demande l'heure et le temps qu'il fait.
8. La bonne travaille bien pendant toute la journée.
9. C'est une moto d'occasion.
10. Un Espagnol de grande taille.
11. Je l'ai rencontrée dans la salle des pas perdus.
12. Le professeur est en train de faire le cours d'anglais.
13. Elle devait faire ses courses en français.

14. Il a mangé sur le pouce.
15. La cloche annonce la fin du marché.

'Exam dislexia'

Under the stress of examination conditions many of us are afflicted by a tendency to misread words, to mistake their gender, or even to ignore them altogether. In the following examples a peculiarly nervous candidate is imagined to have suffered badly in this way, producing the incorrect translations given in brackets after each sentence.

A   Give the correct translation of the following, using the mistaken translations to keep you from falling into the more obvious traps:

1. Les poussins l'ont suivie de près. (*Wrongly translated as*: The fish followed it from the fields.)
2. Il a des chevaux blancs. (He has white hair.)
3. Le savant a levé la main. (The soap has washed his hand.)
4. Le papier à écrire était dans la librairie. (The newspaper to be written was in the library.)
5. Je suis assis sur le banc. (I sat down on the bank.)
6. Ils font le tour de la ville. (They build the tower of the village.)
7. Il étudie l'équitation. (He studies the equation.)
8. Le sol est au-dessous. (The sun is overhead.)
9. Ce matelas va avec mon coussin. (This sailor goes with my cousin.)
10. Hier la journée était chaude et longue. . . . (Here the journey was hot and long. . . .)
11. . . . et aujourd'hui il va rester à la maison. (. . . and today he is having a rest in the house.)
12. La veille la pêcheuse avait vu l'argent. (The old sinner-woman had seen the policeman.)
13. Il y a des chaussettes à vendre dans ce magasin. (There are some shoes advertised for sale in this magazine.)
14. L'ouvreuse fait sa propre tâche. (The workwoman makes the spot clean.)
15. Une souris court sur la roue. (A short smile on the street.)

The context as clue

The possible mis-translations suggested above were mainly due to confusion between words which look similar. There are in French, as in English, many words which have more than one meaning. If the meaning that first comes to mind obviously does not make sense, the context must be used as a guide. This may mean using the word in a way which is unfamiliar; but if the translation does not make sense it must be wrong.

A   Each of the following sentences contains words which can be translated in more than one way. A 'context clue' is given after each in brackets.

Translate each sentence in the way that best fits the context clue, but do not translate the clues themselves.

1. Il a cassé la glace. (un étang en hiver)
2. Il est fier de son adresse. (un homme habile)
3. Il arriva comme prévu. (on parle d'un événement)
4. Les jeunes filles peignent leurs cheveux noirs. (avec un peigne)
5. Il fallait acheter une carte. (on était perdu)
6. Je vais vous montrer une place. (dit l'ouvreuse)
7. Il a beaucoup plu. (un cadeau)
8. Il a vendu le café. (sans lait)
9. Il y a des feuilles partout. (sur la table de l'écrivain)
10. Elle a une mauvaise vue. (et porte des lunettes)
11. Il s'est acheté un ballon. (un joueur de football)
12. Une voiture moderne. (qui roule sur des rails)
13. L'oiseau a volé. (des pierres précieuses, peut-être)
14. Il y a deux pages. (près du roi)
15. Il la conduit bien. (il a un permis)
16. Elle est occupée. (quand papa se rase)
17. Il habite un grand hôtel. (il n'est pas voyageur)
18. Elle découvrit le panier. (pour regarder dedans)
19. Elle la mit sur la coiffeuse. (un nécessaire de toilette)
20. Il met la serviette sur la table. (et en prend du buvard)

B Translate:
1. Dieu a donc oublié tout ce que j'ai fait pour lui?
   (Louis XIV, 1638–1715)
2. Un mauvais général vaut mieux que deux bons.
   (Napoléon, 1769–1821)
3. Plus ça change, plus c'est la même chose.
   (Alphonse Karr, 1808–1890)
4. Quand tout le monde a tort, tout le monde a raison.
   (La Chaussée, 1692–1750)
5. Il faut avoir beaucoup étudié pour savoir peu.
   (Montesquieu, 1689–1755)

Translating prepositions

For English speakers, choosing the correct French preposition when writing or speaking French is often difficult. The problem has been dealt with above, in Part I, pp. 75 ff. But it can also often be difficult to select the appropriate English preposition to translate those commonly used in French, as the following examples show.

de

de can mean any of the following: *about, any, as, at, by, for, from, in, of, on, some, to, with, 's or s'* — or it may not need translating at all. Sense and context are normally sufficient to make its meaning clear, but not always.

A   Each of the following examples contains the word **de**. Although occasionally **de** can be translated in an individual sentence in more ways than one, only one meaning fits all the phrases or sentences in any one group. Write down the number of each group and give the meaning of **de** that best fits its use in all examples in that group. If **de** is not translated, put **de** = X. The answer to No. 1 is given as an example.

1. de = of
   Le toit de la maison.
   Il est mort de faim.
   Il a beaucoup de pain.
2. de = ?
   Ils n'ont pas de sucre.
   Avez-vous du papier buvard?
   A-t-il acheté de l'encre?
3. de = ?
   Un livre avec dessins de l'auteur.
   J'ai lu quelques œuvres de Victor Hugo.
   Un homme généreux est aimé de ses amis.
4. de = ?
   Ils sont venus par le train de Paris.
   C'est une maison qu'il a héritée d'une tante.
   Il arrive de l'étranger.
5. de = ?
   Il prend le train de Paris où il arrivera ce soir.
   Elle portait le deuil de son mari.
   Il le remercia d'avoir pris sa place.
6. de = ?
   Il a acheté des livres.
   Il faut manger du pain.
   Il y a de la neige dans le jardin.
7. de = ?
   Où se trouve le livre de Jean?
   C'est la voiture des Lesage.
   Voici la chambre de la bonne.

8. de = ?
   Il tressaillit de colère.
   Il le menace de sa main.
   Il remplit la boîte de sable.
9. de = ?
   Le Dauphin était l'héritier du trône français.
   Nous avons tenté de le voir.
   Il a pris la route de Lyon et puis le chemin du village.
10. de = ?
    Il parle toujours de ces propres affaires.
    Elle s'indigne de cette idée.
    Il se vante de son adresse.
11. de = ?
    Je l'ai vu passer de l'autre côté de la rue.
    Les arbres se voient de tous côtés.
    Il m'écrit de sa part.
12. de = ?
    Il ne se doute de rien, et s'avance de quelques pas.
    Il jouit d'une bonne santé.
    Je me souviens de lui.
13. de = ?
    On ne doit pas se rire de ses copains.
    Il s'émerveille de son adresse.
    Je m'étonne de ce que tu dis.
14. de = ?
    On le fait d'une façon plus moderne aujourd'hui.
    Il se mêle de mes affaires.
    Je le croyais de parfaite santé.
15. de = ?
    Il servait longtemps d'organiste à l'église.
    Votre permis peut vous servir de passeport.
    Aujourd'hui on traite les femmes d'égal à égal.

à

Although à usually means *to* or *at*, it can have a number of other meanings. Moreover it is often used before a noun which in English we use as an adjective to form a composite noun: **une locomotive à vapeur**, a steam-engine.

A Translate the following, in which **à** = *at*, *in*, *on*, *to* or *for*:

1. Il demeure à Paris, mais il ira à Londres demain.
2. A ta place je ne le ferais pas.
3. J'ai acheté au marché six oranges à quatre-vingt centimes la pièce.
4. Je préfère une place à l'angle du compartiment.
5. Ils participent aux jeux des enfants.
6. Je vois un grand bateau au large.
7. Les visiteurs parlent à voix basse.
8. A quoi sert ceci?
9. Ils sont contents de rentrer à la maison.
10. Ils habitent à la campagne.

B   Translate the following, in which à = *by, by means of, from* or *of*:
1. C'est gentil à vous de le payer.
2. Il l'a acheté à un ami.
3. Les plantes sont toutes mangées aux vers.
4. L'homme en noir a volé le panier à la vieille dame.
5. Il fait de grandes promenades à vélo.
6. On vend ce vin à la bouteille.
7. Elle arrive souvent à cheval.
8. C'est bien bon à vous; merci beaucoup.
9. Je l'ai reconnue à sa voix.
10. Ce doit être vrai, à ce que l'on dit.

C   Translate:
1. L'agent porte une arme à feu.
2. Elle fait la cuisine à la française.
3. Donnez-moi un verre à vin avec de l'eau dedans, s'il vous plaît.
4. Il y a un bateau à voile sur le lac.
5. C'est un ami à moi.
6. Il a mangé une omelette aux champignons.
7. Je souffre d'un mal aux dents affreux.
8. J'ai mis les cartes postales dans la boîte aux lettres.
9. Nous mangeons toujours dans la salle à manger.
10. Mon passe-temps favori est la pêche à la ligne.
11. Nous allons jouer au tennis.
12. Il désobéit à son maître.
13. L'étudiant est entré à l'université.
14. Un bon vin plaît à mon père.
15. Au secours! Au voleur!

D   Translate:
1. Il n'y a rien à craindre.
2. C'est à moi.
3. Elle s'intéresse à tout, mais elle ne croit pas à Dieu.
4. Le directeur est arrivé, le document à la main.
5. C'est à lui à parler à ce moment.
6. Le gymnaste grimpe à la corde, et puis il fait des exercices aux barres parallèles.
7. Il a réussi à le faire à la main.
8. Le livre est à moi, mais les stylos sont à vous.
9. J'ai mangé un œuf à la coque à huit heures, au petit déjeuner.
10. Il y a une vieille maison intéressante à vendre dans le village.

en

When used as a preposition **en** usually means *in*, but it can have other meanings. It must not be confused with the pronoun **en**, used with a verb, meaning *of it, some* etc. (see p. 39).

A   Translate the following, noticing the varied uses of **en**:
1. La révolution a commencé en France en l'an 1789.
2. De jour en jour la situation s'empire.

3. Pendant que j'étais en vacances j'ai voyagé beaucoup en auto-stop.
4. En rentrant à la maison il est monté en haut.
5. Ils sont assis à une petite table en fer sur la terrasse.
6. Le conducteur a mis la voiture en marche.
7. En attendant vous pouvez lire ce livre en silence.
8. De temps en temps quelqu'un arrive en voiture.
9. Je suis allé en France pour les vacances; j'y vais toujours en hiver.
10. Les ouvriers sont en grève, comme toujours en été.

dans

Although **dans** usually means *in*, it must occasionally be translated by another preposition in English, e.g. *from*, *out of*. This is usually made clear by the context.

A   Translate:
1. Le chien mange dans l'assiette et boit dans le verre de son maître.
2. Il a pris un mouchoir dans le tiroir de la commode.
3. Ma voiture m'a coûté dans les huit mille francs.
4. J'ai entendu un bruit dans l'escalier.
5. Je serai prêt dans dix minutes, mais pas avant.

chez

There is no corresponding English preposition for **chez**. It may mean *at the home of*, *at the work place of*, *in the writings of*, *according to the teachings of*, *among the people of*, etc. It is also frequently replaced in English by the possessive *'s* (or *-s'*). Note that **chez** is always used before a noun or pronoun referring to persons.

A   Translate:
1. Je vais passer les grandes vacances chez Jean.
2. Il travaille chez le quincaillier.
3. Chez les Français le vin est plus important que la bière.
4. Faites comme chez vous.
5. D'abord nous allons prendre du thé chez moi.

depuis

Depuis may be variously translated by *since*, *for* or *from*. When the action is considered as still going on at the time, French uses **depuis** with the present tense where English uses the perfect, and **depuis** with the imperfect tense where English uses the pluperfect:
J'habite Paris depuis trois ans. I have been living in Paris for three years.
J'habitais Paris depuis trois ans quand la guerre a éclaté. I had been living in Paris for three years when war broke out.
When the action is already completed, the tense with **depuis** is the same in French as in English.
Depuis is also used with **jusqu'à** to mean *from . . . to* or *from . . . till*.

A   Translate, noting the use of tenses:
1. Je le connais depuis longtemps.
2. Depuis quand l'attendez-vous?

3. Je le savais par cœur à l'école, mais depuis je l'ai oublié.
4. Je vous attendais depuis une heure quand vous êtes arrivé.
5. Je vous avais attendu depuis longtemps avant votre arrivée.
6. D'ici on peut voir depuis le château jusqu'au phare.

où

Où can mean *where*, *in which*, *on which*, and, after a conjunction of time, *when*.

A   Translate:
1. Où est ma règle?
2. Où se trouve la gare?
3. J'ai trouvé la page où on explique ces mots.
4. L'éclair a frappé la maison au moment où il est arrivé.
5. D'où viennent ces gens?
6. Le jour où j'ai acheté ma nouvelle moto était le plus heureux de ma vie.
7. Dites-moi où il se trouve et où il faut le chercher.

sur

Sur usually means *on*, but it can occasionally have other meanings.

A   Translate:
1. Je voudrais demander des renseignements sur la ville.
2. L'espion s'en est allé, le chapeau rabattu sur les yeux.
3. Je suis sûr que je ne me suis pas trompé sur le chemin à suivre.
4. Il est entré, sur quoi tout le monde s'est tu.
5. Il ne faut pas juger les gens sur les apparences.
6. Cette pièce a 5 mètres de long sur 4 mètres de large.

Other preposition problems

The examples given above illustrate some of the difficulties which may arise when translating prepositions. The correct use and translation of prepositions is never easy, and further examples will be constantly met with. The more practice one can have the better.

A   Translate:
1. Je bois toujours du café avant de quitter la maison.
2. Je vous remercie de votre lettre que vous m'avez envoyée de Paris et que j'ai reçue à Lyon.
3. Il y a plus de stations de métro à Paris qu'à Londres.
4. Est-ce que vous avez appris à monter à cheval?
5. Le Louvre n'est pas loin de la place de la Concorde.
6. Ils habitent à la campagne, au pied des Alpes.
7. Ce soir nous mangeons chez les Leroy à huit heures.
8. Il marche le long de la rue de Rivoli.
9. La fête aura lieu au mois de juin dans le jardin de Madame Labelle, à ce qu'on m'a dit.
10. Je suis étudiant ici depuis trois ans.

B   Translate:
1. Il a été soldat dès le commencement de la guerre.
2. Je vous prie d'entrer et de remettre cette lettre entre les mains du directeur.
3. On peut voir depuis les montagnes jusqu'à la mer.
4. Le gosse a reçu un vélo de son grand-père; il est fou de joie.
5. Par un beau jour d'été on peut les voir, couchés par terre au soleil.
6. Il a été très gentil pour nous.
7. Je peux le finir sous très peu de temps.
8. «Venez par ici, s'il vous plaît», m'a-t-il dit. J'ai obéi, à contre-cœur.
9. Il a travaillé jusqu'au commencement du mois; mais dès lors il ne travaille plus.
10. En été j'aime beaucoup me coucher à la belle étoile. Au besoin, je sors dans le jardin à la dérobée, à l'insu de mes parents, et je rentre dans ma chambre au lever du soleil. Ni père ni mère ne s'éveillent jamais à pareille heure, mais je ne sais pas dans quelle mesure ils devinent la vérité.

Translating verbs

The verb is the heart of a sentence. When the meaning of a sentence is not clear, start by finding the verb. Look at its ending, and note the tense, and what it can tell you about its subject — person and number. Ability to recognize which tense is being used is important, but the corresponding tense will not always be correct in translation since French and English tenses are not always used in the same way. A form of verb which is clearly unnatural in English must not be used in translation, whatever may be the form used in the French.

Present tense

The French have only one form for the present tense. The English have three. Two of these forms are used for statements: *I give* and *I am giving*; two are used for questions: *are you giving?* and *do you give?*; and two are used for negatives: *he is not giving* and *he does not give*. Sometimes *do*, used mainly in our interrogative or negative constructions, is also used in English for emphasis: 'He *does* do it!' The French must use some more roundabout way to express this emphasis, such as: **Mais si, il le fait!** or **Bien sûr, il le fait!** This type of expression can often be translated into English using a simple emphatic *do*.

A   Give two alternative translations for each of the following, e.g. **je donne** = I give, I am giving.

1. ils achètent
2. j'aide
3. tu aimes
4. il ajoute
5. elle allume
6. nous amenons
7. vous amusez
8. ils portent
9. elles n'apprennent pas
10. est-ce que j'arrange?
11. arrives-tu?
12. n'attache-t-il pas?
13. est-ce qu'elle attrape?
14. est-ce que nous avançons?
15. ne buvez-vous pas?
16. brûlent-ils?
17. ne cachent-elles pas?
18. est-ce que je chante?
19. est-ce que tu ne cherches pas?
20. est-ce qu'il court?

B   Translate, using the most appropriate form of the verb in English:
1. Je ne choisis pas le jour.
2. Tu ne comprends pas très bien.
3. Il ne finit pas vite.
4. Elle ne le fait pas facilement.
5. Nous ne comptons jamais l'argent.
6. Nous ne connaissons pas encore cette ville.
7. Ne continuez pas votre travail.
8. Ces couteaux ne coupent rien.

9. Elles ne cousent pas bien avec ces mauvaises aiguilles.
10. Ne couvrez pas la soupe.

C Translate:
   1. Tu n'est pas fâché?
   2. Est-ce qu'il ne décharge pas le camion ici?
   3. Est-ce que nous ne déjeunons pas toujours à la maison?
   4. Où est-ce que tu dînes le vendredi?
   5. Comment est-ce qu'on fait ceci?
   6. Regardez! Ma montre marche maintenant.
   7. Je ne peins plus la porte — je peins le mur maintenant.
   8. Tu ne sais pas le faire, mais moi, je sais le faire.
   9. « Tu ne sais rien, toi! » « Mais si! »
  10. « Tu n'aimes pas ce gâteau? » « Mais si! Je l'aime bien. »

Imperfect

The French imperfect (always ending in **-ais, -ais, -ait, -ions, -iez, -aient**)
can be translated by more than one form in English, e.g. **j'écrivais** can
be *I was writing, I used to write, I would write* (as a custom), or *I wrote*.
Before translating an imperfect, make sure you have identified it correctly. It can easily be confused with the conditional, which has the
same endings, but with the future stem. See below p. 118. Also verbs
like **connaître** have the forms **je connais, tu connais** in the present,
which must not be confused with their imperfect: **je connaissais** etc.
Occasionally the imperfect is used to describe actions, where in English
the simple past would be more suitable. Use whichever tense sounds
most natural.

A Translate, using *used to* in your translation:
   1. Quand j'étais en France je dormais dans une tente.
   2. Autrefois une lampe à pétrole éclairait cette pièce.
   3. Au moyen âge on écrivait sur le parchemin.
   4. Avant la télévision nous allions souvent au cinéma.
   5. J'aimais monter à cheval.

B Translate: in the first part of each sentence use a tense to show what
  was happening when the event described in the second part took place.
   1. Il fumait sa pipe quand son ami lui a téléphoné.
   2. Je dormais au moment où le facteur a sonné.
   3. J'écrivais à ma mère quand la lettre est arrivée.
   4. Il étudiait le français lorsque son ami est entré.
   5. Il fermait la porte quand il a entendu quelqu'un dehors.

C Translate:
   1. Il faisait chaud, et j'avais faim.
   2. Il fallait chercher un docteur parce qu'il était très malade.
   3. Il se reposait parce qu'il était fatigué, et je ne voulais pas le déranger.
   4. Une sentinelle gardait le caserne, et la grille était fermée.
   5. Les gens qui faisaient la queue devant le cinéma perdaient patience.

D   Translate:
  1. Quand j'étais jeune, j'allais à l'école à pied.
  2. Le lendemain il voulait continuer le travail qu'il faisait la veille.
  3. Il dormait paisiblement quand le médecin est arrivé.
  4. Je conduisais le camion avec soin, mais je ne pouvais pas éviter l'accident.
  5. Je croyais que c'était un ami — si seulement j'avais su la vérité!
  6. Il ne se rappelait plus ce que faisait la bonne au moment où il est entré dans la pièce.
  7. Après le petit déjeuner elle faisait le ménage avant de sortir.
  8. La nuit tombait. Le vent hurlait dans les arbres; mais l'enfant dans son refuge n'avait plus peur.

Future

Normally when the future is used in French it will be correct to translate it by the future in English. The most frequent exception is after **quand, aussitôt que, dès que**, and similar conjunctions of time. These are followed by the future in French if the future is also used for the main verb of the sentence, but in translation we use the present (p. 16). When translating direct speech, make your English as natural as possible, using *I'll*, *he'll* etc. rather than *I shall* or *he will*: but keep to the more literary English where this reflects a more literary style in the original. Both French and English frequently use **aller**, *to go*, to express the future — especially an immediate or near future.

A   Translate:
  1. «Je vous accompagnerai, si vous voulez», m'a-t-il dit.
  2. Nous le ferons quand nous arriverons.
  3. Je l'achèterai demain; je vais le lui dire maintenant.
  4. Nous allons au cinéma ce soir parce que le cinéma sera fermé demain.
  5. Il ne vous fera pas de mal.
  6. L'avion va partir au lever du soleil.
  7. Ils vont me téléphoner, et ils me diront ce qu'ils vont faire.
  8. Vous viendrez nous voir l'année prochaine, j'espère?
  9. Je vous le montrerai dès qu'il sera ici.
  10. Attendez! Il va vous l'expliquer tout à l'heure.

Conditional

The conditional is formed from the future stem plus the imperfect endings. Confusion between the conditional and the imperfect can arise in verbs which have a basic stem ending in -r, e.g. **courir: je courais** is imperfect, **je courrais** is conditional; **ouvrir: j'ouvrais** is imperfect, **j'ouvrirais** is conditional. Otherwise the endings **-rais** etc. are normally the sign of the conditional.

The French conditional is translated by the English *should* or *would* when this implies a condition: 'I should buy it if I had the money'; 'You would do it if you could'.

The conditional of **devoir** is translated by *ought to*:
Je devrais partir. I ought to leave.
J'aurais dû partir. I ought to have left.
The conditional of **vouloir** is used to express a polite wish:
Je voudrais vous parler. I should like to speak to you.
A conditional used in French after **quand** and other conjunctions of
time is translated by the English imperfect. The conditional is never
used after **si** = *if*.

A   Translate:
1.   Elle disait qu'il ne l'abandonnerait jamais.
2.   «Je le ferais si je pouvais», lui ai-je dit.
3.   Tu aurais dû lui écrire quand tu avais le temps.
4.   Je voudrais une chambre à deux lits, s'il vous plaît.
5.   Je le dirais à mon ami, mais je ne le dirais pas à Monsieur Legros.
6.   On m'a dit que vous iriez à Paris demain s'il était nécessaire.
7.   Ne pourriez-vous pas rouler plus vite? Nous devrions arriver avant
     sept heures.
8.   Nous ne voudrions pas y aller sans vous.
9.   Je serais content si je recevais de leurs nouvelles.
10. Préféreriez-vous travailler le matin ou le soir?

Past historic

The past historic is never used in French in speech or in ordinary letters.
It is, however, used in written French, and it is essential to be able to
recognize and translate it.
In literary French the past historic is generally used where we use our
simple past, as in 'I came, I saw, I conquered'.
The French past historic may also be translated by our past with *did*,
which is used as *do* is used in the present, i.e. mainly in the negative (he
did not come) or the interrogative (did he come?), and also sometimes
for emphasis (but I *did* do it, I tell you!).

The past historic in French has the following forms:

All -er verbs	Regular -ir and -re verbs	Venir, tenir and their compounds	All -evoir verbs including devoir
e.g. aller	e.g. finir	e.g. devenir	e.g. recevoir
j'allai	je finis	je devins	je reçus
tu allas	tu finis	tu devins	tu reçus
il alla	il finit	il devint	il reçut
nous allâmes	nous finîmes	nous devînmes	nous reçûmes
vous allâtes	vous finîtes	vous devîntes	vous reçûtes
ils allèrent	ils finirent	ils devinrent	ils reçurent
	vendre: je vendis tu vendis, etc.		devoir: je dus tu dus, etc.

For -er verbs, to keep the sound soft, e must be inserted after g, and c must take a cedilla when these are followed by a: **je mangeai, je plaçai,** etc. See p. 6.

All irregular past historics have one of the sets of endings shown above: **-is, -it** or **-us, -ut,** etc. The only exception is **croître,** to grow, which takes û throughout: **je crûs, tu crûs,** etc. The 1st person singular must be known for each. Once this is known the rest of the tense follows the pattern given above.
Some important irregular past historics are:
être, **je fus**
avoir, **j'eus**
faire, **je fis**
mourir, **je mourus**
naître, **je naquis**
vivre, **je vécus**
and -aindre, -eindre, -oindre verbs:
craindre, **je craignis**
Note that in **-ir** verbs, and in **dire,** the singular of the present and of the past historic is identical; thus in translation (and this occurs very often with **dit-il**) the context must be used to see whether to translate in the present or the past, e.g. by *he says* or *he said.*

A   From the following passage select all the verbs in the past historic and rewrite them in the perfect, remembering to make the past participle agree if necessary.

A ce moment mon frère vint me chercher. Il me dit qu'une jeune fille qui s'appelait Claire, et qu'il avait rencontrée la veille, venait d'arriver pour déjeuner chez nous. Il me demanda de venir faire sa connaissance.
   Nous descendîmes au salon. Dès que je la vis, je sus que je l'avais déjà rencontrée quelque part. Mais elle me regarda d'une manière anxieuse et me fit signe de ne rien dire. Je fis donc semblant de la rencontrer pour la première fois.
   Quand elle partit après le déjeuner, je la suivis à quelque distance. Je fus étonné de la voir entrer dans un vieux bâtiment délabré. J'attendis pendant dix minutes, mais comme elle ne reparut pas, je montai l'escalier. Tout était noir et silencieux. Je m'arrêtai devant une porte au premier étage. Soudain j'entendis un cri affreux.

B   Translate the above.

C   Translate:

Pendant une période de grand froid une panne de chauffage me contraignit de me réfugier à un hôtel. Je choisis un petit hôtel près de mon bureau.
   Le premier soir je montai peu après le dîner à ma chambre, car je voulais lire au lit.
   Mais, fatigué, après très peu de temps je mis le livre sur la table de chevet, et éteignis la lampe suspendue au-dessus de ma tête.

J'avais dormi peut-être deux heures quand un bruit m'éveilla. Il y avait quelqu'un dans ma chambre. Je cherchai à tâtons l'interrupteur, mais je ne pus pas le trouver.

Soudain la porte s'ouvrit et l'intrus sortit à pas de loup. Trouvant enfin l'interrupteur, j'allumai, et je sautai de mon lit. Je cherchai parmi les affaires que j'avais apportées avec moi à l'hôtel, mais rien ne manquait. Ma serviette et mon portefeuille étaient toujours sur la commode.

Le matin, avant d'aller au bureau, je racontai au directeur ce qui m'était arrivé.

Il ne s'étonna pas. C'était lui-même, m'expliqua-t-il, qui était entré dans ma chambre. Il avait trouvé ma serviette dans la salle à manger, et il voulait me la rendre. Il frappa à la porte, mais évidemment je dormais, car je ne répondis pas. Ainsi il entra doucement, posa la serviette sur la commode, et ressortit, sans savoir qu'il m'avait réveillé.

D   Rewrite the passage in French as far as ' . . . sur la commode' as if you were writing a letter, using the perfect instead of the past historic.

E   Rewrite the last paragraph of the passage in French as direct speech, i.e. as what the manager said to you, starting:
Je ne m'étonne pas. C'était moi qui suis entré dans. . . .

Perfect and other compound tenses

The differences between the English perfect and the French passé composé have already been mentioned in Part 1, pp. 19–20.
There are, besides the perfect, other compound tenses. Like the perfect, these have the auxiliary **être** for reflexive verbs and verbs of motion (p. 20), and both **avoir** and **être** must be translated by the relevant English form of *to have*.

Perfect (passé composé):

J'ai parlé. I have spoken.
Elle est arrivée. She has arrived.
Ils se sont lavés. They have washed.

Pluperfect (plus-que-parfait):

J'avais parlé. I had spoken.
Elle était arrivée. She had arrived.
Ils s'étaient lavés. They had washed.

Another tense, called the past anterior, sometimes replaces the pluperfect. This is used only in clauses of time (introduced by e.g. **quand, après que, dès que, aussitôt que**), and only in sentences where the verb of the main clause is in the past historic. The past anterior is formed from the past historic of **avoir** or **être**, plus the past participle. It is translated in the same way as the pluperfect:
Dès que j'eus parlé, je partis. As soon as I had spoken, I left.
Quand elle fut arrivée, nous dînâmes. When she had arrived, we dined.

Future perfect:

J'aurai parlé. I shall have spoken.
Elle sera arrivée. She will have arrived.
Ils se seront lavés. They will have washed.

Conditional perfect:

J'aurais parlé. I should have spoken.
Elle serait arrivée. She would have arrived.
Ils se seraient lavés. They would have washed.

Translating the perfect

As the French use the perfect instead of the past historic in everyday speech and in correspondence, special care must be taken to choose the correct English tense, especially when translating speech, letters or other passages that do not employ the past historic. The French perfect may, according to circumstances, have any of the following meanings:
J'ai parlé. I have spoken. I spoke. I did speak.
Il n'a pas mangé. He has not eaten. He did not eat.
Est-elle arrivée? Has she arrived? Did she arrive?

Translating the future and conditional perfects

After conjunctions of time such as **quand, lorsque, dès que**, the future and conditional perfects are translated by the English perfect and pluperfect (see p. 16):
Je partirai dès que le facteur aura apporté la lettre.
I shall leave as soon as the postman has brought the letter.
Il m'a dit qu'il rendrait visite à sa sœur seulement quand elle l'aurait invité.
He told me that he would visit his sister only when she had invited him.

A   Translate:

Cher Jean-Marc,
   Quand tu recevras cette lettre, j'aurai quitté Paris. J'en ai assez d'étudier, et je sais que je n'aurais jamais réussi à mes examens même si je les avais passés cet été. Je n'ai pas fait mes adieux à mes amis, parce que je savais qu'ils auraient essayé de me persuader de rester, et moi, j'étais sûre qu'il fallait partir.
   Je suis venue en Amérique parce que j'ai toujours voulu visiter New York, où j'ai des parents. J'ai très peu d'argent, car le voyage m'a coûté presque tout ce que j'avais épargné. J'ai dû donc chercher du travail tout de suite. Pour le moment j'ai accepté un emploi comme serveuse dans un restaurant, mais j'espère que bientôt j'aurai trouvé un emploi plus intéressant.
   Tu m'as dit l'été dernier que tu aurais aimé passer les vacances à New York, si tu avais connu quelqu'un qui y habitait: pourquoi pas venir me voir cet été? Cela me ferait plaisir.
   Écris-moi bientôt,

                              Isabelle

B The verbs in the following are in the past historic and in a variety of compound tenses. Translate into the most natural English past tenses:

1. Le professeur lui demanda s'il avait fini sa version. «Quand vous l'aurez finie, montrez-la-moi», dit-il.
2. Nous écoutâmes encore une fois, mais sa voix était devenue trop faible; nous n'entendîmes plus rien.
3. Dès qu'ils seront arrivés, nous irons au restaurant. Ils auraient pu nous téléphoner plus tôt pour nous dire qu'ils venaient.
4. Les enfants s'installèrent devant la télévision dès que leurs parents furent partis.
5. Soudain il s'arrêta. Il avait entendu un bruit derrière lui. Il n'aurait pas eu peur s'il n'avait pas été seul dans la forêt.
6. S'il avait gagné le gros lot à la loterie, il aurait pu acheter la voiture qu'il avait vue; mais il n'avait gagné que cinquante francs.
7. Après que Monsieur Lesage fut reparti les élèves recommencèrent à faire du tapage.
8. Les ouvriers décidèrent qu'on aurait dû envoyer des délégués pour discuter le problème avec le patron.
9. Il m'avait dit qu'il serait déjà parti avant mon arrivée.
10. Je ne l'aurais jamais fait s'il m'avait averti à temps; mais il arriva trop tard.

Reflexives

The French frequently use reflexive verbs, the English equivalents of which are not reflexive. Be careful not to put in reflexive pronouns (*myself*, *yourself*, etc.) in English translations where they are not necessary. The French also sometimes use a reflexive verb where we would use a passive, e.g. **Je m'appelle** ('I call myself') corresponds to the English *I am called*.

Remember, when translating reflexive verbs, that in French **être** is always used in compound tenses. This must be changed to the corresponding tense of *to have* in English:

Je me serai lavé. I shall have washed.

A Translate into normal English:

1. Comment vous appelez-vous?
2. Ils s'amusent bien chez leurs amis.
3. L'enfant s'est blessé avec le canif.
4. Mon frère s'est marié hier.
5. Asseyez-vous, messieurs. Le café se sert ici.
6. Je m'excuse de m'être endormi; je vais me lever aussitôt.
7. Les journaux se vendent chez le marchand qui se trouve là-bas.
8. Ne vous moquez pas des pauvres.
9. Il se promène dans le parc où, chaque jour, il promène son chien.
10. Les deux garçons se regardent, s'approchent l'un de l'autre, et se mettent à se battre.

Passives and impersonals

Besides using the reflexive to avoid a passive, as explained above, the French frequently use the impersonal pronoun **on**, corresponding to the English *one*, but more often translated by the impersonal *they* or *you*:

On dit qu'il est riche.
They say he is rich/It is said that he is rich.
D'ici on peut voir la mer.
From here you can see the sea/From here the sea can be seen.
As a general rule the translation of **on** by *one* should be avoided, especially in speech, where it sounds formal and stilted to English ears.

A   Translate:
  1. On a mis une enseigne dans la vitrine: «Ici on parle français».
  2. Qu'est-ce qu'on va faire maintenant?
  3. Comment est-ce qu'on dit ça en anglais?
  4. On n'a pas encore envoyé les billets. Qu'est-ce qu'on va faire?
  5. Si on se met ici on peut voir l'entrée de la caverne.
  6. Le prisonnier fit ce qu'on lui ordonna.
  7. On est heureuse, m'a-t-elle expliqué, quand on est aimée de son mari.
  8. J'entends des pas dans l'escalier; je crois que l'on vient enfin.
  9. Savez-vous où on a mis la clef?
  10. Si on prend ce train on arrive à Paris à deux heures dix.

Put -ing where needed

The French present participle, which ends in **-ant**, is nearly always translated by the English *-ing* form:
en parlant, while speaking
un film amusant, an amusing film
The English present participle, ending in *-ing*, can also often be used to translate a French infinitive (e.g. **Il aime lire.** He likes reading.
See p. 32), but this does not mean that the French infinitive must always be translated by the English present participle. The English infinitive may be preferable in some cases, and often there can be two ways of translating different infinitives occurring in the same sentence:
Vivre sans aimer n'est pas proprement vivre. (Molière, 1622–1673)
To live without loving is not really living.

A   Translate:
  1. Il est en train d'écrire une lettre.
  2. Après avoir parlé, il partit.
  3. Tout en mangeant son déjeuner il a continué à lire la lettre.
  4. Je l'ai entendu parler, sans le voir.
  5. Vivre n'est pas respirer; c'est agir. (Rousseau, 1712–1778)

Notes on the subjunctive

Although it is rarely used in speech, it may be necessary to recognize verbs in the subjunctive mood. The indicative mood represents facts. The subjunctive mood indicates an attitude of emotion towards or doubt about facts. Compare:

Il est venu. (Indicative)

He has come.

Je regrette qu'il soit venu. (Subjunctive)

I'm sorry that he has come,

Subjunctive forms are very rarely used in English, and French subjunctive forms should be translated by whatever English form best fits the context. As a rule this will cause no problem, provided that the verb being used is recognized. In many cases the subjunctive form is identical with the corresponding indicative form.

The present subjunctive is normally formed by adding the endings **-e**, **-es**, **-e** in the singular, and **-ent** in the 3rd person plural, to the stem of the 3rd person plural of the present indicative. The **nous** and **vous** lines are identical with those of the imperfect indicative:

Regular present subjunctives

donner	finir	vendre	recevoir
je donne	je finisse	je vende	je reçoive
tu donnes	tu finisses	tu vendes	tu reçoives
il donne	il finisse	il vende	il reçoive
nous donnions	nous finissions	nous vendions	nous recevions
vous donniez	vous finissiez	vous vendiez	vous receviez
ils donnent	ils finissent	ils vendent	ils reçoivent

A few irregular verbs have present subjunctives which occur quite frequently and which may be difficult to recognize. These are:

aller: aille, ailles, aille; allions, alliez, aillent
être: sois, sois, soit; soyons, soyez, soient
faire: fasse, fasses, fasse; fassions, fassiez, fassent
avoir: aie, aies, ait; ayons, ayez, aient
pouvoir: puisse, puisses, puisse; puissions, puissiez, puissent
savoir: sache, saches, sache; sachions, sachiez, sachent
valoir: vaille, vailles, vaille; valions, valiez, vaillent
venir: vienne, viennes, vienne; venions, veniez, viennent
vouloir: veuille, veuilles, veuille; voulions, vouliez, veuillent.

The *imperfect subjunctive* is based on the past historic form of the verb. In all persons other than the third person singular, -ss- is present:

je donnasse	nous donnassions	ils donnassent
tu donnasses	vous donnassiez	

Similarly, **je finisse**, etc., **je vendisse**, etc., **je reçusse**, etc. The imperfect subjunctive of être is **je fusse**, etc., and of avoir, **j'eusse**, etc.

The third person singular of the imperfect subjunctive can nearly always be recognized by its ending in -ˆt:
il donnât, il finît, il vendît, il reçût
être: **il fût**
avoir: **il eût**

The subjunctive is used only in certain specific conditions. An idea of these may make it easier to recognize subjunctive forms.

(a) The subjunctive is used in subordinate clauses introduced by **que**, when the main verb is one of the following:

  (i) a verb of emotion, e.g.
      regretter que, être content que, douter que
  (ii) a verb of wishing, ordering or fobidding, e.g.
      vouloir que, ordonner que, défendre que
  (iii) a verb of fearing, e.g.
      avoir peur que, craindre que
  (iv) a verb of saying or thinking used negatively or interrogatively,
      e.g. dire que, penser que
  (v) an impersonal expression, e.g.
      il faut que, il est possible que

  Examples:
  Je veux qu'ils s'en aillent.
  I want them to go away.
  Pensez-vous qu'il soit arrivé?
  Do you think he has come?
  Je crains qu'il ne le sache.
  I'm afraid that he knows.
  Note the insertion of **ne** before the subjunctive verb; this is used after certain verbs and expressions without making the subjunctive negative.

(b) The subjunctive is used in adverb clauses introduced by certain conjunctions, e.g. **avant que**, before; **bien que**, although; **pour que**, in order that; **sans que**, without.
  Bien qu'il ne soit pas riche, il est généreux.
  Although he is not rich, he is generous.

(c) The subjunctive is occasionally used in a main clause to express a wish, prayer or command:
  Vive le roi!
  Long live the king! — literally, May the king live!

(d) The subjunctive is used in a relative clause, to qualify a superlative or a negative expression:
  C'est la femme la plus belle que j'aie jamais vue.
  She is the most beautiful woman I have ever seen.

A Copy the following sentences; underline the subjunctive in each and
then translate into natural English:
1. Pensez-vous qu'ils le sachent?
2. Il faut qu'il le fasse.
3. Il semble qu'il l'ait trouvé.
4. Donnez-moi de l'argent afin que je puisse l'acheter.
5. Je ne connais personne qui soit toujours aimable.
6. Que Dieu ne m'abandonne pas!
7. Je craignis qu'il ne parlât.
8. De crainte qu'il ne revînt, elle a fermé la porte à clé.
9. Je regrette qu'il le fît avant les autres.
10. Il partit sans qu'elle le sût.

Some awkward verbs

The following is a list of verbs which can prove awkward in translation or which have more than one meaning. Several of them appear elsewhere, but they have been listed here for easy reference.

aller, s'en aller: Allons! Let's go! Come now! I say! **allez-vous-en!** Go away! **Aller** + infinitive is used to form the near future.

arriver: to arrive; to happen

s'agir de: il s'agit de, it is a question of; it has to do with; it concerns

s'asseoir: to sit down (the action of sitting)
  être assis(e)(s): to be seated — **assis** is the past participle used as an adjective.

(se) blesser: to wound (oneself)

brûler: usually to burn, but note **brûler un feu rouge,** to jump the traffic lights

charger: to load, put a load on someone or something; **se charger de,** to take upon oneself (some task)

composer un numéro: to dial a number (telephone)

conduire: to lead, conduct; frequently used for to drive (a car or other vehicle); **se conduire,** to behave

connaître: to know, in the sense of to be acquainted with. See also **savoir.**

coucher: to put to bed; **se coucher,** to go to bed

croire: to believe; also to think, consider

se débrouiller: to manage, get out of difficulties; **être débrouillard,** to be the kind of person who gets round difficulties

défendre: to defend; to forbid

dégoûter: to disgust. Do not confuse with **déguster,** to taste, sample.

devenir: to become. Do not confuse with **deviner,** to guess.

dire: to say, to tell (but not to speak)

se diriger: to go (**vers,** in the direction of); turn in the direction (of)

se dresser: to stand, rise up (usually refers to buildings, monuments, trees, mountains, etc.)

échapper: to escape (something); **s'échapper:** to escape, to get away; **l'échapper belle,** to have a narrow escape

ennuyer: to annoy, bore, tease; **s'ennuyer,** to be bored, grow weary

entendre: to hear; to understand; **s'entendre,** to understand each other, agree; **Entendu!** Agreed!

faillir: to fail. Frequently used to mean to have just escaped doing something, almost to have done something.

faire: to do, to make. Used in many idioms, including weather expressions. **Faire la cuisine,** to cook; **faire le ménage,** to do the housework; **faire semblant** (de), to pretend (to)
  se faire: to be, to take place, to occur. **Il se fait tard,** it is growing late; **il se fait (bâtir une maison),** he has (a house built) for himself, etc.

falloir: to be necessary, must. Always used with the impersonal subject **il. Il me faut,** I must

s'inquiéter: to worry

laisser: to let, allow, leave, permit; **laisser tomber,** to drop

manquer: to miss, fail, to nearly (do something)

se mettre à: to start (to do something); **(se) mettre au courant,** to get (oneself) or make (someone else) acquainted with the facts

se moquer de: to laugh at, make fun of (someone)

passer: to pass; for exams also means to sit; **se passer,** to take place, to happen

payer: to pay; to pay for

penser à: to think about, bear in mind; **penser de:** to think of, have an opinion about

porter: to carry; to wear; **se porter,** to be (in health)

promener: to take for a walk; **se promener,** to go for a walk; to go for a ride, drive, sail, flight, trip, etc., according to means of travelling — always with idea of recreation, exercise, pleasure, etc.

savoir: to know (as a fact); to know by heart (See **connaître,** above.)

servir: to serve; **servir à,** be used for, as; **se servir de,** to make use of, to use

sortir: to go out; when used with a direct object, it means to take out, and is then conjugated with **avoir** in compound tenses.

se souvenir de: to remember, to call to mind

se taire: to keep silent; not to speak

tenir: to hold. **Tiens! Tenez!** Well now! **tenir à,** to hold to, insist on, want very much; **se tenir droit,** to hold oneself upright, sit up straight

tirer: to pull, to draw (in sense of pull); to draw a line (but not to draw a picture); also used to mean to shoot (originally, to draw a bow)

travailler: to work (*not* to travel — **voyager**)

se trouver: to find oneself, to be located, or simply to be, when speaking of the position of something.

valoir: to be worth; frequently used as an impersonal verb meaning to be worth while: **Il vaudrait mieux ne pas le faire.** It would be better not to do it. **Il vaut la peine d'y aller.** It's worth going there.

venir de + infinitive: is used to mean to have just done something. **Il vient de parler.** He has just spoken. **Il venait de parler.** He had just spoken, etc. This construction is used in the present and the imperfect.

vouloir: to wish, to want; **en vouloir à,** to be angry with, to feel ill disposed towards (someone); **vouloir bien,** to be willing (to do something); **vouloir dire,** to mean

A   The verbs listed above are included in the following. Use the list where necessary to translate:

1. De sa poche il a sorti un mouchoir et un anneau à clés. «Il faut que je me dépêche», s'est-il dit en sortant de la maison. «Je ne veux pas manquer le train.»

2. Napoléon a fait bâtir l'Arc de Triomphe à Paris pour célébrer ses victoires.

3. «Il vaut mieux finir tes devoirs avant de te coucher», déclara son père d'une voix sévère. «Allons! Mets-toi au travail!»

4. Cet objet curieux sert à ouvrir les bouteilles.

5. Il m'en veut parce que je me suis servi de son vélo pour faire une promenade à la campagne hier — mais, que voulez-vous? — je m'ennuyais à la maison, et il ne s'en sert presque jamais.

6. Il m'a demandé si ma femme voudrait bien recevoir une jeune étudiante allemande qui venait d'arriver en Angleterre.

7. «Tu as bien raison de t'inquiéter», m'a dit le professeur. «Je viens de parler de toi au directeur. Il avait l'air plus irrité que jamais. Tu vas certainement être fortement réprimandé.»

8. Je voudrais bien faire visite à ton grand-père. Peut-être me permettra-t-il de chasser les lapins — je sais bien tirer au fusil de chasse.

9. — Est-ce que vous avez payé la chambre?
— Pas encore. Je ne peux pas trouver mon portefeuille. Je crois que je l'ai laissé tomber quelque part.
— Mais non — je sais où il se trouve. Vous l'avez mis dans votre autre veston, celui que vous portiez hier soir. — Le voila!

10. Louise, qui était toujours maladroite, a laissé tomber le bol de soupe chaude et a failli tuer le chat.

11. — Le tirage de la loterie a eu lieu hier, mais nous avons manqué de gagner un lot.
— Allons! Nous risquons de nous faire tuer si nous nous tenons ici, au milieu de la rue, en bavardant comme deux vieilles filles!

12. Son père ne manqua pas de remarquer sa mine inquiète.
«Tu t'es conduit mal, cela se voit. Qu'est-ce que tu as fait, alors?» lui demanda son père.
Charles se mit à trembler, mais il ne répondit pas.
Son père se mit en colère. «Je peux bien deviner», dit-il. «Tu as fait quelque chose que je t'ai défendu, n'est-ce pas?»
Son père avait beau demander. Charles persista dans sa résolution de ne rien dire.

13. — Je vous ai fait venir parce que je voulais vous parler.
— De quoi s'agit-il, mon capitaine?
— Il s'agit de vous approcher de l'ennemi pendant la nuit pour écouter ce qu'on dit, dans l'espoir d'apprendre ses plans. Ce sera dangereux!
— N'importe. Je sais me débrouiller.
— Alors, c'est entendu?
— Oui, mon capitaine. Je me charge de tout. Ne vous inquiétez pas.

14. L'auto démarra et, conduite à une vitesse folle, elle brûla un feu rouge, écrasa un poulet, et finit par se jeter contre un arbre. Le chauffeur faillit se tuer — mais il l'échappa belle, et il vit toujours.

15. Parce qu'elle ne pouvait pas trouver l'emploi qu'elle souhaitait, une jeune fille sauta du premier étage de la tour Eiffel. Elle tomba sur une vieille bagnole — c'était celle-ci et non pas la jeune fille qui fut écrasée. Elle, elle se fit si bien connaître qu'elle se fit offrir l'emploi qu'elle cherchait, car elle ne se blessa que légèrement. On affirme que cette histoire est vraie.

16. Il se faisait tard. Un silence profond s'est fait dans la chambre. Fermant les yeux, Jean a fait semblant de dormir — mais il ne dormait pas: il écoutait. Il était sûr que quelque chose se passait dans la chambre à côté.

17. Il lui arrivait souvent de s'endormir devant la télé en attendant l'arrivée de son mari, qui revenait tard si le train arrivait en retard à la gare.

18. Il avait mal au cœur. La pensée qu'il allait devenir malade encore une fois se dressait devant lui comme un spectre menaçant. Il devait appeler le médecin. Il composa son numéro, mais personne ne répondit. Qu'est-ce qu'il fallait faire? Il s'assit de nouveau dans son fauteuil pour attendre ce qui devait arriver. On avait beau lui dire qu'il n'était pas malade — lui, il savait la vérité, car ce n'était pas la première fois qu'il avait connu ces symptômes.

19. L'agent se dirigea vers la foule.
   « Qu'est-ce qui se passe ici? demanda-t-il.
   — C'est le camion, quelqu'un lui expliqua. Ce camion-ci. Il est monté sur le trottoir et a failli écraser ce pauvre monsieur.
   — Ce n'est pas un pauvre monsieur, celui-là, s'écria l'agent. C'est Jean Tuetout, l'assassin. Je le cherche depuis des mois. Le conducteur du camion a bien fait — sans le savoir, du reste.»

20. Ce que vous pensez d'autrui est votre affaire; mais quelquefois il est plus sage de se taire, et de garder ses pensées pour soi. On ne peut guère blâmer les gens s'ils vous en veulent parce que vous leur dites la vérité à propos des choses qu'ils ont faites et desquelles ils ne veulent plus se souvenir.

3
Aural and oral

Aural refers to hearing, and an aural test is one intended to find out how well the spoken language is understood. Tests include dictation, and questions on a passage read in French without the written text being seen.

Oral refers to speech, and an oral test should strictly be one that tests the ability of the candidate to speak or pronounce the language, as in a reading test. In practice the term is applied also to a conversation between examiner and candidate in which both aural and oral skills are needed.

Dictation

Dictation is not only an important aural test; it also tests knowledge of spelling rules, agreements, verb endings and accents.

During the dictation, remember the following rules:
(a) Watch the mouth of the reader. This may help you to distinguish between similar sounds, such as n and m, b and v.
(b) Do not worry about the meaning of individual words if this is not grasped during the actual dictation. Leave this until the dictation has been completed.
(c) Make no attempt to correct anything written while the dictation is still in progress. To do so will mean missing what follows. Wait until the dictation is over.

After the dictation is over, read through what you have written very carefully. Correct your work, bearing in mind the following points:
(a) Check that you have used the right word or ending where the sound alone could be written in different ways. Among words and endings easily confused are:
mais/mes/mai
ces/ses/c'est
on/en/ont
son/sont
dont/dans
l'eau/le haut
l'auteur/la hauteur
-is/-it/-i/-ie/-ies
-e/-es/-ent
-ai/-ais/-ait/-aient/-ez/-é/-ée/-és/-ées/-er
(b) Check that you have made all necessary agreements. For the agreements of verbs, see p. 5; for past participles, see p. 24, and for adjectives, see p. 51.
Where the sound alone cannot tell you the gender and/or number of a word, other elements of the sentence or of the passage as a whole may do so. For example:
  (i) **Son amie est partie hier.** It is impossible to tell from the sound of this whether **ami** and **parti** are masculine or feminine; but if the next sentence starts with **Elle** . . . , or the friend has already been mentioned and named as feminine, the spelling becomes clear.
  (ii) **C'est une jolie bague qu'il lui a achetée.** Here the article **une** shows the gender of **bague**, and therefore the spelling of **jolie** and **achetée** in agreement.
  (iii) Possessive or demonstrative adjectives may give the necessary information about number:
    Il a mis ses crayons dans son sac. **Ses** shows that **crayons** must be plural; **son** shows that **sac** must be singular.
    Regardez ces images. **Ces** shows that **images** must be plural.

(c) Never put a past participle or an infinitive directly after the subject (noun or pronoun): **Jean 'été'** must be **Jean était**; **vous 'parler'** must be **vous parlez**.

(d) Except with **avoir** and **être** used as auxiliaries in compound tenses, a verb following the main verb of a sentence will be an infinitive: **il veut 'parlé'** must be **il veut parler**.

(e) Distinguish between such constructions as **il l'a fait** and **il la fait**. In such cases the context must be used as a guide unless the last verb is clearly a past participle: **'il la vendu'** must be **il l'a vendu(e)**, because the sound **vendu** only occurs as the past participle of **vendre**.

(f) A hard **k** sound may be **ca-, co-, cu-**, or **qu-**: **car, comme, curé, qui, quelque**. If a known **c** is sounded softly before **a, o** or **u** it must have a cedilla: **ça, façon, reçu**.
Similarly if a known **g** is sounded softly before **a, o** or **u**, an **e** must be inserted to keep the **g** soft: **mangeais, plongeons**. If an **e** is added to a **g** at the end of an adjective to make it feminine, **u** is inserted to keep it hard: **long, longue**.

(g) **S** sounded like **z** between two vowels is always one **-s-**: **il disait**; **s** sounded softly between two vowels is double: **ils finissent**.

(h) The **t** of **et** is never sounded; thus where the choice is between e.g. **elle et une amie** and **elle est une amie**, the first would be correct if the **t** was not sounded, the second correct if the **t** of **est** was sounded.

(i) **Quand** sounds like **quant** before a vowel, as in **quand il vient**. **Quant** is almost always used before **à**: **quant à moi**, and so is easy to recognize.

(j) There is no accent on **cela** or its abbreviation **ça**; there is no hyphen in **parce que, quelque chose** or any of the phrases with **tout**, e.g. **tout à l'heure, tout à fait**; there are hyphens in **c'est-à-dire**.

(k) Accents must be treated as being as important as letters, since in words where the accent is used incorrectly the meaning may be completely changed: **du** = some, **dû** = owed; **la** = the, **là** = there; **ou** = or; **où** = where; **sur** = on, **sûr** = sure; **pécher** = to sin, **pêcher** = to fish, etc.

(l) Never write **è** at the beginning or end of a word. The only words starting with **ê** are **être** and **êtes**. No words end in **-ee**, but you can have feminine forms ending **-ée**.

(m) In a very large number of cases when there is the combination of **e** + consonant + mute **-e** the first **e** takes a grave accent: **mère, première mènent**, etc. The same applies if there is **-ch-** between the two **es**: **pèche, sèchent**, etc. The main exceptions are words which formerly had an **s** before **t**, often related to an English word which retains the old **-st-**: **arrête, bête, fête**, etc.

(n) Among words commonly misspelt the following should be noted: **adresse, arbre, bleu, danser, exercice, grand-mère, professeur, tante, vieil** and **vieille**; the phrase **s'il vous plaît**, and the numbers **treize, seize** and **quatorze**.

(o) Pairs of words which sound slightly different but which are nevertheless frequently confused include:
agent, argent; chevaux, cheveux; minuit, minute; rue, roue.

Punctuation

The following are the names used in dictation for punctuation marks:
point . full stop
virgule , comma
deux points : colon
point-virgule ; semicolon
point d'exclamation ! exclamation mark
point d'interrogation ? question mark
trait d'union - hyphen
tiret — dash
ouvrez les guillemets « open inverted commas
fermez les guillemets » close inverted commas
ouvrez les parenthèses (open brackets
fermez les parenthèses) close brackets
à la ligne begin a new paragraph

A   Rewrite the following, using the correct alternatives:
1. ses/ces livres-ci
2. sept/cette table-là
3. en/on hiver
4. Ne faites pas ça/sa
5. leur/leurs chevaux
6. Vous l'a/la mangiez.
7. Elle l'a/la mangée.
8. la veille/vieille de Noël
9. Où/Ou est mon livre?
10. Avez-vous finit/fini?
11. Il n'a pas obéi/obéit.
12. Donnez-moi/Donnais-moi quelque-chose/quelque chose.
13. Il vient quelque-fois/quelquefois parce-que/parce que tu le veut/veux.
14. As-tu fais/fait ton devoir?
15. Il a été/était ici en été/était.

B   Rewrite the following, using the correct alternatives:
1. Il a amener/amené   c'est/ses/ces   frères.
2. Quand/Quant   est-ce que vous   allait/allez   me rendre   mes/mais livres?
3. Mon mari   ma donnait/m'a donné   une nouvelle montre.
4. Il vous   donnez/donnait   les journaux au moment ou/où   la mer/mère est entrée   dans/dont   la maison   avec ses/ces enfants.
5. La voiture roule sur quatre roues/rues   au milieu de la rue/roue.
6. Il/Ils ne faut pas donner/donné   l'argent/agent   à l'argent/agent.
7. Ces/Ses cheveux/chevaux   en/ont   tiré/tiret   sa charrette.
8. Elle peigne/Elles peignent   les cheveux/chevaux   de sa fille pour l'a faire/la faire   aussi belle que possible.
9. Il et/est arrivé   dont/dans la ville   avec l'amie/ami qu'il espère épousé/épousée/épouser.
10. La route est longe/longue,   mes/mais   elle est facile/façile   et/est tout-à-fait/tout à fait   son/sans/sont   difficulté/difficultais.

Aural comprehension

When listening to a passage which is being read in French, remember the following:
(a) Watch the lips and expression of the reader.
(b) Do not worry if there are difficult words you have not met before; you will probably not be asked about them.
(c) Never try to make a mental translation while listening — you will miss what comes next.

When answering questions designed to test your understanding of a passage of spoken French, make sure that your answers are concise, and include only the relevant details.

Answer in English the questions below the two passages which follow, after they have been read to you by a teacher or a friend. Do not refer to the passages themselves.

A Mathieu voulait acheter une chaîne stéréo. Pendant les vacances il avait travaillé comme garçon dans un restaurant pour gagner l'argent nécessaire. Mais les chaînes coûtent cher. Mathieu n'avait toujours pas assez d'argent pour acheter le modèle qu'il voulait. Il cherchait dans les magasins, et enfin il trouva une chaîne qui était beaucoup moins cher, mais qui ressemblait un peu à celle qu'il voulait. Il demanda au vendeur pourquoi ce modèle coûtait si peu.

«C'est une offre spéciale, une occasion», dit le vendeur. «Voulez-vous l'écouter?»

Il mit un disque et Mathieu écouta avec plaisir la musique. Il était bien content. Quelle chance d'avoir trouvé une si bonne chaîne à un prix si bas! Il acheta la chaîne et la rapporta chez lui dans sa vieille voiture.

Mathieu installa la chaîne dans sa chambre et donna son vieil électrophone à son petit frère. Au début la chaîne marchait très bien. Mais après quelques jours elle commença à faire un bruit curieux, un bruit grinçant, qui devenait de plus en plus fort. Mathieu demanda à un ami, qui avait étudié l'électronique, ce qu'elle avait. Celui-ci examina la chaîne et trouva qu'il y avait une faute très grave, et qu'il ne valait pas la peine de la réparer.

Mathieu était furieux. Il rapporta la chaîne au magasin où il l'avait achetée, et raconta au vendeur ce qui c'était passé. Le vendeur s'excusa, mais dit qu'il ne pouvait rien faire: cette chaîne n'avait pas de garantie.

1. What did Mathieu want to buy?
2. How had he earned the money?
3. Why could he not buy the model he wanted?
4. Why was the model he did buy so cheap?
5. How did Mathieu take it home?
6. What did he do with his old record player?
7. What happened to the new stereo?
8. Whom did Mathieu ask for advice, and what was he told?

9. What did Mathieu do then?
10. What did the shopkeeper say?

B   J'avais toujours horreur d'aller chez le dentiste. Je me souviens de ma
première visite. La salle d'attente était très sombre, peinte en brun foncé,
avec de vieilles chaises en bois peu confortables. On se sentait déjà mal
à l'aise en y entrant. Sur les murs il y avait des affiches qui vous préve-
naient de votre sort, si vous ne soigniez pas vos dents.

La petite fille qui me précédait dans la queue entra dans le cabinet de
consultation. Bientôt je pouvais entendre des cris affreux. Qu'est-ce qui
se passait là-dedans? Je l'écoutais, je tremblais, et je savais que ce serait
bientôt mon tour. Mais je ne me souviens plus de rien, car je m'évanouis.

Quelques années plus tard, un nouveau dentiste arriva. Celui-ci était
différent. Il avait fait peindre la salle d'attente en bleu clair. Il y avait
des fauteuils confortables et des journaux à lire. On entendait de la
musique dans son cabinet de consultation. Le dentiste m'expliqua ce
qu'il allait faire et pourquoi il allait le faire. Il me montra les instruments
qu'il utilisait. Je n'avais plus peur. Tout me paraissait simple, nécessaire,
et même intéressant. C'est probablement à cause de ce dentiste — dont
je ne me rappelle plus le nom — que je commençai à m'intéresser à la
médecine, et que je devins enfin médecin. C'est toujours la question des
rapports entre le médecin et ses clients qui m'intéresse le plus; la
manière dont le médecin — ou le dentiste — peut expliquer à ses clients
les mystères du cabinet de consultation et les mettre à leur aise.

1. What was the narrator's attitude towards going to the dentist's?
2. What was the waiting-room like on his first visit?
3. What type of posters were there on the walls?
4. What were the narrator's feelings while the little girl was in the
   surgery?
5. What happened to the narrator?
6. What changes did the new dentist make to the waiting-room?
7. How did the new dentist treat his patient?
8. How did the narrator respond to this?
9. What is the narrator's profession?
10. What particular aspect of his profession most interests the
    narrator?

Reading

Most French exams include the reading aloud of a short passage. Usually the candidate is given the opportunity of reading it through in advance. If such preparation is possible, only a general idea of the meaning is necessary, sufficient to know which words should be grouped together to make sense, and where it is possible to pause for breath.

Syllables and stress

Single consonants between syllables belong to the following syllable. Where there are more than one consonant these may be divided between syllables: **é/lé/men/taire**.
Stress is put on the final syllable of a word or of a group of words spoken together:
Une gram/**maire**
Une gram/maire   é/lé/men/**taire**
Une gram/maire   é/lé/men/**taire**   //   est vrai/ment né/ces/**saire**.

Intonation

The intonation of a short sentence normally shows a steadily falling pattern.
A longer sentence will be broken up into word groups. There will be a slight rise at the end of each word-group, except the last, where the tone will fall:
C'est lui/qui m'a demandé/de venir/vous voir.
In commands there is a falling pattern:
Donnez-moi ça!
Questions end with an upward turn:
Qu'est-ce qu'il a dit?

Pronunciation of e-mute

(a) A mute **e** occurring inside a word of more than one syllable should not be sounded, unless the **e** precedes two consonants. Thus **maintenant** is pronounced **main/t'nant**, and **médecin** is pronounced **méd'cin**, but the **e** in **collection** is sounded.

(b) Before **n** or **m** the **e** often combines to make a nasal sound, e.g. **attend**. In **-emment**, and also in **femme** and **solennel** the **e** sounds like **a**.

(c) A double consonant usually has the same effect as a grave accent: **appelle**.

(d) The **e** at the beginning of a word is always sounded, whether or not it has an accent: **est, et, essayer**.

(e) **E** is always mute when it ends a word: **grande, fille**. It is sounded if it is combined with a consonant at the end of the word, unless the word is a plural or the second person singular of a verb. Thus it is sounded in **parler, portez, gilet, met**, but not in **pommes** or **donnes**.

A Write out the words below and then mark them as follows:
1. Underline each **e** that sounds like **è**.
2. Cross out each **e** inside a word that is not sounded or merely breathed.
3. Do not touch any **e** at the beginning or end of a word.

acheté, appartement, appelé, entrerai, universelle, proprement, queue, jouet, genou, geler, omelette, terre, rechercher, toutefois, tiennent

B Write out the words below and then mark them as follows:
1. Underline any nasal combination of **en** or **em**.
2. Put brackets round any **e** which sounds like **a**.
3. Do not touch any other **e**.

tellement, demain, solennel, prudemment, viennent, menacer, semence, renouveler, rentrer, femme, septembre, semelle, sensible, commence, semaine

Vowels

Vowels (with the exception of the mute **e**) must be enunciated clearly and roundly, without the slurring which is common to English pronunciation.
Many French words have combinations of vowels which make a single sound, e.g.:
eau in beau, cadeau
eu in heureux, feu
oi in fois, trois
ou in sous, fou; but note the 'w' sound in ouest and Edouard.
A distinction should be made between the sound é as in **les, manger, allé**; and the sound è as in **lait, jette, frère**. These two sounds distinguish, for example, the 1st person of the future from the 1st person of the conditional: **j'irai (é); j'irais (è)**.

Some consonants

In order to pronounce **r**, **k** and **t** correctly it helps to keep the tip of the tongue against the lower part of the mouth, below the lower gum. If this is done, only moving the tongue away when necessary, the sound of these consonants, especially the **r**, will be greatly improved.
Remember also:
ch is always sounded like the English *sh*, as in *share* (never *tch* as in our *chair*), e.g. **marcher, chaise**;
-s- between vowels is sounded like -*z*-; e.g. **raser**;
-ss- between vowels is soft as in *hiss*; e.g. **essayer**;
qu is always like our *k*, thus **qui** is sounded like *key*.

Liaison

Liaison is the sounding of the final consonant of a word as if it were the initial consonant of a following word, if that word starts with a vowel

or h-mute, or before **y**. If syllables are read in an even continuous
'stream' this will often come naturally.

Rules are complicated and usage differs widely. The following guide-
lines will be sufficient:

(a) Never make a liaison after a pause for breath. There can only be
liaison between words which are actually spoken in the same breath.

(b) Never make a liaison after **et**, but do after **est**.

(c) Never make a liaison after a noun which ends in a consonant unless
that consonant is always sounded. There is no liaison after **forêt** —
La forêt // est vaste, but there will be liaison after **cheval** — **Le
cheval‿est beau**.

(d) Liaison is made between a pronoun and the following verb, **il‿est**,
and between subject and object pronouns before verbs, **il‿y a**;
nous‿en mangeons, vous‿en avez.

(e) Liaison is made between a verb in the 3rd person when this ends in
-t and a following object, infinitive, complement or preposition:
elle fait‿un gâteau; il doit‿arriver, il paraît‿ennuyé, il vient‿avec moi.

(f) Liaison is made between adjectives and also the articles **un, une, les**
and **des** and the following noun: **un bon‿ami, un‿encrier, les‿eaux,
des‿hommes**.

(g) Liaison is made between prepositions and the nouns of other words
they govern: **devant‿une maison, dans‿une grande rage, après‿avoir
parlé**.

(h) Liaison is made after **pas** when this is used as part of the negative:
il n'est pas‿arrivé, and between words forming common phrases, such
as **de temps‿en temps, tout‿à fait, en‿hiver**, or words which the sense
requires to be spoken as one close group: **un mois‿après, très‿aimé,
très bien‿aimé**, etc.

A Using the rules given above as a guide, mark a liason sign ‿ between words in the following, assuming that each group is spoken in
one breath:

1. Le chien est un animal; et l'homme est aussi un animal.
2. Le col entre les montagnes // est plus haut que le tunnel.
3. Elle n'est pas arrivée // et elle n'a pas téléphoné.
4. Il nous en a parlé.
5. Vous avez fini?
6. Nous étions tous dans un coin de la salle.
7. Un grand oiseau descendait vers le plus petit des arbres.
8. C'était un petit enfant // qui commençait à chanter.
9. Devant un hôtel // un homme se tenait immobile, et attendait en
silence.
10. Il ouvrit à trois heures, pas un moment trop tôt.

The oral

The oral examination provides the candidate with an opportunity to show that he is able to understand simple spoken French, and to make himself understood.

The examiner will want the candidate to be successful, and will be only too glad to make things as easy as possible.

The candidate should return the examiner's initial greeting with a polite **Bonjour, monsieur** or **Bonjour, madame**, and when asked to sit down should do so saying **Merci, monsieur**. The French are invariably polite on such occasions, and these preliminaries will not only establish a French atmosphere, but also help to put the candidate at his ease.

For the conversation with the examiner remember the following points:

(a) Questions should be answered as naturally as possible. There is no need to repeat the question or always to give a complete sentence. For certain questions, a short answer such as **Oui, monsieur** or **Quelquefois, madame**, will be appropriate. The addition of **monsieur** or **madame** makes such short answers less abrupt. Most questions will, however, ask for more than this, and when it is natural to do so, answers can be made as full as possible.

(b) If you miss a word or do not understand a question, then say so, and ask for the question to be repeated. Do not leave long pauses. Useful phrases are:
Je ne comprends pas tout à fait, monsieur/madame.
Voulez-vous me répéter la question, s'il vous plaît?
Pardon, monsieur, je n'ai pas compris.

(c) Do not learn pieces of French on certain topics by heart, and then recite them. The examiner will be aware of this and will interrupt and ask you about something else. It is far better to answer spontaneously.

(d) Do not worry too much about making mistakes. The examiner is not looking for faults; he is looking for the ability to understand and to make oneself understood.

Short answers

Be careful when giving short answers.
You cannot answer the question **Êtes-vous élève ici?** Are you a pupil here? by saying 'Oui je suis'. Acceptable answers would be **Oui, monsieur,** or **Oui, je suis élève ici, monsieur.** The verb être cannot be used alone. The same applies to the verbs **faire** and **avoir.** The English answers 'Yes I do' and 'Yes I have' have no direct equivalent in French.

For example, a question such as **Aimez-vous le français?** Do you like French? can be answered by **Oui, monsieur, beaucoup,** or **Non, monsieur, je ne l'aime pas.**

Avez-vous visité la France? Have you ever been to France? can be answered by **Oui, monsieur, une fois,** or **Non, monsieur, je ne l'ai jamais visitée.**

Avoir plus a number cannot be used alone. To answer the question **Combien de disques avez-vous?** How many records have you got? one can say **J'ai vingt disques**, or **J'en ai vingt**, but not '**J'ai vingt**'. Similarly, **Je n'en ai pas**, I have none.

A   Give short answers to the following questions:
1. Est-ce que vous jouez au football?
2. Est-ce que vous aimez les oranges?
3. Est-ce que vous avez un vélo?
4. Est-ce que vous comprenez ceci?
5. Est-ce qu'il fait beau aujourd'hui?
6. Savez-vous nager?
7. Entendez-vous les voitures dans la rue?
8. Est-ce que vous êtes allé à Londres hier?
9. Peut-on voir la lune pendant le jour?
10. Est-ce que vous avez traversé la Manche?
11. Avez-vous des frères?
12. Avez-vous froid?
13. Vous n'apprenez pas le français, n'est-ce pas?
14. Vous ne savez pas lire, n'est-ce pas?
15. Combien de doigts avez-vous (y compris les pouces)?

General questions

Whether or not a 'prepared' topic has been set, every oral exam is likely to include a number of questions of a personal, though general, nature. The following questions are representative of those a candidate might be asked. Answers should not, however, be learnt by heart and recited. There are many ways of asking the same question, and the answer must be formed accordingly.

A   Give answers to the following questions, remembering that they are intended to represent spoken answers:
1. Comment vous appelez-vous?
2. Quel âge avez-vous?
3. Est-ce que vous avez des sœurs ou des frères?
4. Depuis quand êtes-vous élève à cette école?
5. Depuis combien de temps apprenez-vous le français?
6. Avez-vous toujours habité l'Angleterre?
7. Quel jour de la semaine est-ce aujourd'hui?
8. Quelle date sommes-nous aujourd'hui?
9. Quel temps fait-il aujourd'hui?
10. Quel temps a-t-il fait hier?
11. Quelle langue parlons-nous en ce moment?
12. Quelle est la date de votre anniversaire?
13. A quelle heure vous êtes-vous levé ce matin?
14. Qu'est-ce que vous avez mangé au petit déjeuner ce matin?
15. Comment est-ce que vous êtes venu à l'école ce matin?
16. Décrivez les vêtements que vous portez aujourd'hui.
17. Décrivez votre meilleur(e) ami(e).

18. Quelle saison de l'année préférez-vous? Pourquoi?
19. Qu'est-ce que vous avez fait hier soir?
20. Qu'est-ce que vous ferez ce soir?

Topics

The following are a selection of topics which may be touched on in an oral examination. If candidates have been given certain topics to prepare, care must be taken not to recite passages learnt by heart, and even then any other subject may also be included. The answers to the following questions should be prepared as if spoken in normal conversation.

Daily life

1. A quelle heure vous levez-vous d'habitude?
2. Est-ce que vous vous levez plus tard le samedi et le dimanche?
3. Qu'est-ce que vous mangez au petit déjeuner?
4. A quelle heure est-ce que vous mangez chez vous le soir?
5. Qu'est-ce que vous faites pendant la soirée?
6. Pendant le trimestre, est-ce que vous avez des devoirs à faire à la maison?
7. A quelle heure vous couchez-vous pendant la semaine?
8. Préférez-vous prendre une douche ou un bain?
9. Qui est-ce qui vous réveille le matin?
10. Qu'est-ce que vous avez fait ce matin avant de venir à l'école?

Home and family

1. Combien de personnes y a-t-il dans votre famille?
2. Est-ce que vous êtes le seul enfant dans votre famille?
3. Comment s'appellent vos frères/vos sœurs? Quel âge ont-ils?
4. Est-ce que vous avez des animaux chez vous? Lesquels?
5. Est-ce que vous aidez à faire le ménage? Qu'est-ce que vous faites pour aider?
6. Décrivez votre maison/votre appartement. Combien de pièces y a-t-il chez vous? Est-ce que le bâtiment est ancien ou moderne?
7. Avez-vous une chambre à vous seul?
8. Décrivez votre chambre.
9. Avez-vous un jardin? Comment est-il?
10. Est-ce que vous allez souvent voir des parents? Où habitent-ils?

Sports, pastimes, hobbies

1. Quel sport préférez-vous? Pourquoi?
2. Quels sports pratiquez-vous à l'école?
3. Quel est votre passe-temps favori?
4. Est-ce que vous aimez la musique? Jouez-vous d'un instrument de musique?
5. Est-ce que vous avez jamais essayé de faire du ski ou de la voile?
6. Est-ce que vous allez souvent au cinéma? Quel est votre film préféré?

7. Est-ce que vous collectionnez quelque chose?
8. Aimez-vous faire des promenades à pied, à vélo ou à cheval?
9. Préférez-vous regarder la télévision à la maison, ou sortir avec vos copains?
10. Êtes-vous membre d'un club de jeunes?

Holidays

1. Préférez-vous les vacances au bord de la mer, à la campagne, à l'étranger, à la maison ou ailleurs?
2. Préférez-vous les vacances en famille, chez un ami ou chez un parent?
3. Qu'est-ce que vous faites pendant les vacances de Noël?
4. Où comptez-vous aller en vacances cette année?
5. Avez-vous jamais passé des vacances dans une ferme?
6. Est-ce que vous aimez faire du camping?
7. Préférez-vous voyager en voiture, en train, en bateau ou en avion?
8. A votre avis, quelle saison de l'année est la meilleure pour les vacances?
9. Combien de semaines durent les vacances de Pâques à l'école?
10. Est-ce que vous trouvez les grandes vacances trop longues?

School

1. A quelle distance de l'école habitez-vous? Comment arrivez-vous à l'école?
2. Il y a combien d'élèves dans votre classe?
3. Quelles sont les matières que vous étudiez à l'école?
4. Quelle est votre matière préférée? Pourquoi?
5. Combien de temps dure chaque cours de français?
6. A quelle heure se terminent les cours d'habitude?
7. Pourquoi faut-il aller à l'école quand on est jeune?
8. Pendant combien de temps êtes vous libre pendant l'heure du déjeuner?
9. Prenez-vous le déjeuner à l'école, apportez-vous des sandwichs, ou déjeunez-vous à la maison?
10. Savez-vous déjà ce que vous voulez faire quand vous quitterez l'école?

Reading

1. Pour acheter un livre en France, est-ce qu'il faut aller dans une librairie ou dans une bibliothèque?
2. Et où faut-il aller si vous voulez simplement emprunter un livre?
3. Aimez-vous mieux lire, écouter la radio ou regarder la télévision?
4. Quel est votre livre préféré? Décrivez-le.
5. Lisez-vous au lit avant de vous endormir?
6. Pouvez-vous nommer un auteur ou un livre français?
7. Aimez-vous les bandes dessinées? Connaissez-vous Astérix?
8. Est-ce que vous lisez un journal ou est-ce que vous regardez les informations à la télévision?
9. Aimez-vous la science-fiction?
10. Préférez-vous les ouvrages d'imagination ou les histoires vraies?

Town and traffic

1. Est-ce que vous habitez près du centre d'une ville, loin du centre, ou à la campagne?
2. Qu'est-ce que l'on peut faire dans votre ville pour s'amuser?
3. Quels sont les avantages et les désadvantages d'une grande ville?
4. Décrivez la ville où vous habitez, ou la ville la plus proche de chez vous.
5. Si vous pouviez choisir, voudriez-vous acheter une maison au centre d'une ville, ou à la campagne?
6. Dans quelle région d'Angleterre voudriez-vous habiter?
7. Quels sont les moyens de transport public où vous demeurez?
8. Qu'est-ce que c'est que le Métro?
9. A quoi servent les feux rouges?
10. Qu'est-ce que c'est qu'une autoroute?

Travel

1. Est-ce que vous avez voyagé à l'étranger? Décrivez votre voyage.
2. Est-ce que vous avez déjà visité la France? Quand? Où?
3. Avant d'aller à l'étranger qu'est-ce qu'il faut obtenir?
4. Qu'est-ce qu'il faut faire à la douane si on a quelque chose à déclarer?
5. Qu'est-ce qu'on peut voir à Paris?
6. De quel côté de la route faut-il rouler en France?
7. Comment voyagent les gens qui arrivent en France (i) au Havre? (ii) à Orly? (iii) et à la Gare du Nord?
8. Qu'est-ce que c'est qu'un bureau de change?
9. Qu'est-ce que c'est qu'un syndicat d'initiative?
10. Quel pays préféreriez-vous visiter si vous aviez tout le temps et tout l'argent nécessaires?

Jobs

1. Que vend un boucher? un boulanger? un épicier? un charcutier?
2. Que fait un coiffeur?
3. Qui faut-il faire venir si quelqu'un est très malade à la maison?
4. Qui a les vacances les plus longues, croyez-vous: un professeur d'école ou un fermier?
5. Qui est-ce qui vous apporte des lettres?
6. A votre avis, quel est le travail le plus dangereux?
7. Et quel est le travail le plus intéressant?
8. Quelle sorte de travail chercherez-vous quand vous quitterez l'école?
9. Aimeriez-vous travailler à l'étranger? Dans quel pays?
10. Décrivez en quelques mots ce que fait:
   un agent de police   un marin   un fermier
   un mécanicien   une dactylo.

Food and restaurants

1. Qu'est-ce que vous aimez manger? Qu'est-ce que vous n'aimez pas?
2. Avez-vous jamais mangé des escargots? des cuisses de grenouille?
3. Qu'est-ce que vous mangerez ce soir?

4. Qui est-ce qui fait la cuisine chez vous?
5. Comment s'appelle un homme qui sert dans un restaurant?
6. Aimeriez-vous travailler dans un restaurant? Pourquoi (pas)?
7. Quelle est la différence entre un repas table d'hôte et un repas à la carte?
8. Après un repas dans un restaurant vous voulez payer. Qu'est-ce que vous demandez au garçon?
9. Qu'est-ce que c'est qu'un 'restaurant self'?
10. Est-ce que l'alcool se vend dans les cafés en Angleterre? Et en France?

Describing a picture

In describing a picture, the various areas can be identified as follows:
au premier plan, in the foreground
au fond, in the background
au milieu, in the middle
à droite, on the right
à gauche, on the left

The following terms can be used to describe the relative positions of objects in the picture:
sur, on
sous, under
au-dessus (de), above
au-dessous (de), below
entre, between
devant, in front of
derrière, behind
à côté (de), by the side (of)
de l'autre côté (de), on the other side (of)
en face (de), opposite

The following verbs can be used to describe positions and attitudes:
être assis, to be seated
être couché, to be lying
se tenir, to stand
se dresser, to rise up (of things, trees, mountains, etc.)

A   Look at picture 1 and answer the following questions:
1. Qu'est-ce que vous voyez au fond de l'image?
2. Décrivez la maison.
3. Que vend la vendeuse à l'étalage à gauche?
4. Qu'est-ce qui est attaché au réverbère?
5. Que fait le garçon?
6. Qui parle au conducteur de la voiture? Qu'est-ce qu'il dit, croyez-vous?
7. Que fait la dame dans le jardin?
8. Combien d'animaux peut-on voir? Que font-ils?
9. A quoi sert un passage clouté?
10. Décrivez la voiture.

B Picture 2 shows the Place du Tertre in Paris. This is a well-known square in the Montmartre district, famous for its artists. In the background the large white dome is that of the basilica of the Sacred Heart usually known as **le Sacré Cœur**. In the square itself many artists line the pavements, hoping to sell their work to the tourists, and in the centre are tables where one can eat. Many famous artists have patronized the local cafés, often paying for their drinks and food with their pictures and sculptures.

Describe the scene in French in words suitable for an oral description, adding information from the details given above.

1.

Verb tables

Tense endings for all verbs:

Future	Imperfect & Conditional	Past historic Always one of these sets:			
-ai	-ais	-ai	-is	-ins	-us
-as	-ais	-as	-is	-ins	-us
-a	-ait	-a	-it	-int	-ut
-ons	-ions	-âmes	-îmes	-înmes	-ûmes
-ez	-iez	-âtes	-îtes	-întes	-ûtes
-ont	-aient	-èrent	-irent	-inrent	-urent

For the subjunctive, see pp. 125 ff.

Regular verbs

1st conjugation

Infinitive and meaning	Participles (and auxiliary)	Present	Future	Imperfect	Past Historic
donner	donnant	je donne	je donnerai	je donnais	je donnai
	donné	tu donnes	tu donneras	tu donnais	tu donnas
		il donne	il donnera	il donnait	il donna
to	(avoir)	nous donnons	nous donnerons	nous donnions	nous donnâmes
give		vous donnez	vous donnerez	vous donniez	vous donnâtes
		ils donnent	ils donneront	ils donnaient	ils donnèrent

-er verbs with stem modifications in present and future (see p. 6):

like **mener** to lead	like **céder** to yield	-oyer & -uyer like **employer**, to employ	
je mène	je cède	j'emploie	**-cer** verbs
tu mènes	tu cèdes	tu emploies	N.B. nous plaçons
il mène	il cède	il emploie	
nous menons	nous cédons	nous employons	**-ger** verbs
vous menez	vous cédez	vous employez	N.B. nous mangeons
ils mènent	ils cèdent	ils emploient	
			appeler & jeter see list below
Future:			
je mènerai	je céderai	j'emploierai	

2nd conjugation

Infinitive and meaning	Participles (and auxiliary)	Present	Future	Imperfect	Past Historic
finir	finissant fini	je finis tu finis il finit	je finirai tu finiras il finira	je finissais tu finissais il finissait	je finis tu finis il finit
to finish	(avoir)	nous finissons vous finissez ils finissent	nous finirons vous finirez ils finiront	nous finissions vous finissiez ils finissaient	nous finîmes vous finîtes ils finirent

3rd conjugation

Infinitive and meaning	Participles (and auxiliary)	Present	Future	Imperfect	Past Historic
vendre	vendant vendu	je vends tu vends il vend*	je vendrai tu vendras il vendra	je vendais tu vendais il vendait	je vendis tu vendis il vendit
to sell	(avoir)	nous vendons vous vendez ils vendent	nous vendrons vous vendrez ils vendront	nous vendions vous vendiez ils vendaient	nous vendîmes vous vendîtes ils vendirent

*Verbs which do not have stems ending in -d take -t: e.g. **il rompt.**

4th conjugation: only **-evoir** verbs are like **recevoir,** all other **-oir** verbs are irregular.

Infinitive and meaning	Participles (and auxiliary)	Present	Future	Imperfect	Past Historic
recevoir	recevant reçu	je reçois tu reçois il reçoit	je recevrai tu recevras il recevra	je recevais tu recevais il recevait	je reçus tu reçus il reçut
to receive	(avoir)	nous recevons vous recevez ils reçoivent	nous recevrons vous recevrez ils recevront	nous recevions vous receviez ils recevaient	nous reçûmes vous reçûtes ils reçurent

Infinitive	Participles (and auxiliary)	Present	Future	Imperfect	Past Historic
aller to go	allant allé (être)	je vais tu vas il va nous allons vous allez ils vont	j'irai	j'allais	j'allai
appeler to call (s'appeler: to be called)	appelant appelé (avoir; reflexive: être)	j'appelle tu appelles il appelle nous appelons vous appelez ils appellent	j'appellerai	j'appelais	j'appelai
apprendre to learn	like prendre				
s'asseoir to sit down	s'asseyant assis (être)	je m'assieds tu t'assieds il s'assied nous nous asseyons vous vous asseyez ils s'asseyent	je m'assiérai *or* je m'assoirai	je m'asseyais	je m'assis
avoir to have	ayant eu (avoir)	j'ai tu as il a nous avons vous avez ils ont	j'aurai	j'avais	j'eus
battre to beat (se battre, to fight)	battant battu (avoir; reflexive: être)	je bats tu bats il bat nous battons vous battez ils battent	je battrai	je battais	je battis
boire to drink	buvant bu (avoir)	je bois tu bois il boit nous buvons vous buvez ils boivent	je boirai	je buvais	je bus
commencer to begin	commençant commencé (avoir)	je commence tu commences il commence nous commençons vous commencez ils commencent	je commencerai	je commençais	je commençai

Infinitive	Participles (and auxiliary)	Present	Future	Imperfect	Past Historic
comprendre to understand	like prendre				
conduire to conduct; drive (a vehicle)	conduisant conduit (avoir)	je conduis tu conduis il conduit nous conduisons vous conduisez ils conduisent	je conduirai	je conduisais	je conduisis
connaître to know; be acquainted with	connaissant connu (avoir)	je connais tu connais il connaît nous connaissons vous connaissez ils connaissent	je connaîtrai	je connaissais	je connus
convaincre to convince, convict	convainquant convaincu (avoir)	je convaincs tu convaincs il convainc nous convainquons vous convainquez ils convainquent	je convaincrai	je convainquais	je convainquis
courir to run	courant couru (avoir)	je cours tu cours il court nous courons vous courez ils courent	je courrai	je courais	je courus
craindre to fear	craignant craint (avoir)	je crains tu crains il craint nous craignons vous craignez ils craignent	je craindrai	je craignais	je craignis
croire to believe	croyant cru (avoir)	je crois tu crois il croit nous croyons vous croyez ils croient	je croirai	je croyais	je crus
devenir to become	like venir (être)				
devoir to owe, have to	devant dû, due (avoir)	je dois tu dois il doit nous devons vous devez ils doivent	je devrai	je devais	je dus

Infinitive	Participles (and auxiliary)	Present	Future	Imperfect	Past Historic
dire to say, tell	disant dit (avoir)	je dis tu dis il dit nous disons vous dites ils disent	je dirai	je disais	je dis
dormir to sleep	dormant dormi (avoir)	je dors tu dors il dort nous dormons vous dormez ils dorment	je dormirai	je dormais	je dormis
écrire to write	écrivant écrit (avoir)	j'écris tu écris il écrit nous écrivons vous écrivez ils écrivent	j'écrirai	j'écrivais	j'écrivis
envoyer to send	envoyant envoyé (avoir)	j'envoie tu envoies il envoie nous envoyons vous envoyez ils envoient	j'enverrai	j'envoyais	j'envoyai
être to be	étant été (avoir)	je suis tu es il est nous sommes vous êtes ils sont	je serai	j'étais	je fus
faire to do, make	faisant fait (avoir)	je fais tu fais il fait nous faisons vous faites ils font	je ferai	je faisais	je fis
falloir to be necessary, must	fallu (avoir)	il faut	il faudra	il fallait	il fallut
jeter to throw	jetant jeté (avoir)	je jette tu jettes il jette nous jetons vous jetez ils jettent	je jetterai	je jetais	je jetai
joindre to join	like peindre				

Infinitive	Participles (and auxiliary)	Present	Future	Imperfect	Past Historic
lever to raise (se lever: to get up)	levant levé (avoir; reflexive: être)	je lève tu lèves il lève nous levons vous levez ils lèvent	je lèverai	je levais	je levai
lire to read	lisant lu (avoir)	je lis tu lis il lit nous lisons vous lisez ils lisent	je lirai	je lisais	je lus
mentir to (tell a) lie	like dormir				
mettre to put (se mettre à: to start to)	mettant mis (avoir; reflexive: être)	je mets tu mets il met nous mettons vous mettez ils mettent	je mettrai	je mettais	je mis
mourir to die	mourant mort (être)	je meurs tu meurs il meurt nous mourons vous mourez ils meurent	je mourrai	je mourais	je mourus
naître to be born	naissant né (être)	je nais tu nais il naît nous naissons vous naissez ils naissent	je naîtrai	je naissais	je naquis
offrir to offer	like ouvrir				
ouvrir to open	ouvrant ouvert (avoir)	j'ouvre tu ouvres il ouvre nous ouvrons vous ouvrez ils ouvrent	j'ouvrirai	j'ouvrais	j'ouvris
paraître to seem	like connaître				
partir to depart, leave	partant parti (être)	je pars tu pars il part nous partons vous partez ils partent	je partirai	je partais	je partis

Infinitive	Participles (and auxiliary)	Present	Future	Imperfect	Past Historic
peindre	peignant peint	je peins tu peins il peint	je peindrai	je peignais	je peignis
to paint	(avoir)	nous peignons vous peignez ils peignent			
permettre to allow	like mettre				
plaire	plaisant plu	je plais tu plais il plaît	je plairai	je plaisais	je plus
to please	(avoir)	nous plaisons vous plaisez ils plaisent			
pleuvoir to rain	pleuvant plu (avoir)	il pleut	il pleuvra	il pleuvait	il plut
pouvoir	pouvant pu	je peux (puis) tu peux il peut	je pourrai	je pouvais	je pus
to be able can	(avoir)	nous pouvons vous pouvez ils peuvent			
prendre	prenant pris	je prends tu prends il prend	je prendrai	je prenais	je pris
to take	(avoir)	nous prenons vous prenez ils prennent			
rire	riant ri	je ris tu ris il rit	je rirai	je riais tu riais il riait	je ris
to laugh	(avoir)	nous rions vous riez ils rient		nous riions vous riiez ils riaient	
savoir	sachant su	je sais tu sais il sait	je saurai	je savais	je sus
to know (as a fact)	(avoir)	nous savons vous savez ils savent			
sentir to feel	like sortir (avoir)				
servir to serve	like sortir (avoir)				

Infinitive	Participles (and auxiliary)	Present	Future	Imperfect	Past Historic
sortir to go out	sortant sorti (être)	je sors tu sors il sort nous sortons vous sortez ils sortent	je sortirai	je sortais	je sortis
souffrir to suffer	like ouvrir				
sourire to smile	like rire				
suivre to follow	suivant suivi (avoir)	je suis tu suis il suit nous suivons vous suivez ils suivent	je suivrai	je suivais	je suivis
tenir to hold	tenant tenu (avoir)	je tiens tu tiens il tient nous tenons vous tenez ils tiennent	je tiendrai	je tenais	je tins tu tins il tint nous tînmes vous tîntes ils tinrent
valoir to be worth	valant valu (avoir)	je vaux tu vaux il vaut nous valons vous valez ils valent	je vaudrai	je valais	je valus
vaincre to vanish	like convaincre				
venir to come	venant venu (être)	je viens tu viens il vient nous venons vous venez ils viennent	je viendrai	je venais	je vins tu vins il vint nous vînmes vous vîntes ils vinrent
vivre to live (be alive)	vivant vécu (avoir)	je vis tu vis il vit nous vivons vous vivez ils vivent	je vivrai	je vivais	je vécus
voir to see	voyant vu (avoir)	je vois tu vois il voit nous voyons vous voyez ils voient	je verrai	je voyais	je vis

Infinitive	Participles (and auxiliary)	Present	Future	Imperfect	Past Historic
vouloir to want, wish	voulant voulu (avoir)	je veux tu veux il veut nous voulons vous voulez ils veulent	je voudrai	je voulais	je voulus

Answers

Answers are given to those exercises where only one answer is correct. Suggested renderings are given for translations, although obviously there will be several acceptable versions. No answers are given to open-ended exercises. Page number references to the exercises are given in italic.

A
3

1. aussitôt qu'
2. donc
3. mais
4. parce que
5. ni . . . ni
6. si (= whether)
7. quand
8. pendant que
9. ou
10. si (= if)

B
3

Ma chambre n'est pas très grande, mais elle est claire parce qu'elle a deux grandes fenêtres. Chaque matin mon réveil sonne à sept heures, mais je reste au lit jusqu'à sept heures et demie, parce que je n'aime pas me lever le matin. J'écoute la radio, pendant que je me lève et que je m'habille. Ensuite je bois du café, mais je ne mange ni pain ni œufs, parce que je n'ai jamais faim à cette heure du matin. Aussitôt que j'arrive au bureau, je commence à avoir faim.

A
6

1. ils aboient
2. je m'appelle
3. tu jettes
4. nous préférons
5. ils amènent
6. il dégèle
7. vous réussissez
8. j'achète
9. elle envoie
10. nous mangeons
11. il rompt
12. nous saisissons
13. elles choisissent
14. je pêche
15. il reçoit
16. nous apercevons
17. tu paies (*or* payes)
18. ils emploient
19. tu rappelles
20. nous plaçons

B
6

1. arrête . . . empêche
2. finissent
3. amène
4. gêne . . . balaye (*or* balaie)
5. mangeons
6. jettent . . . jetons
7. guérissent
8. plaçons
9. mélange . . . préfère
10. aboient . . . aperçoivent
11. sèchent
12. se promène
13. vend
14. marche . . . traverse
15. prête
16. rend
17. rangeons
18. réussissez
19. aperçoit
20. appelles

A
7

1. j'ai
2. tu es
3. il va
4. elle a
5. on dit
6. nous faisons
7. vous êtes
8. ils font
9. elles écrivent
10. je peux
11. tu veux
12. il sait
13. elle voit
14. on doit
15. nous recevons
16. vous tenez
17. ils offrent
18. elles retiennent
19. je prends
20. tu dors
21. Il ment
22. elle ouvre
23. on sert
24. nous sortons

25. vous connaissez
26. ils reconnaissent
27. elle craint
28. il peint
29. nous joignons
30. vous faites
31. ils vont
32. elles ont
33. je vois
34. tu peux
35. il couvre
36. elle reconnaît
37. on interrompt

38. nous sommes
39. vous craignez
40. ils aperçoivent
41. elles prennent
42. je reçois
43. tu dois
44. il souffre
45. elle prend
46. on sait
47. nous écrivons
48. vous savez
49. ils sont
50. elles veulent

B
8

1. est
2. va
3. vient
4. voulez
5. comprennent . . . dis

6. dort
7. fait
8. connaît
9. craignons
10. offrent

C
8

1. sait . . . souffre
2. savez-vous . . . veut
3. dois . . . veux
4. peins . . . peignent
5. réussissent . . . réussis

6. peux . . . vois?
7. dois . . . puis-je
8. sais . . . connaît
9. connaissez . . . sais . . . allez
10. jouent . . . font . . . sont

A
9

1. je peux; puis-je?
2. tu reconnais
3. il est
4. nous voyons
5. vous vivez
6. ils paraissent
7. je m'assieds
8. tu mens
9. elle s'appelle
10. nous rions
11. vous suivez
12. elles fuient
13. je m'endors
14. tu mets
15. on meurt
16. nous cédons
17. vous découvrez
18. ils réussissent
19. je suis
20. tu sens
21. il me plaît
22. nous écrivons
23. vous buvez
24. ils sourient
25. elles peuvent

26. . . . meurt.
27. . . . s'enfuit.
28. . . . court
29. . . . suit
30. . . . viennent
31. . . . est
32. . . . lisons
33. . . . riez
34. . . . courent
35. . . . souffrons
36. . . . savent
37. . . . deviennent
38. . . . boit
39. . . . se trouve
40. . . . craint
41. Écrivez . . .
42. . . . paraît
43. . . . sourit
44. . . . conduit
45. . . . joint
46. . . . ment . . . crois
47. Asseyez-vous . . .
48. . . . boivent
49. . . . lisent
50. . . . vit

B
10

1. mangeons — vends
2. aperçois — placez
3. envoie — envoyez
4. peignons — crains
5. finissent - · prête

6. connaît — faites
7. jetons — jette
8. appelle — appelez-vous
9. préfère — achètes
10. était — êtes

A   1. Il lit un livre.
11 2. Je vais à Paris.
    3. Parlez-vous anglais?
    4. Comment allez-vous?
    5. Comment fait-on ceci?
    6. L'arbre meurt.
    7. Ils peignent la cuisine.
    8. Je n'aime pas le café, mais j'aime bien le thé.
    9. Aimez-vous le sport?
   10. Anne et Marie font beaucoup d'erreurs.

B   1. Vous ne le faites pas, n'est-ce pas?
11 2. Je ne veux pas boire ce que vous buvez.
    3. Savez-vous conduire? Moi, je conduis très bien.
    4. Je connais quelqu'un qui sait le poème par cœur.
    5. — Pierre, Charles, Jean: est-ce que vous riez?
       — Mais non, Monsieur. Nous lisons.
    6. Je ne peux pas faire ce que vous voulez.
    7. Nous faisons la cuisine pour les autres.
    8. Je ne peux pas le faire et je ne veux pas essayer.
    9. -- Vous pouvez faire ceci pour moi.
       — Mais non! Je ne peux pas.
   10. — Qu'est-ce que vous faites ce soir?
       — Nous voulons aller au cinéma.

A   1. . . . travaille . . .
13 2. . . . mange . . .
    3. . . . regarde . . .
    4. . . . allez-vous . . .
    5. . . . vient . . .
    6. . . . en écoutant . . .
    7. . . . voyant . . .
    8. . . . en étudiant . . .
    9. En rentrant . . .
   10. . . . en courant.
   11. . . . en souriant . . . en sifflant . . .
   12. . . . tout en conduisant . . .
   13. Etant descendu . . .
   14. Après avoir acheté . . .
   15. S'étant couché . . .

B   1. Elle sort en portant son parapluie à la main.
13 2. Il commence à manger sans attendre.
    3. Couché sur mon lit j'entends passer les voitures.
    4. Sachant la vérité je ne peux pas répondre sans rire.
    5. Il écoute avec attention le guide qui explique l'histoire du château.
    6. Regardez! Voilà le facteur qui arrive maintenant.
    7. J'écris mes lettres tout en regardant la télévision.
    8. Ayant beaucoup voyagé, il raconte des histoires amusantes.
    9. D'ici elle peut voir jouer les enfants.
   10. Quand je travaille je n'aime pas être dérangé par des gens qui posent des questions agaçantes.

C   1. une mère aimante   4. un maillot de bain*
13 2. un arbre mourant   5. un escalier roulant
    3. une langue vivante   6. des lettres intéressantes

D   (a)
14   **Present participles**   **Infinitive**
     pouvant   pouvoir
     différant   différer
     aimant*   aimer
     suivant*   suivre
     sachant   savoir
     ayant   avoir

     (b)
     Not present participles   **Meaning**
     suffisant (adj)   sufficient
     pourtant (adv)   yet, however
     différent (adj)   different
     enfant (noun)   child
     aimant* (noun)   magnet
     cependant (adv, conj)   however, meanwhile
     instant (adj, noun)   instant
     suivant* (adj)   following
     savant (adj, noun)   learned, learned man
     avant (prep, adv)   before
     diamant (noun)   diamond

     * these appear in both columns

A   1. je menais   11. vous riiez
14   2. tu dansais   12. ils disaient
     3. elle rougissait   13. je comprenais
     4. nous nagions   14. tu ouvrais
     5. vous buviez   15. il partait
     6. ils vivaient   16. nous tenions
     7. je voulais   17. vous réussissiez
     8. tu pouvais   18. ils choisissaient
     9. elle voyait   19. elles plongeaient
     10. nous placions   20. tu lançais

B   Je devais toujours me coucher après le dîner. J'étais obligé de quitter maman, qui
15   restait à causer avec ses amies, au jardin s'il faisait beau, dans le salon s'il faisait
     mauvais.
        Une fois couché, j'avais l'habitude de lire un des livres que je recevais chaque
     année à Noël. Je ne comprenais pas toujours tout ce que je lisais, mais souvent, après
     avoir posé le livre sur ma table de nuit, je fermais les yeux, je réfléchissais sur ce que
     je venais de lire, et les phrases commençaient à me devenir intelligibles.

C   1. Mathieu me rendait toujours visite quand il était à Paris.
16   2. Pendant l'hiver nous allions au cinéma tous les samedis.
     3. Étiez-vous en Grèce au même temps que moi?
     4. Je buvais toujours du thé, mais maintenant je préfère le café.
     5. Nous savions que sa maison se trouvait quelque part dans le bois, mais nous ne
        pouvions pas la trouver.
     6. Ils mangeaient un repas énorme et nous n'avions rien à manger.
     7. Est-ce que tu rougissais à cause de ce qu'il disait?
     8. Connaissiez-vous déjà Alain?
     9. Marie a dit qu'elle voulait venir avec nous, mais qu'elle ne pouvait pas.
     10. J'étais dans la cuisine et je faisais la vaisselle, quand un homme a mis sa main
        sur mon épaule.

A   1. ... mangerai ...   3. ... donnerez ...
17   2. ... vendra ...   4. ... porteras ...

5. ... craindrons ...
6. ... essuierez ...
7. ... essayerai (or essaierai)

8. ... amènera ...
9. ... choisiront ...
10. ... voudrons ...

B
17
1. ... apprendra ...
2. ... neigera ...
3. ... achètera ...
4. ... vendront ...
5. ... cueillerons ...

6. ... mangeront ...
7. ... pourrai ...
8. ... sera ...
9. ... saurai ...
10. ... reconnaîtrai ...

C
17
1. Il boira du vin si vous buvez aussi.
2. Quand il arrivera, je quitterai la maison.
3. Est-ce que vous allez au cinéma cet après-midi?
4. Nous allons passer les vacances chez ma tante.
5. J'achèterai deux billets.
6. S'il rentre de bonne heure nous pourrons partir avant le dîner.
7. Nous ouvrirons la porte seulement s'il amène le prêtre.
8. J'ouvrirai la porte quand il apportera le paquet.
9. Voulez-vous vous asseoir?
10. Quand est-ce que vous allez chez le boulanger?

A
19
1. ... viendrait ...
2. ... voudrait ...
3. ... pourrais ...
4. ... rendraient ...
5. ... espérerait ...

6. ... mangerions ...
7. ... auriez ...
8. ... lâcherait ...
9. ... aiderait.
10. ... rendrait ...

B
19
1. Le contrôleur m'a dit que je devais payer.
2. L'agent nous a répondu qu'il faudrait attendre.
3. Elles nous ont demandé quand notre père reviendrait.
4. Le directeur m'a demandé quand je pouvais commencer.
5. Je lui ai répondu que je pourrais commencer le lendemain.
6. Jean m'a dit que nous devrions partir à six heures.
7. Elle nous a demandé combien de temps nous passerions en Grèce.
8. Je lui ai dit que je ne viendrais pas samedi.
9. Il m'a assuré qu'on ne m'attendrait pas ce jour-là.
10. Je lui ai promis que je ferais mieux la prochaine fois.

C
19
1. Paul a dit qu'il jouerait pour l'équipe s'il avait le temps.
2. Anne nous a dit que nous aurions dû voir le film.
3. Tu aurais pu venir avec nous si tu avais fini à cinq heures.
4. Nous ne savions pas si vous pourriez venir.
5. Il vaudrait mieux aller en Grèce plus tard.
6. Pourriez-vous nous dire l'heure, s'il vous plaît, Monsieur?
7. Ils préféreraient aller chercher une glace au café.
8. Si je pouvais entendre, je répondrais.
9. — Tu devrais aller faire tes devoirs.
   — Mais non! J'aimerais beaucoup mieux regarder la télévision.
10. Chaque jour le guide leur montrait des vues extraordinaires, et ils savaient que le lendemain il leur montrerait des vues encore plus spectaculaires.

A
21
1. Il a mangé ...
2. J'ai fini ...
3. Nous avons vendu ...
4. Vous avez manqué ...
5. Ils ont menti ...

6. Tu as rendu ...
7. J'ai conduit ...
8. Ils ont aperçu ...
9. Elle n'a jamais souri.
10. Il n'a plus plu.

B
21
1. J'ai tenu ma promesse.
2. Ils n'ont pas peint le mur.

3. Le film n'a pas plu au visiteur.
4. Ils ont bu le thé.
5. Je n'ai pas offert de bière à l'ouvrier.
6. N'avez-vous pas écrit la lettre?
7. Nous avons pris la chambre pour dix jours.
8. Il n'a pas lu le journal.
9. Ils ont lu le livre, mais ils n'ont pas cru chaque mot.
10. Nous avons ouvert la porte.

C
22
1. Je suis arrivé.
2. Il est entré dans la chambre.
3. Est-il mort?
4. Il est passé me voir.
5. Je suis retourné à six heures.
6. Il est devenu très riche.
7. Je suis tombé en sortant.
8. Il est parti de bonne heure.
9. Pierre est monté à sa chambre.
10. Jean est resté en bas.

D
22
1. N'est-il pas encore arrivé?
2. Il est descendu dans l'ascenseur.
3. Je suis revenu parce que je suis sorti sans argent.
4. L'enfant est devenu très difficile — c'est pourquoi je suis sorti.
5. Je suis resté ici parce que mon chien est mort.
6. Il est arrivé à la tour Eiffel; il est monté au premier étage.
7. Il est descendu très vite.
8. Il est né à Paris.
9. Je suis passé à l'hôpital.
10. Il a plu toute la journée.

E
22
Il est né à Dijon. Il est allé à Paris, où il a étudié l'anglais. Il est devenu professeur des langues étrangères à la Sorbonne — l'université de Paris. Il a écrit beaucoup de livres, et a acheté un appartement très moderne au centre de la ville, où son fils est né. Il est mort à Londres, où il est allé rendre visite à la famille de sa femme anglaise.

A
23
1. Ayant parlé ainsi, il est sorti.
2. Etant arrivé tard, il s'est mis à travailler sans délai.
3. S'étant couché de bonne heure, il s'est endormi immédiatement.
4. S'étant levé trop tard il ne s'est pas lavé.
5. Ayant pris son stylo il s'est mis à écrire.

A
23
1. Il était tombé . . .
2. Nous avions ouvert . . .
3. Vous aviez mis . . .
4. Ils avaient couru . . .
5. Il était mort . . .
6. Il avait sauté . . .
7. Vous aviez bu . . .
8. Ils avaient rompu . . .
9. Ils avaient été . . .
10. Ils avaient eu . . .
11. Vous aviez vu . . .
12. Elles avaient aperçu . . .
13. J'avais craint . . .
14. Tu n'avais jamais cru . . .
15. Il lui avait fallu faire . . .
16. Avions-nous lu . . .
17. Quand aviez-vous écrit . . .
18. J'étais parti . . .
19. Ceci m'avait beaucoup plu.
20. Il avait plu . . .

B
23
1. J'avais mangé . . .
2. Tu étais sorti . . . je suis arrivé . . .
3. Je ne pouvais pas . . . il avait vendu . . .
4. . . . ont protesté . . . avait donné.
5. Je savais . . . je l'avais conduit . . .
6. Il est venu . . . ils avaient découvert . . .

7. Il était né . . .
8. . . . avait ouvert . . . je suis entré . . .
9. . . . avons trouvé qu'il n'était pas sorti . . . croyions . . .
10. . . . ai demandé . . . il avait dit

A
25

1. . . . arrivée . . .
2. . . . sorti(e)s . . .
3. . . . tombés . . .
4. . . . couchée . . .
5. . . . appelée . . .

6. . . . dit . . .
7. . . . raconté . . . racontées
8. . . . lavée . . .
9. . . . resté(e)s . . .
10. . . . sorti . . .

B
25

1. Jean et Marie sont arrivés ici cet après-midi.
2. Une troupe de soldats était partie par avion.
3. Il lui a parlé.
4. Ils avaient voyagé de pays en pays.
5. Je n'ai pas cassé l'assiette — c'est toi qui l'as cassée!
6. Je n'ai pas cru les choses qu'il m'a racontées.
7. Tous les livres ont disparu.
8. Je croyais que j'avais perdu ma règle, mais je l'ai trouvée sous la table.
9. Les fleurs qu'elle avait mises dans le vase étaient tombées sur le plancher.
10. L'eau qu'elle a apportée n'est pas très chaude.
11. Les feuilles, tombées des arbres, ont couvert la terre.
12. Ils se sont souvent battus, mais je ne sais pas qui gagnait d'habitude.
13. La vieille voiture que mon père a peinte brille maintenant.
14. Je n'ai pas mis à la poste la lettre que vous m'avez donnée, parce que je l'ai oubliée.
15. Il a essuyé l'encre qu'il avait renversée.

C
25

Hélène s'est levée tard le jeudi matin. Elle n'a pas eu le temps de boire son café, car elle était arrivée en retard au bureau la veille et son chef l'avait grondée. Elle a couru jusqu'à l'arrêt d'autobus, mais le bus était déjà parti. Elle ne pouvait pas se décider s'il vaudrait mieux attendre le prochain autobus ou aller au bureau à pied. A ce moment-là une Peugeot s'est arrêtée tout près d'elle, et elle a vu son chef qui lui a fait signe, mais qui ne l'a pas prise avec lui dans sa voiture. Hélène était furieuse et elle a décidé de rentrer chez elle.

A
26

1. Le repas sera préparé par le cuisinier.
2. La fenêtre a été réparée par son voisin.
3. Les gâteaux ont été mangés par l'âne.
4. La nouvelle école sera ouverte par le maire.
5. Le sol a été chauffé par le soleil.

B
26

1. L'explosion avait blessé un passant.
2. Ici on parle français.
3. On dit qu'elle est très intelligente.
4. On sonne.
5. On a sonné.

C
26

1. Un prix a été donné au gagnant. *Or:* On a donné un prix au gagnant.
2. On a posé beaucoup de questions au prisonnier.
3. On a offert du pain et du fromage aux mendiants.
4. On a montré la chambre au visiteur.
5. On a enseigné son rôle à l'acteur.
6. On a vendu aux touristes une carte de la ville.
7. Garçon! On m'a donné un mauvais œuf.
8. On a offert au Prince la main de la Princesse.
9. On a apporté des grappes de raisin au malade.
10. On m'a demandé le nom de mon dentiste.

A
28

1. Il se promène dans le parc.
2. Je m'appelle Leroy. Comment vous appelez-vous?
3. Au revoir! Amusez-vous bien!
4. Elle s'est excusée et s'en est allée.
5. Dépêche-toi et couche-toi.
6. Je me déshabillerai, et puis je me baignerai.
7. Pardon, monsieur, je me suis réveillé trop tard.
8. Les soldats se sont battus, et se sont blessés.
9. Pour s'asseoir sur cette chaise il faut se baisser.
10. Il s'est marié, et tous ses amis se sont moqués de lui.

A
29

1. Donne!
2. Saisissez!
3. Vendons!
4. Reçois!
5. Mettons!
6. Dites!
7. Faites!
8. Viens!
9. Allons!
10. Allons-y!
11. Va-t'en!
12. Asseyez-vous!
13. Taisez-vous!
14. Sache-le!
15. Lavez-vous!
16. Mange-le!
17. Manges-en!
18. Vas-y!
19. Donnez-le-moi!
20. Achetons-le!
21. Veuillez me suivre.
22. Soyez sage!
23. Ne me le rends pas!
24. N'ayez pas peur!
25. Ne sois pas si bête!

B
29

1. Asseyez-vous, s'il vous plaît.
2. Donnez-moi votre tasse, s'il vous plaît.
3. Sois sage!
4. Attention!
5. Entrez! N'attendez pas sur le palier.
6. Laissez-la venir avec nous!
7. Parlez plus lentement, s'il vous plaît. Ne parlez pas si vite.
8. Donnez-m'en deux.
9. Poussez. Tirez.
10. Tais-toi et fais attention!
11. Téléphonez à la police.
12. Apportez-le ici.
13. Allez-vous-en!
14. Va chercher le médecin.
15. Venez voir cette belle vue.

A
31

1. Je n'ai pas fini.
2. Il ne travaille plus.
3. Nous n'avons jamais mangé des escargots.
4. Ils n'ont guère commencé.
5. Je n'ai vu personne dans la rue.
6. Vous n'y trouverez rien.
7. Ils n'en ont mangé que deux.
8. Elle n'a plus de papier.
9. Je n'ai vu aucun des films.
10. Ne lui donnez ni vin ni bière.

B
31

Quand je suis entré dans la maison la lampe n'était pas allumée et je ne pouvais rien voir. J'étais certain que personne n'était arrivé avant moi, et je n'ai rien entendu. Soudain, quelqu'un s'est approché de moi; je n'ai entendu aucun bruit, mais cette personne m'a frappé sur la tête. Dès ce moment-là je ne savais plus rien.

C
31

1. Personne n'y est.
2. Non, je n'y ai rien acheté.

3. Non, je n'en ai mangé aucune(s).
4. Non, je ne l'ai jamais visitée.
5. Non, je ne parle ni l'un ni l'autre.
6. Non, je n'y vais plus.
7. On ne les voit nulle part.
8. Non, elle n'est guère commencée.
9. Il n'y a rien là-dedans.
10. Personne ne s'y trouve.

A
34

1.	de	6.	d'
2.	—	7.	à
3.	d'	8.	—
4.	à, —	9.	de
5.	—, de	10.	de, à

B
34

1. J'ai appris à nager l'année dernière.
2. Nous allons visiter le musée cet après-midi.
3. Il a peur de perdre.
4. Je m'intéresse à collectionner les vieilles bouteilles.
5. Le professeur a oublié d'apporter ses lunettes.
6. Je préfère ne pas les aider.
7. Il vaut mieux ne rien dire.
8. Ils viendront demain pour réparer l'ascenseur.
9. Commencez par lire ce dossier, ensuite vous rencontrerez le client.
10. Je n'ose pas le laisser se servir de ma moto.

A
34

1. Il demande à son père de lui donner un vélo.
2. Son père lui défend de conduire sa moto.
3. J'ai mes devoirs à finir.
4. Elle a promis à sa fille de lui donner une nouvelle robe.
5. On vous invite à dîner chez nous.

B
34

Paul apprenait à jouer de la trompette. Il jouait très mal. Dès qu'il commençait à jouer, sa famille essayait de l'empêcher de continuer. Sa mère faisait semblant d'avoir mal à la tête, son père lui demandait d'aller faire quelque course, et sa sœur lui disait qu'elle ne pouvait supporter le bruit. Mais Paul refusait de les écouter; il espérait devenir un grand musicien un jour.

A
35

1. Est-ce que vous venez? Venez-vous?
2. Est-ce que vous avez de la monnaie? Avez-vous de la monnaie?
3. Savez-vous l'heure? Est-ce que vous savez l'heure?
4. Puis-je sortir, s'il vous plaît? Est-ce que je peux sortir, s'il vous plaît?
5. Est-ce que Jean sait conduire? Jean sait-il conduire?
6. Parlez-vous anglais, Madame? Est-ce que vous parlez anglais, Madame?
7. N'avez-vous pas fini vos devoirs? Vous n'avez pas fini vos devoirs?
8. Voudriez-vous ouvrir la porte? Est-ce que vous voudriez ouvrir la porte?
9. Est-ce que vous avez trouvé mon stylo? Avez-vous trouvé mon stylo?
10. Pourriez-vous faire ceci pour moi? Est-ce que vous pourriez faire ceci pour moi?

A
36

1. «Bon», dit-il.
2. «Jamais!», a-t-il répondu.
3. «Et vous?», demande-t-il.
4. «Tu viens?», a-t-elle demandé.
5. «Doucement!», a-t-elle chuchoté.
6. «Je dois essayer», s'est-il dit.
7. «Pas encore!», ont-ils crié.
8. «C'est trop dangereux», ai-je pensé.
9. «Venez ici!», a commandé le portier.
10. «Et vous aussi!», a répondu Pierre.

B   1. «Quand est-ce que vous viendrez?», a demandé Marie.
36   2. «Mange-le!», m'a ordonné ma mère.
      3. «Tuez-le!», a ordonné le général.
      4. «Je ne veux pas le faire!», s'est-elle écriée.*
      5. «Je ne sais pas encore», m'a avoué Georges.
      6. «Puis-je sortir?», a demandé Pierre au professeur.
      7. «C'est toujours beaucoup trop dangereux», me suis-je dit de nouveau.
      8. «Doucement! Ne faites pas de bruit», leur ai-je dit à voix basse.
      9. «Mais si! — Je comprends très bien», ai-je contredit.
     10. «Qui est là? Qu'est-ce qu'il y a?», s'est demandé Charles.

*The past participle always agrees with the reflexive pronoun in s'écrier.

A   Je m'approchais d'un hôtel à Paris quand un homme qui regardait une carte m'a
37   arrêté et m'a dit:
     — Excusez-moi, Monsieur. Je cherche une pharmacie.
     — Prenez la première rue à droite, et la deuxième à gauche.
        Il m'a remercié et il est parti. Un moment plus tard je suis entré dans l'hôtel, et
     j'ai demandé à l'employé une chambre.
     — Oui, Monsieur, a dit l'employé; mais il faut la payer maintenant.
     — Pourquoi? lui ai-je demandé.
     — Parce qu'il y a tant de gens qui s'en vont sans payer.
        Je lui ai dit que je prendrais la chambre, et je lui ai demandé la clé. Avant de
     monter, j'ai téléphoné à mon bureau, et ensuite j'ai dû attendre l'ascenseur. Je
     pouvais entendre la radio dans la grande salle. Je voulais écouter la musique, mais
     d'abord j'avais besoin de me reposer.

A   Monsieur Dubois voulait laver sa voiture. Il l'avait décrottée. Il a appelé son fils
39   Pierre, et il lui a demandé de chercher de l'eau chaude. Pierre est allé à la maison. Il
     y en a trouvé. Il l'a rapportée à son père.
        A ce moment Madame Dubois les a appelés.
     — Venez vite, a-t-elle dit, la soupe est chaude. Elle est sur la table. Il faut venir en
     manger vite. Elle est si bonne.

B   1. On l'achète à la boucherie.
39   2. Oui, je l'ai vue.
      3. Oui, on lui en donne.
      4. Oui, on peut y en acheter.
      5. Il y en a sept.
      6. Non, je ne les ai pas comptées.
      7. Oui, je lui parle souvent.
      8. Non, on ne peut pas l'entendre.
      9. Oui, je l'ai goûtée souvent.
     10. Oui, (Non) elle (ne) l'a (pas) visitée.

C   1. Rendez-la-moi; je l'ai achetée.
39   2. Est-ce que vous les avez trouvées dans le tiroir?
      3. Nous en avons six. Combien en avez-vous acheté?
      4. Les deux dames s'y sont promenées avec leurs chiens.
      5. Donnez-le-moi! Je veux en manger.
      6. Pourquoi Georges les y a-t-il mises?
      7. Je ne vais pas le leur donner.
      8. Personne n'y habite plus.
      9. Allez-vous-en! Ne les touchez pas!
     10. Je lui ai demandé ce qu'il en pensait.

D   — Tu peux m'emmener en ville cet après-midi, Michèle?
40   — Oui, j'y vais de toute façon. Qu'est-ce que tu veux y faire?
        — Je dois aller chez Jean-Luc chercher mes livres. Je les y ai laissés la semaine
     dernière. Jean-Luc voulait les emprunter et il a promis de me les rendre, mais

maintenant j'en ai besoin, et je ne l'ai pas vu et je ne peux pas lui téléphoner.
— Il n'a pas de téléphone?
— Non, il n'en a pas et il n'en veut pas. Il dit qu'un téléphone le dérangerait quand
il essaie de travailler.
— Bon, allons-y.

A
41

1. Après vous, messieurs.
2. Ils travaillent pour nous.
3. Partez sans moi.
4. Nous voulons venir avec toi.
5. Nous chantons comme elles.
6. Ils travaillent pour lui.
7. Pensez à moi.
8. Tu es aussi stupide qu'eux.
9. Moi, je ne reviendrai pas.
10. Nous, nous sommes riches.

B
41

1. — C'est toi?
   — Oui, c'est moi.
2. Pourquoi moi? Pourquoi pas elle?
3. Lui et moi, nous pouvons le faire ensemble.
4. Vous et moi, nous allons le réparer nous-mêmes.
5. On ne peut pas le faire soi-même.
6. Les mères enseignent leurs enfants elles-mêmes.
7. Il pense à elle, mais elle ne pense pas à lui.
8. Derrière vous, mesdames, vous verrez un portrait du roi lui-même.
9. — Qui a cassé la fenêtre — toi?
   — Non, papa, pas moi.
10. Lui-même, il n'oserait pas le dire.

C
41

— Tu vas payer, toi!
— Qui? Moi?
— Mais oui, toi!
— Pourquoi pas lui?
— Parce qu'il va payer pour elle.
— Pour elle? Elle ne paye jamais, elle. C'est toujours nous, n'est-ce pas?
— Pas nous, cette fois — toi seul!

A
43

1. la, le
2. le, le
3. —, —, à l'
4. la, les
5. des, au
6. le, un
7. de, le
8. la, de l'
9. les, le, des
10. les, une

B
43

1. Le frère et la sœur savent conduire tous les deux, mais la famille n'a pas de voiture.
2. Des enfants jouaient au football dans la cour de récréation.
3. La cuisinière fait des gâteaux avec de la farine, des œufs et du sucre.
4. Il y a de la neige au sommet de la montagne, mais il n'y a pas de neige dans la vallée.
5. Il parle anglais et il apprend le français.
6. Le roi Henri II a régné de 1547 à 1559.
7. La pauvre petite Marie-Louise: elle n'aime pas l'école!
8. Paris est la capitale de la France: c'est une très belle ville.
9. Il va au restaurant au coin de la rue.
10. Les avions modernes peuvent transporter beaucoup de passagers.

C
44

Hier soir, pendant que je regardais les actualités à la télévision, on a sonné à la porte.
J'ai ouvert la porte et j'ai vu une vieille femme qui portait un grand panier. Je lui ai

demandé ce qu'elle voulait. Elle m'a dit qu'elle avait des fruits à vendre — des pommes, de bonnes poires, et beaucoup des meilleures cerises.

J'ai acheté les pommes et quelques poires, mais je n'ai pas acheté de cerises. Je n'aime pas les cerises.

A
47
un honneur, une peur, une personne, un malheur, un bonheur, un prix, une paix, un beurre, un groupe, un verre, une terre, une sentence, un silence, un étage, une encre, un village, une plage, une rage, une couleur, un problème, un reste, un légume, un pouce, une tour, un tour, une radio, un livre, une livre, un poste, une poste

B
47
Le roi a envoyé un serviteur amener la fille du duc. La jeune fille est arrivée, accompagnée de sa mère.

« Votre fille doit épouser mon fils, le prince, a dit le roi à la duchesse. Comme ça elle deviendra reine un jour. »

La duchesse savait que sa fille n'aimait pas le prince, qui était laid et très gros. Elle est donc allée voir son amie, la reine.

« Ma fille ne veut pas se marier avec le prince, a expliqué la duchesse. Elle aime un acteur, et veut devenir actrice. L'idée de devenir reine, ou même duchesse, ne lui plaît pas.

— Je comprends, a dit la reine. Mais le roi est un homme âgé, et il ne comprend pas les jeunes. Il a oublié que je suis la fille d'un paysan, et que ma nièce est fermière. J'étais danseuse; ce n'était qu'après avoir épousé mon mari qu'on m'a donné le titre de princesse.

— Il me semble, madame, a dit la duchesse, que la vie est plus facile pour le serviteur qui aime une servante, ou pour un paysan qui aime une paysanne, qu'elle est pour les dames et les messieurs de la cour.

— C'est vrai, a dit la reine, mais il y aura toujours des jeunes filles qui aimeraient devenir la femme d'un prince — comme si tous les princes étaient beaux et charmants et très, très riches! »

A
48

1. un portefeuille
2. une boîte aux lettres
3. un porte-monnaie
4. un bateau à vapeur
5. un arc-en-ciel
6. une arme à feu
7. une salle de classe
8. une salle à manger
9. au rez-de-chaussée
10. une salle de bains
11. un bateau à voiles
12. un porte-plume
13. un rouge-gorge
14. une salle d'attente
15. une montre d'or
16. un agent de police
17. un bain de soleil
18. une chambre à coucher
19. une agence de voyages
20. un bureau de change

A
50
Quand nous voulions aller du côté de Lyon pour rendre visite aux Lebrun, nous y sommes toujours allés à cheval, même si les chevaux gris étaient fatigués. Il nous fallait prendre avec nous des vêtements chauds, peut-être de vieux anoraks bleus, pour les fils des Lebrun, ou bien des blue-jeans, car les Lebrun étaient très pauvres, et ils souffraient toujours du froid pendant les hivers interminables. Nous nous rappelons très bien les nez rouges des enfants qui guettaient notre arrivée derrière les vitres des fenêtres de la chaumière.

B
50

1. Les deux vieillards lisaient des journaux français.
2. L'actrice portait des bijoux magnifiques, des bagues, des bracelets et un collier de diamants.
3. Les chevaux couraient à travers les champs et par-dessus les ruisseaux.
4. Mes neveux sont des jumeaux et ils ont les cheveux noirs.
5. Je ne me souviens pas de tous les détails du plan.
6. Deux des enfants avaient le visage rouge.
7. Mes grand-mères étaient très belles toutes les deux.
8. Au marché j'ai acheté deux choux-fleurs et trois choux.

9. Mettez les verres à vin sur la table s'il vous plaît, et cherchez les tire-bouchons.
10. J'ai rencontré les Lecomte à une soirée la semaine dernière.

A
53
1. ... un bel homme
2. Les méchants enfants ... chien méchant
3. ... un brave homme ... gens pauvres
4. Le pauvre chat ... jeune fille allemande
5. La vieille dame danoise ... maison ancienne
6. une jolie robe bleue ... une chère amie
7. ... la dernière année
8. ... semaine dernière ... un nouveau film français
9. Cette vieille table carrée ... italienne
10. ... grand jardin magnifique ... de beaux arbres étrangers ... de petites fleurs rouges, bleues, et jaunes

C
53
1. Napoléon a été un grand soldat, mais il n'était pas un homme grand.
2. Il a acheté une nouvelle maison, une jolie maison, très ancienne.
3. La maison neuve qu'ils construisent est très laide.
4. Les hommes ont l'air très cruels, mais les femmes sont gentilles.
5. Elle était furieuse quand elle a vu que les chaises étaient si chères.
6. Cette histoire est fausse, mais elle est très amusante.
7. La terre était couverte de neige blanche et fraîche.
8. Au bout de la longue rue, il y a une petite place publique.
9. Elle était assise sur l'herbe fraîche et verte sous le vieil arbre.
10. Elle n'était pas très contente quand elle a trouvé que la boîte en bois était vide.

A
55
1. L'été dernier, quand il faisait beau, nous sommes allés à la plage chaque jour.
2. Les Français disent qu'en Angleterre il fait toujours du brouillard ou bien qu'il pleut toujours.
3. Il faut conduire lentement parce qu'il gèle.
4. Quand j'ai faim, je mange du chocolat.
5. Moi, j'avais raison et il avait tort, mais j'avais peur de le lui dire.
6. Mon frère boit beaucoup de bière quand il a soif.
7. J'ai besoin de beaucoup d'argent pour acheter une nouvelle moto.
8. Mon amie est venue me voir hier; elle avait l'air d'être très contente.
9. Cette soupe est froide, et moi, j'ai froid; j'ai demandé de la soupe chaude.
10. Il avait l'air furieux quand je lui ai demandé s'il avait eu peur.

A
60
bien — well
mal — badly
peu — little
lentement — slowly
vite — quickly
constamment — constantly
honnêtement — honestly
aveuglément — blindly
prudemment — prudently, discreetly
doucement — quietly, softly, gently
mieux — better
pis — worse
heureusement — happily, fortunately
follement — foolishly, madly
nouvellement — newly, recently

B
60
Hier ... très tot ... Après ...
doucement ... Malheureusement ... donc ...
à pied ... heureusement ... souvent ... très ...
très (fort) ... déjà là ... lentement ...
puis ... beaucoup plus vite ...

bientôt ... extrêmement (fort) ... presque toujours ...
en retard ... très longtemps

C
60

1. Beaucoup de gens visitent ce château chaque éte.
2. Avez-vous assez d'argent?
3. La plupart des livres sont trop anciens.
4. Sa femme est assez jolie.
5. Cette pièce est beaucoup trop petite.
6. Le fermier a autant de vaches que son voisin.
7. Peu de gens mangent ici; c'est un peu trop coûteux (cher).
8. Il fait tant de fautes la plupart du temps.
9. La salle est certainement trop noire.
10. Cette malle est assez grande; je n'ai plus tant d'affaires.

D
61

1. Les jours ont passé vite/sont vite passés.
2. Nous visiterons le musée demain.
3. Il avait vraiment peur.
4. Vous voilà enfin!
5. Donnez-nous d'abord quelque chose à manger, s'il vous plaît.
6. Malheureusement ils sont bientôt partis.
7. Elle est morte soudainement quelques jours plus tard.
8. Il a tant voulu le remettre immédiatement.
9. Soudain le voleur s'est enfui.
10. Lentement Jean a sorti de l'argent; ensuite il a remis son portefeuille dans sa poche.
11. Très bien. Après tout, moi, je le fais souvent aussi.
12. Tout va très bien aujourd'hui.
13. Je l'ai tout simplement cherché dans le dictionnaire.
14. Heureusement on l'a vite attrapé.
15. «Puisque vous êtes ici, vous pouvez rester», a-t-elle dit froidement.

E
61

1. Combien de gens vont venir demain?
2. Est-ce que nous aurons assez de poires? Pourquoi avez-vous acheté autant de pêches?
3. Après avoir lu un peu il était assez fatigué.
4. Ça suffit pour le moment; venez me voir demain.
5. Vous m'avez donné trop de sucre et pas assez de lait.
6. La plupart des Parisiens prennent le métro; il n'y a pas assez d'autobus, et ceux-ci roulent trop lentement.
7. J'ai toujours quelques-unes des pommes que vous m'avez données hier.
8. On vend les fruits ici; achetez des oranges, s'il vous plaît.
9. Je ne sais pas comment il est allé aux États-Unis, parce qu'il avait très peu d'argent.
10. Il a eu au moins trente leçons de conduite, mais il conduit aussi mal qu'au début.

A
63

1. plus grand	2. plus petite	3. moins grande
4. aussi long	5. moins court	6. si petit
7. plus froid	8. moins grande	9. aussi lourde
10. plus haute	11. la plus grande ... le plus petit	
12. plus mauvais	13. le plus petit ... le moins	
14. la moindre	15. le mieux ... les meilleurs	

B
63

1. Elle est la meilleure chanteuse de Paris.
2. Des deux frères le plus âgé est devenu le plus célèbre.
3. Nous habitions en Allemagne quand j'étais plus jeune.
4. Qui est le plus jeune des enfants? Marie est la plus jeune.
5. Ce livre est meilleur que l'autre, n'est-ce pas?
6. Si vous voulez réussir vous devez travailler mieux.

7. La tour est plus haute que l'église, mais l'église est plus belle.
8. Je suis aussi intelligent que Paul, mais j'ai étudié moins.
9. Une demi-heure plus tard il dormait plus profondément que jamais.
10. Il devenait de plus en plus difficile à comprendre.

A
65

1. mon livre	2. ma livre	3. mes livres	4. mes livres
5. ton ami	6. ton amie	7. sa mère	8. son frère
9. ses sœurs	10. son encre	11. notre maison	12. vos maisons
13. votre femme	14. votre mari	15. vos enfants	16. leur œuf
17. leurs œufs	18. leur os	19. leurs os	20. leurs amies

B
66

1. C'est la mienne; elle est à moi.
2. C'est le tien; il est à toi.
3. C'est la sienne; elle est à lui.
4. C'est la sienne; elle est à elle.
5. Ce sont les miennes; elles sont à moi.
6. Ce sont les siens; ils sont à elle.
7. Ce sont les siens; ils sont à lui.
8. Ce sont les siennes; elles sont à elle.
9. Ce sont les nôtres; elles sont à nous.
10. Ce sont les vôtres; ils sont à vous.
11. Ce sont les leurs; ils sont à elles.
12. Ce sont les nôtres; elles sont à nous.
13. Ce sont les leurs; elles sont à eux.
14. Ce sont les vôtres; ils sont à vous.
15. Ce sont les leurs; ils sont à elles.
16. C'est la nôtre; elle est à nous.

C
66

1. Ces livres sont les leurs.
2. Mes idées ne sont pas les mêmes que les vôtres.
3. Veux-tu échanger mon vélo contre le tien?
4. Les jeunes filles ont dit que les tasses n'étaient pas les leurs.
5. Gratte-moi le dos et je te gratterai le tien.
6. Il a mis tous mes mouchoirs dans son tiroir.
7. Votre amie attend en bas avec la mienne.
8. Je ne sais pas si cet argent est à moi ou à lui.
9. C'est à vous de lire, pas à moi.
10. Il a levé la tête et il m'a demandé si j'avais vu son père.

D
66

1. Il a trouvé sa place.
2. A sa grande surprise sa mère était là.
3. Il est monté, une bougie à la main.
4. Il a ouvert la porte pour sa mère et son ami(e).
5. Ils sont venus chercher leurs vélos mais ils ont pris les nôtres.
6. A qui est ce manteau? C'est à moi.
7. Qu'est-ce que vous faites dans ma chambre?
8. Le juge condamne l'homme pour ses crimes.
9. «A qui est cette voiture?» a demandé l'agent.
10. J'ai trouvé vos chaussettes, mais je ne peux pas trouver les miennes.

A
68

1. qu'
2. que
3. lesquels . . . laquelle
4. qu' . . . dont
5. qui . . . qui

B
68

1. Ce soldat qui porte un revolver est un officier.
2. Voilà la vache qui donne tant de lait.
3. Il est midi à l'horloge qui se trouve au-dessus de la porte d'entrée.

4. J'ai trouvé le carnet dans lequel il a écrit ses mémoires.
5. Voilà la jeune fille avec qui je suis allé au cinéma hier.
6. C'était l'hiver de 1921, pendant lequel beaucoup de neige est tombée.
7. L'enfant qui a perdu sa balle est malheureux.
8. Ils habitent un appartement moderne, qui se trouve près du parc.
9. Je n'ai pas mis de timbre sur la lettre que vous venez de mettre à la poste.
10. Voici la clef avec laquelle il a ouvert la porte de sa chambre.

C
69
1. La voiture qui est devant la maison est une vieille Renault.
2. Le garçon qui poursuit le ballon est mon frère.
3. La femme que j'ai vue hier est revenue aujourd'hui.
4. J'ai perdu la règle que vous m'avez prêtée.
5. Dans laquelle de ces rues est-ce que vous demeurez?
6. Pour qui avez-vous acheté les pommes que j'ai vues sur la table de la cuisine?
7. J'ai écrit à l'agence dont j'ai parlé.
8. Anne a perdu le paquet dans lequel j'avais mis le collier.
9. Il a volé tout ce qu'il y avait dans la maison.
10. Ce qui est curieux, c'est qu'il n'est jamais revenu.

A
71
1. ce livre	2. cette fleur	3. cet arbre	4. ces maisons
5. ces ennemis	6. cette tasse	7. ces chaises	8. cette eau
9. ces rues	10. ces hommes		

B
71
1. cette table-ci	2. cette montagne-là
3. cette horloge-ci	4. ces chemises-là
5. ces idées-ci	6. ce tableau-ci
7. cette araignée-là	8. ces œufs-ci
9. cet os-ci	10. cette tomate-là

C
71
1. Je prendrai ce livre-ci, mais pas celui-là.
2. Ceux qui n'ont pas d'argent ne peuvent pas faire ceci.
3. Ne parlez pas comme ça!
4. Voici deux crayons — prenez celui-ci.
5. J'aime les chiens, mais pas celui du fermier.
6. Prenez des pommes; non, pas celles-là, celles-ci!
7. Ces pièces sont aussi grandes que celles dans notre maison.
8. Vous pouvez entrer par cette porte, mais celle-là est fermée à clef.
9. — Comment ça va?
   — Très bien, merci!
10. J'ai lu tous les livres dans ma chambre, mais pas ceux qui sont dans le salon.

D
71
«Entrez, messieurs-dames. Je vais vous montrer cette belle maison, que la nation vient d'acheter. Vous êtes mes premiers visiteurs.
— Merci, a dit un des touristes — celui à la barbe noire.
— Voici la grande salle.
— C'est magnifique, s'est écrié le touriste à la barbe noire.
— Et celle-ci est la salle à manger.
— Celle-ci? a demandé une dame. J'aimerais bien avoir une salle à manger aussi grande que celle-ci.
— Quelle belle table! s'est écrié un autre touriste. Cette fois ce n'était pas celui à la barbe noire.
— Et qu'est-ce que c'est que ceci? a demandé un petit garçon qui était avec une dame — celle qui avait admiré la salle à manger.
— Ça? a dit le guide. C'est un vieux phonographe.
— Est-ce qu'il marche?
— Mais oui, très bien. On collectionne les choses anciennes ici. Regardez donc ici: ceci, c'est un vieux poste de radio.
— Ce doit être celui que j'ai vu sur l'affiche près de l'entrée, a dit le garçon.
— C'est un garçon intelligent, celui-là, a dit le guide à la mère du garçon. Et

maintenant, continuons la visite, messieurs-dames. D'abord la cave. . . . Nous voici! Entrez, s'il vous plaît.

— Cette porte-ci est tres solide, a dit l'homme à la barbe noire.

— Naturellement! Nous avons plus de sept cents bouteilles des meilleurs vins de France dans cette cave.

— Et cette clef? Est-ce qu'elle fonctionne?

— Mais oui! Naturellement.

— Allez en avant. Je vais l'essayer. Un moment, s'il vous plaît. Voilà, la porte est fermée à clef.»

Une voix s'est fait entendre de l'autre côté de la porte:«Mais monsieur, nous sommes enfermés!

— Mais oui! Vous comprenez, moi aussi, je collectionne les choses. Amusez-vous bien! Vous avez plus de sept cents bouteilles des meilleurs vins de France — ça devrait suffire pour le moment.»

Le guide et ses visiteurs ont crié: mais en vain. Comme l'homme à la barbe noire avait dit, c'était une porte bien solide!

A   Pièce Nocturne:
74   *Femme*: quelque chose?
    Mari: je n'entends rien.
    F.   Rien? . . . quelqu'un . . .
    M.   Je n'entends personne.
    F.   Personne? . . .
    M.   . . . quelques-unes . . .
    M.   . . . quelque chose.
    F.   On . . . tout le monde . . .
    M.   On . . .
    . . . quelque chose

B   1. Quelqu'un a fermé la porte à clef et a caché la clef.
74   2. — Vous avez acheté quelque chose?
        — Non, rien.
    3. Je crois qu'il y a quelque chose dans mon lit — quelque chose d'horrible!
    4. Il ne fait jamais rien de pratique.
    5. Quelques-uns de mes amis sont français, quelques-uns sont anglais.
    6. Il y a quelqu'un ici qui veut vous parler.
    7. Tout le monde écoute, mais personne n'ose parler.
    8. Il a quelque chose d'important à nous dire.
    9. Ils disent qu'on est fou si on parle à soi-même.
    10. — Est-ce qu'il y a quelqu'un là-bas?
         — Non, personne.

A
80

¹D	E	R	R	I	²E	R	³E		
E					N		N		
⁴P	A	R			F				
U					A				⁵P
I					⁶C	O	M	M	E
⁷S	O	U	S		E				N
					⁸D	E			D
	⁹J	U	¹⁰S	T	E				A
			U						N
¹¹P	O	U	R		¹²A	V	A	N	T

B   1. le long de . . .
80 2. en . . . comme . . . sans
    3. à . . . en . . . à . . . de . . . sans . . . devant
    4. à . . . aux . . . au . . . de . . . en face de
    5. de . . . en . . . à . . . de
    6. par . . . sans . . . à . . . à
    7. de . . . à
    8. dans . . . de . . . de
    9. sans . . . pour . . . dans
    10. en . . . de . . . en . . . par . . . au

D   1. De temps en temps on peut les voir par la fenêtre.
81 2. L'écureuil a couru à travers la rue, juste devant mon vélo.
    3. Il est arrivé par avion, mais il va retourner par (le) train.
    4. Il y a un petit jardin devant la maison, et un autre plus grand par derrière.
    5. Il s'est promené le long de la rue, son parapluie à la main.
    6. Il a écouté en silence l'homme à ses côtés.
    7. À mon avis, il vaut mieux travailler dans la cuisine que dans la boutique.
    8. En été je prends une douche au lieu d'un bain.
    9. On peut voir la lumière du phare de loin quand il fait beau.
    10. Je l'ai entendu parler à la radio de ses voyages en Chine.
    11. Il partira après le déjeuner, vers une heure et demie.
    12. Le cambrioleur s'est enfui, laissant sa valise derrière lui.
    13. Je le ferai pour vous, mais après mon propre travail.
    14. Je suis venu à Paris pour six mois, mais je suis ici depuis deux ans.
    15. J'aimerais parler français comme un Français.

A   1. C'est agréable ici, n'est-ce pas?
84 2. — Ce doit être le facteur.
       — Non, c'est un agent!
    3. On dit qu'il est le meilleur photographe de la ville.
    4. —Qu'est-ce que c'est? C'est un antivol, et en voilà la clef.
    5. — Il neige.
       — Mais non! Il pleut.
    6. Je le ferai maintenant, pendant que j'y pense.
    7. J'en voudrais un peu, s'il vous plaît.
    8. L'entrée est par ici, n'est-ce pas?
    9. — Quelle heure est-il?
       — Il est une heure et demie.
    10. — Il ne gèle plus, n'est-ce pas?
        — Mais si!
    11. — Qu'est-ce qu'il y a?
        — Ce n'est rien de sérieux.
    12. — Où est mon café?
        — Le voilà. Il n'y a pas de sucre dedans.
    13. — C'est jeudi aujourd'hui?
        — Non, c'est déjà vendredi.
    14. — Buvez votre thé.
        — Non, il est trop chaud.
    15. — C'est agréable ici, dans le jardin, n'est-ce pas?
        — Pas quand il fait froid, comme aujourd'hui.
    16. — Est-ce que ça fait mal?
        — Oui, ça fait très mal.
    17. Il est possible qu'ils l'ont vendu.
    18. Dans la vallée il y a un bois, et au milieu il y a une chaumière.
    19. Son cheval? Je ne sais pas où il se trouve, mais il n'est pas vrai qu'il a été vendu.
    20. Regardez mon pauvre vélo! Regardez-le donc! Qu'est-ce qui lui est arrivé?

B
84
C'était le jour de Noël. C'était aussi mon anniversaire. En général, il n'est pas très agréable si on a son anniversaire le jour de Noël, parce que les gens vous donnent un cadeau en disant: Voici quelque chose pour Noël — c'est pour ton anniversaire aussi — comme si ça rend le cadeau meilleur. Mais cette fois on m'avait promis quelque chose d'exceptionnel, assez bon pour Noël et pour mon anniversaire ensemble.

J'avais attendu depuis longtemps pour découvrir ce que c'était — et enfin le moment était arrivé. Il se trouvait là, un grand colis sur la table, avec mon nom dessus.

Il était difficile de l'ouvrir — mais enfin j'ai réussi. Et voilà! tout comme j'avais espéré: un magnétophone stéréo. C'était vraiment, cette fois, «exactement ce que je désirais».

A
87
1. Chacun des soldats porte un fusil.
2. Tous mes amis étaient là.
3. Il est très riche, et il a beaucoup de possessions.
4. Tout ce qu'il fait est bien fait.
5. Je n'ai pas tout l'argent que je voudrais, mais j'en ai assez.
6. Vous pouvez vendre tous ces livres — je les ai tous lus.
7. Je l'aime beaucoup: il a beaucoup d'amis.
8. Elle a trouvé un mari pour chacune de ses filles.
9. — Tout est prêt.
— Très bien; nous pouvons tous partir maintenant.
10. Le jardin est assez grand, mais je ne peux pas y planter tout ce que je voudrais.

A
89
1. Il fait beau.
2. Nous sommes lundi aujourd'hui.
3. Il est dix heures moins dix.
4. Il était au lit.
5. Il en a trois.
6. Il en a vingt et un.
7. Marie est la plus jeune.
8. Il se trouve dans le verger.
9. C'était une place au coin, près de la fenêtre, dans un compartiment de première classe.
10. (a) Oui, il y croit. (b) Il n'y a pas toujours cru.

B
90
1. Il est descendu à sept heures vingt.
2. Parce qu'il était en retard.
3. Il s'est lavé le visage et les mains.
4. Non, il a pris du café noir.
5. Il a mis du beurre et de la confiture sur son croissant.
6. Non, il est arrivé juste à temps.

C
90
1. Comment s'appelle l'ami de Jean?
Il s'appelle François.
2. De quel côté Jean met-il le livre rouge?
Il le met à droite.
3. De quelle couleur est l'autre livre?
Il est bleu.
4. Que représente son stylo à bille?
Il représente le train.
5. Est-ce que François comprend ce que son ami essaie de lui expliquer?
Non, il ne comprend pas encore.

D
91
1. Avez-vous un frère ou une sœur?
2. Qu'est-ce que vous avez fait hier soir?
3. Qu'est-ce que vous avez pris pour le petit déjeuner ce matin?
4. Quand faut-il envoyer chercher le médecin?

    5. Pourquoi les gens lisent-ils les journaux?

E
91
1. Il est mon ami.
2. C'était en hiver.
3. Nous sommes allés à pied parce que le vélo de Louis avait une crevaison.
4. Nous voulions aller ensemble.
5. Nous avons trouvé un homme, couché sur la neige.
6. J'ai dit que je croyais qu'il était ivre.
7. Il sentait l'alcool.
8. Il pouvait mourir parce qu'il faisait si froid.
9. Oui, nous l'avons secoué.
10. Non, nous n'avons pas réussi à le réveiller.
11. Nous avons vu approcher le camion de M. Meunier.
12. Oui, il s'est arrêté.
13. Il nous a aidé à hisser l'ivrogne dans son camion.
14. Oui, je suis allé dans le camion et Louis aussi.
15. Nous l'avons déposé au poste de police.

F
92
Cher Alain,

    Comment vas-tu? Est-ce que tu as reçu ma dernière lettre? Je l'ai envoyée il y a trois semaines, et je n'ai pas encore reçu une réponse. Tu n'es pas malade, j'espère? Est-ce que tu as été en vacances?

    Je voudrais bien te demander: Est-ce que tu pourras venir ici à Pâques? Et est-ce que je pourrais te rendre visite plus tard, peut-être au mois d'août ou à Noël?

    Est-ce que tu veux parler anglais pendant que tu seras ici? Tu m'aideras à parler français en France, n'est-ce pas?

    Écris-moi bientôt.
                Ton ami,
                Mark

A
95
1. Cent quatre-vingt-dix-huit
2. Cinq mille quatre cent seize
3. Six milles
4. Neuf
5. Celle de Jean

B
95
1. Ma deuxième sœur a trois fils et une fille.
2. Les juges ont donné le premier prix à Louise.
3. Si vous voulez téléphoner il faut composer le numéro zéro deux, dix-huit, quatre-vingt-dix-sept.
4. Il y a une vingtaine de pommiers dans le jardin.
5. La rivière a trois mètres de profondeur, mais le lac est beaucoup plus profond que la rivière.
6. La grande muraille de Chine a environ trois mille kilomètres de long.
7. Il mesure cent soixante et un centimètres.
8. Il y travaille depuis une dizaine d'années.
9. Quand je prends le train je voyage en seconde.
10. Il y a des milliers de gens dans cette ville, mais je n'en connais qu'une dizaine.

A
97
1. dix heures du matin
2. trois heures de l'après-midi
3. Quelle heure est-il?
4. Il est neuf heures.
5. Il ne travaille pas le dimanche.
6. Il y a un marché dans la ville tous les jeudis.
7. Le voyage a duré toute la journée.
8. Prenez ce médicament trois fois par jour: à huit heures, à midi, et à six heures et demie du soir.

9. Je viendrai vous voir encore une fois demain en huit, à cinq heures moins le quart.
10. Si vous venez mercredi le vingt et un février, je serai là.
11. Pendant la première année il a dû prendre ses vacances au printemps ou en automne.
12. Il a dix-sept ans; son anniversaire est le jour de l'an.
13. J'aurai seize ans le onze septembre.
14. Je ne peux pas le faire aujourd'hui, mais je le ferai demain ou après-demain.
15. Le lendemain de mon arrivée je me suis levé de bonne heure, et je me suis couché tard.

B Les deux jeunes hommes se sont couchés un peu après minuit. Le lendemain Paul
98 s'est réveillé le premier — après huit heures. Jean dormait toujours.

« Lève-toi, a dit Paul, en le secouant. Nous devons partir aujourd'hui, comme je t'ai dit hier soir.

— Je le sais bien, a dit Jean, en ouvrant un œil. C'est aujourd'hui samedi le vingt et un juin, n'est-ce pas? Ah! J'ai bien dormi cette nuit! As-tu compté l'argent?

— Mais oui! a répondu Paul. Nous avons huit billets de cinquante francs — ça fait quatre cents francs; et nous avons aussi trente et un francs en monnaie.

— Quelle heure est-il? a demandé Jean. J'ai oublié de remonter ma montre hier.

— Il est déjà huit heures moins le quart — non, je veux dire huit heures et quart. Dépêche-toi! Le train part dans une heure, à neuf heures quinze.

— Ce sera la troisième fois que nous partons sans manger, a grommelé Jean.

— Tant pis! Ce sera un long voyage.

— Ce sera une longue journée, aussi. Espérons qu'il y aura une voiture-restaurant dans le train.»

Quelques minutes plus tard les deux jeunes hommes sont partis à pied vers la gare de Lyon. Leur destination — Florence, en Italie. Et pourquoi? Hier ils ont visité le Louvre, à Paris. Mais ils ont visité le Louvre un peu avant minuit.

Aujourd'hui ils partent, par le train, avec un seul gros paquet, d'environ deux mètres de long sur un mètre cinquante de large. Ce paquet contient quelque chose qu'ils espèrent vendre pour cent millions de francs: la Joconde, la Mona Lisa.

99 1. Je ne connais pas très bien Pierre; mais je sais qu'il habite en France, à Dijon je crois, et qu'il écrit des livres.
2. Les Français disent qu'ils ont le pays le plus beau du monde, la langue la plus belle, les meilleures voitures, la meilleure cuisine et les meilleurs vins. Les Anglais ne seraient pas d'accord — sauf pour les vins.
3. Dans un restaurant self il n'y a ni garçon ni serveuse, mais on peut obtenir, par exemple, de la bonne soupe, du bon pain, des petits pains frais, et du poulet avec des petits pois. On y vend aussi du vin et de la bière.
4. La reine cruelle était furieuse.
   «Décapitez-la!», s'est-elle écriée.
   La pauvre Alice pensait qu'on allait vraiment la décapiter — mais elle s'est réveillée en sursaut — ce n'était qu'un rêve!
5. — Tu as combien de timbres dans ta collection?
   — J'en ai plus de trois cents, et j'en aurai encore davantage quand mon oncle m'en enverra. Il voyage assez souvent, et cette fois il va en Suède, au Japon et aux États-Unis. J'aimerais beaucoup y aller aussi.
6. Tous les jeudis je dois prendre l'autobus pour aller au marché. J'aime acheter des fruits et des légumes frais, mais il y a très peu de choix dans le petit magasin du village. Après avoir fait mes courses, je passe souvent voir une amie et nous allons au cinéma ensemble.
7. Hier j'avais un mal de tête affreux et je ne voulais pas sortir, mais j'avais promis à Philippe que j'irais avec lui faire de la voile s'il faisait beau. Comme je mettais

mon anorak, j'ai entendu un coup de tonnerre, et en regardant par la fenêtre j'ai vu qu'il pleuvait à verse. Deux minutes plus tard Philippe m'a téléphoné pour me dire qu'il vaudrait mieux attendre jusqu'au lendemain.

8. Au-dessus du portail de la cathédrale de Saint-Marc, à Venise, il y a quatre grands chevaux dorés. Les Vénitiens les ont rapportés d'Istanbul, autrefois Constantinople, il y a plus de sept cents ans — en l'an 1204. Napoléon les a volés, et il les a placés sur l'Arc de Triomphe qu'il était en train d'édifier à Paris. Mais pendant la Première Guerre mondiale les Français les ont envoyés en Italie, pour les préserver des Allemands. Naturellement les Italiens les ont gardés, et les ont remis en place au-dessus du portail de la cathédrale de Saint-Marc.

9. Pendant que mon oncle me parlait, je regardais, non pas sans émotion, le petit salon que je n'avais pas vu depuis si longtemps. Rien n'était changé. Toujours le canapé à carreaux jaunes, les deux fauteuils rouges, la Vénus sans bras sur la cheminée, le portrait de grand-papa sur le mur, et, dans un coin, près de la fenêtre, le bureau, tout chargé de vieux bouquins et de dictionnaires. Au milieu de ce bureau j'ai aperçu un gros cahier ouvert, sans doute le roman que mon oncle écrivait depuis au moins sept ans.

10. La veuve est entrée dans la cuisine où son fils l'attendait. Péniblement elle a posé son panier de vivres sur la table. Après un long silence elle a dit:

«J'ai vu dans la rue des femmes qui n'ont pas de quoi nourrir leurs petits enfants. La misère est partout.

— Il n'y a pas de temps à perdre, a dit son fils. Nous devons guillotiner ceux qui volent la nourriture du peuple. Nous devons établir un tribunal pour ceux qui nous volent.

— Laisse-le, lui a répondu sa mère. Tu es jeune; tu a des illusions. Il ne faut plus guillotiner les gens — pas même les ennemis de la République.

— Mais si! s'est écrié le jeune homme, en se levant. La Révolution fera pour les siècles le bonheur du genre humain. Vive la Révolution!»

A   1. He goes for a boat trip.
107 2. He studies medicine.
    3. He is going there now.
    4. She does the washing-up.
    5. He was an orphan whom the sisters had adopted.
    6. He has hidden the wine in the cellar.
    7. How stupid he is!
    8. The beggar's clothes are ragged.
    9. This engine does not work well.
    10. There is a well-worn carpet in this room.

B   1. He feels sick.
107 2. I follow my father with some bits of wire.
    3. The W.C. is opposite.
    4. He says that he has just taken his exam.
    5. He claims he has succeeded.
    6. Waiter! Give me some potato crisps.and a light ale.
    7. He likes reading very much.
    8. They chat a lot.
    9. They were all wearing blue jackets.
    10. The invalid sat up in bed.

C   1. A paraffin lamp.
107 2. He loads it.
    3. He is going to watch a football match.
    4. The car goes better on these wide tyres.
    5. The photographer is very clever.

6. He gropes for the switch.
7. She asks what the time is and what the weather is like.
8. The maid works well throughout the day.
9. It is a second-hand motorbike.
10. A tall Spaniard.
11. I met her in the main hall of the station.
12. The teacher is busy giving the English lesson.
13. She had to do her shopping using French.
14. He had a quick snack.
15. The bell announces the end of the market.

A   1. The chicks followed close behind her.
108 2. He has some white horses.
     3. The scholar raised his hand.
     4. The writing-paper was in the book-shop.
     5. I am sitting on the bench.
     6. They do the tour of the town.
     7. He studies horsemanship.
     8. The ground is underneath.
     9. This mattress matches my cushion.
    10. Yesterday the day was hot and long . . .
    11. . . . and today he is going to stay at home.
    12. The previous day the old fishwife had seen the money.
    13. There are some socks for sale in this shop.
    14. The usherette does her own task.
    15. A mouse runs on the wheel.

A   1. He broke the ice.
108 2. He is proud of his skill.
     3. It happened as foreseen.
     4. The young girls comb their black hair.
     5. They had to buy a map.
     6. I'll show you a seat.
     7. It gave great pleasure.
     8. He sold the cup of coffee.
     9. There are sheets of paper everywhere.
    10. Her sight is poor.
    11. He has bought himself a football.
    12. A modern railway coach.
    13. The bird has stolen.
    14. There are two page-boys.
    15. He drives it well (a car).
    16. It (i.e. the bathroom) is engaged.
    17. He lives in a big mansion.
    18. She uncovered the basket.
    19. She put it on the dressing-table.
    20. He puts the brief-case on the table.

B   1. Has God forgotten all I've done for Him?
109 2. One bad general is better than two good ones.
     3. The more things change the more things remain the same.
     4. When everyone is wrong everyone thinks he is right.
     5. Only those who have studied much know how little they really know.

A	1. of	2. any	3. by	4. from
110	5. for	6. some	7. 's	8. with
	9. to	10. about	11. on	12. X
	13. at	14. in	15. as	

A   1. He lives in Paris, but he will go to London tomorrow.
111 2. In your place I should not do it.
    3. I bought six oranges in the market for eighty centimes each.
    4. I prefer a seat in the corner of the compartment.
    5. They share in the children's games.
    6. I can see a big ship out at sea.
    7. The visitors speak in whispers.
    8. What's this for?
    9. They're glad to get home.
    10. They live in the country.

B   1. It's kind of you to pay for it.
112 2. He bought it from a friend.
    3. The plants are all worm-eaten.
    4. The man in black has stolen the basket from the old woman.
    5. He goes for long cycle rides.
    6. This wine is sold by the bottle.
    7. She often turns up on horseback.
    8. That's very kind of you. Thanks very much.
    9. I recognized her by her voice.
    10. It must be true, from what they say.

C   1. The policeman is armed.
112 2. She cooks in the French style.
    3. Please give me a wine-glass with some water in it.
    4. There's a sailing-boat on the lake.
    5. He's one of my friends.
    6. He ate a mushroom omelette.
    7. I have terrible toothache.
    8. I have posted the cards in the letter-box.
    9. We always eat in the dining-room.
    10. My favourite pastime is fishing.
    11. We are going to play tennis.
    12. He disobeys his master.
    13. The student has entered the university.
    14. A good wine pleases my father.
    15. Help! Stop thief!

D   1. There is nothing to fear.
112 2. It's mine.
    3. She is interested in everything, but she does not believe in God.
    4. The Headmaster arrived with the document in his hand.
    5. Now it's his turn to speak.
    6. The gymnast climbs up the rope, and then he does exercises on the parallel bars.
    7. He has managed to do it by hand.
    8. The book's mine, but the pens are yours.
    9. I ate a boiled egg at 8 o'clock, at breakfast.
    10. There's an interesting old house for sale in the village.

A   1. The Revolution started in France in the year 1789.
112 2. From day to day the situation grows worse.
    3. While I was on holiday I did a lot of hitch-hiking.
    4. On returning home he went upstairs.
    5. They sat down at a little iron table on the terrace.
    6. The driver started the car.
    7. Whilst waiting you can read this book in silence.
    8. From time to time someone arrives by car.

9. I went to France for the holidays; I always go there in winter.
10. The workmen are on strike, as they always are in summer.

A   1. The dog eats from his master's plate and drinks out of his glass.
113   2. He took a handkerchief out of the drawer of the chest of drawers.
      3. My car cost me somewhere around 8 thousand francs.
      4. I heard a noise on the stairs.
      5. I shall be ready in ten minutes, but not before.

A   1. I am going to spend the summer holidays at John's.
113   2. He works at the ironmonger's.
      3. For the French, wine is more important than beer.
      4. Make yourself at home.
      5. First of all we'll go and have tea at my place.

A   1. I have known him for a long time.
113   2. How long have you been waiting for him?
      3. I knew it by heart at school, but since then I've forgotten it.
      4. I had been waiting for you for an hour when you arrived.
      5. I had waited for you for a long time before your arrival.
      6. From here you can see from the castle to the lighthouse.

A   1. Where is my ruler?
114   2. Where is the station?
      3. I've found the page where these words are explained.
      4. At the very moment he arrived lightning struck the house.
      5. Where do these people come from?
      6. The day I bought my new motorbike was the happiest of my life.
      7. Tell me where he is, and where to look for him.

A   1. I should like to ask for some information about the town.
114   2. The spy went off, his hat pulled down over his eyes.
      3. I'm sure I have not made a mistake about which road to take.
      4. He entered, whereupon everyone fell silent.
      5. You must not judge people by appearances.
      6. This room is 5 metres long by 4 metres wide.

A   1. I always drink coffee before leaving home.
114   2. Thank you for your letter which you sent me from Paris, and which I received
         in Lyons.
      3. There are more stations on the Metro in Paris than on the Underground in
         London.
      4. Have you learnt to ride a horse?
      5. The Louvre is not far from the Place de la Concorde.
      6. They live in the country, at the foot of the Alps.
      7. This evening we are going to eat at the Leroys' at 8 o'clock.
      8. He walks along the rue de Rivoli.
      9. From what I have heard, the fête will take place in June in Madame Labelle's
         garden.
     10. I have been a student here for three years.

B   1. He has been a soldier since the beginning of the war.
115   2. Please come in and hand this letter to the director.
      3. You can see from the mountains to the sea.
      4. The lad has been given a bike by his grandfather; he is wild with delight.
      5. On a fine summer's day you can see them, lying on the ground in the sunshine.
      6. He has been very kind to us.
      7. I can finish it in a very short time.
      8. 'Come this way, please', he told me. I obeyed, grudgingly.

9. He worked up to the beginning of the month, but from then on he has done no more work.

10. In summer I very much like sleeping in the open. If needs be, I go into the garden secretly, without my parents knowing, and I return to my room at sunrise. Neither my father nor my mother ever wake up at such an hour, but I don't know to what extent they guess the truth.

A
116
1. They buy. They are buying.
2. I help. I am helping.
3. You like. You do like.
4. He adds. He is adding.
5. She lights. She is lighting.
6. We bring. We are bringing.
7. You amuse. You are amusing.
8. They carry. They are carrying.
9. They do not learn. They are not learning.
10. Am I arranging? Do I arrange?
11. Are you coming? Do you come?
12. Doesn't he attach? Isn't he attaching?
13. Is she catching? Does she catch?
14. Are we advancing? Do we advance?
15. Don't you drink? Aren't you drinking?
16. Do they burn? Are they burning?
17. Don't they hide? Aren't they hiding?
18. Do I sing? Am I singing?
19. Aren't you seeking? Do you not seek?
20. Does he run? Is he running?

B
116
1. I don't choose the day.
2. You don't understand very well.
3. He doesn't finish quickly.
4. She doesn't do it easily.
5. We never count the money.
6. We don't yet know this town.
7. Don't go on with your work.
8. These knives don't cut anything.
9. They don't sew well with these bad needles.
10. Don't put a cover on the soup.

C
116
1. Aren't you angry?
2. Doesn't he unload the lorry here?
3. Don't we always have lunch at home?
4. Where do you dine on Fridays?
5. How do you do this?
6. Look! My watch is working now.
7. I'm not painting the door any more — I'm painting the wall now.
8. You don't know how to do it, but I do.
9. 'You don't know anything!' 'Oh yes, I do!'
10. 'Don't you like this cake?' 'Yes I do. I like it very much.'

A
117
1. When I was in France I used to sleep in a tent.
2. Formerly an oil lamp used to light this room.
3. In the Middle Ages people used to write on parchment.
4. Before the days of television we often used to go to the cinema.
5. I used to like horse riding.

B
117
1. He was smoking his pipe when his friend phoned him.
2. I was asleep when the postman rang.
3. I was writing to my mother when the letter arrived.

    4. He was studying French when his friend entered.

    5. He was shutting the door when he heard someone outside.

C   1. It was hot, and I was hungry.

117 2. We had to fetch a doctor because he was very ill.

    3. He was resting because he was tired, and I didn't want to disturb him.

    4. A sentry was guarding the barracks, and the gate was closed.

    5. The people standing in a queue in front of the cinema were becoming impatient.

D   1. When I was young I used to go to school on foot.

118 2. The next day he wanted to go on with the work which he had been doing the day before.

    3. He was sleeping peacefully when the doctor arrived.

    4. I was driving the lorry carefully, but I could not avoid the accident.

    5. I believed he was a friend — if only I had known the truth!

    6. He could no longer remember what the maid was doing when he entered the room.

    7. After breakfast she used to do the housework before going out.

    8. Night was falling. The wind was howling through the trees; but the child in his shelter was no longer afraid.

A   1. 'I'll take you, if you like', he told me.

118 2. We'll do it when we get there.

    3. I'll buy it tomorrow; I'm going to tell him so now.

    4. We are going to the cinema this evening because the cinema will be shut tomorrow.

    5. He won't hurt you.

    6. The plane will leave at daybreak.

    7. They're going to phone me, and they'll tell me what they are going to do.

    8. I hope you will come and see us next year.

    9. I'll show it to you as soon as he arrives.

  10. Wait! He'll explain it to you presently.

A   1. She used to say that he would never abandon her.

119 2. 'I would do it if I could', I told him.

    3. You ought to have written to him when you had the time.

    4. I'd like a room with two beds, please.

    5. I'd say it to my friend, but I wouldn't say it to M. Legros.

    6. They told me you would go to Paris tomorrow if it were necessary.

    7. Couldn't you drive faster? We ought to get there before seven.

    8. We should not like to go there without you.

    9. I should be pleased if I had news of them.

  10. Would you prefer to work in the morning or in the evening?

A   mon frère est venu . . . Il m'a dit . . . Il m'a demandé . . . Nous sommes descendus

120 . . . je l'ai vue, j'ai su . . . elle m'a regardé . . . elle m'a fait signe . . . J'ai fait . . . elle est partie . . . je l'ai suivie . . . J'ai été . . . J'ai attendu . . . elle n'est pas reparue . . . j'ai monté . . . Je me suis arrêté . . . j'ai entendu . . .

B   At that moment my brother came to fetch me. He told me that a girl called Claire,

120 whom he had met the day before, had just arrived to have lunch with us. He asked me to come and meet her.

      We went down to the living room. As soon as I saw her, I knew that I had already met her somewhere. But she looked at me in a strange way and motioned me to say nothing. So I pretended to be meeting her for the first time.

      When she left after lunch, I followed her at some distance. I was astonished to see her enter an old tumble-down building. I waited for ten minutes, but as she did not reappear, I went up the stairs. All was dark and silent. I stopped in front of a door on the first floor. Suddenly I heard a terrible scream.

C   During a very cold period, a breakdown in the central heating forced me to take
120 refuge in an hotel. I chose a small hotel near my office.

The first evening I went up to my room shortly after dinner, because I wanted to
read in bed.

But as I was tired, I soon put the book back on the bedside table, and put out
the light which hung above my head.

I had slept for perhaps two hours when a noise woke me up. There was someone
in my room. I groped for the light switch but could not find it.

Suddenly the door opened, and the intruder crept stealthily out of the room.
Finding the switch at last, I turned on the light, and jumped out of bed. I searched
among the things which I had brought with me to the hotel, but nothing was missing. My brief-case and my wallet were still on the chest of drawers.

In the morning, before going to the office, I told the manager what had happened.

He was not surprised. It was he himself, he explained, who had entered my room.
He had found my brief-case in the dining-room, and he wanted to give it back to
me. He knocked on the door, but evidently I was asleep, for I did not answer. So he
entered quietly, put the brief-case on the chest of drawers, and went out without
knowing that he had awakened me.

D   Rewritten as a letter the past historic tenses will become perfect; the text remains
121 otherwise the same:

. . . m'a contraint . . . j'ai choisi . . . je suis monté . . . j'ai mis . . . et j'ai éteint . . .
m'a éveillé . . . J'ai cherché . . . je n'ai pas pu le trouver . . . la porte s'est ouverte . . .
l'intrus est sorti . . . J'ai allumé . . . j'ai sauté . . . j'ai cherché . . .

E   Je ne m'étonne pas, Monsieur. C'était moi qui suis entré dans votre chambre. J'ai
121 trouvé votre serviette dans la salle à manger, et j'ai voulu vous la rendre. J'ai frappé
à la porte, mais évidemment vous dormiez, car vous n'avez pas répondu. Ainsi je
suis entré doucement, j'ai posé la serviette sur la commode, et je suis ressorti, sans
savoir que je vous avais réveillé.

A   Dear Jean-Marc,
122   When you receive this letter, I shall have left Paris. I've had enough of studying,
and I know that I wouldn't have passed my exams even if I had taken them this
summer. I didn't say goodbye to my friends because I knew that they would have
tried to persuade me to stay, and I was sure that I had to go.

I came to America because I've always wanted to visit New York, where I have
relatives. I've got very little money, as the journey cost me almost all that I had
saved. So I had to look for work straight away. For the moment I've accepted a job
as a waitress in a restaurant, but I hope that I'll have found a more interesting job
soon.

You told me last summer that you would have liked to spend the holidays in
New York if you had known someone who lived there. Why not come to see me
this summer? I'd like that.

Write soon.
Isabelle

B   1. The teacher asked him if he'd finished his translation. 'When you've finished it,
123   show it to me', he said.
      2. Once more we listened, but his voice had become too faint; we could no longer
          hear anything.
      3. As soon as they arrive we'll go to the restaurant. They could have phoned us
          earlier to say they were coming.
      4. The children settled down in front of the television as soon as their parents had
          left.

5. Suddenly he stopped. He had heard a noise behind him. He would not have been afraid had he not been all alone in the forest.
6. If he had won the big prize in the lottery he would have been able to buy the car he had seen; but he'd only won 50 francs.
7. After Monsieur Lesage had left the pupils started to kick up a row again.
8. The workmen decided that they ought to have sent delegates to discuss the problem with the boss.
9. He had told me that he would have already left before I arrived.
10. I would never have done it if he had warned me in time; but he arrived too late.

A
123
1. What is your name?
2. They have a good time at their friends'.
3. The child hurt himself with the penknife.
4. My brother got married yesterday.
5. Sit down, gentlemen. Coffee is served here.
6. I'm sorry I fell asleep; I'm going to get up at once.
7. Papers are sold at the news-agent's over there.
8. Don't make fun of the poor.
9. He walks in the park where he takes his dog for a walk every day.
10. The two boys eye each other, draw close, and start to fight.

A
124
1. A sign has been put in the shop window: 'French is spoken here'.
2. What shall we do now?
3. How do you say that in English?
4. They haven't sent the tickets yet. What are we going to do?
5. If you stand here you can see the entrance to the cave.
6. The prisoner did as he was ordered.
7. A woman is happy, she explained to me, when her husband loves her.
8. I can hear steps on the stairs; I think someone's coming at last.
9. Do you know where they've put the key?
10. If you take this train you'll get to Paris at ten past two.

A
124
1. He is busy writing a letter.
2. After he had spoken he left.
3. Whilst eating his lunch, he continued to read the letter.
4. I heard him speak, without seeing him.
5. To live is not just breathing — it's doing something.

A
127
1. sachent: Do you think they know it?
2. fasse: He must do it.
3. ait: It appears he has found it.
4. puisse: Give me some money so that I can buy it.
5. soit: I don't know anyone who is always nice.
6. abandonne: May God not desert me!
7. parlât: I feared he might speak.
8. revînt: Fearing that he might return, she locked the door.
9. fît: I'm sorry he did it before the others.
10. sût: He left without her knowing it.

A
129
1. From his pocket he took out a handkerchief and a key-ring. 'I've got to hurry up', he said to himself as he left the house. 'I don't want to miss the train.'
2. Napoleon had the Arc de Triomphe built in Paris to celebrate his victories.
3. 'You had better finish your homework before going to bed', his father told him severely. 'Come along, now. Get to work!'
4. This strange object is used for opening bottles.
5. He's annoyed with me because I used his bike to go for a ride in the country yesterday — but, after all, I was getting bored at home, and he hardly ever uses it.

6. He asked me whether my wife would be kind enough to take in a young German girl student who had just arrived in England.

7. 'You have every reason to be worried', the master told me. 'I have just spoken to the headmaster about you. He appeared to be in a worse mood than ever. You will certainly get at least a good scolding.'

8. I should very much like to visit your grandfather. Perhaps he'd let me go rabbit hunting — I know how to use a shot-gun.

9. 'Have you paid for the room?' 'Not yet. I can't find my wallet. I think I've dropped it somewhere.' 'No you haven't. I know where it is. You left it in your other jacket, the one you were wearing yesterday evening. — Here it is!'

10. Louise, who was always clumsy, dropped the bowl of hot soup and almost killed the cat.

11. 'The draw for the lottery took place yesterday, but we didn't win a prize.' 'Come along! We risk being killed, standing here in the middle of the road, gossiping like two old maids.'

12. His father did not fail to notice how he looked.
    'You've been behaving badly, I can see that much. What have you been up to, eh?' his father asked him.
    Charles started to tremble, but he did not answer.
    His father grew angry. 'I can well guess,' he said. 'You've done something I've told you not to, haven't you?'
    Well might his father ask. Charles stuck to his resolution to say nothing.

13. 'I sent for you because I wanted to speak to you.'
    'What's it about, sir?'
    'We want you to go up to the enemy lines during the night to listen to what is being said, in the hope of learning their plans. It will be risky.'
    'I don't mind. I can manage.'
    'So, it's agreed then?'
    'Yes, sir. I'll take care of everything. Don't worry. Tomorrow I'll return and tell you all I've heard.'

14. The car started off and, driven at a mad speed, it jumped the lights, ran over a chicken, and ended up by crashing into a tree. The driver nearly killed himself — but he had a narrow escape and is still alive.

15. Because she was not able to find the job she wanted, a girl jumped from the first floor of the Eiffel Tower. She fell on to an old banger — and it was the car, not the girl, who was crushed. As for her, she became so well known that someone offered her the job she wanted, for she was only slightly hurt. It is said that this actually happened.

16. It was growing late. A deep silence filled the room. Closing his eyes, John pretended to be asleep, but he was not asleep — he was listening. He was sure that something was happening in the next room.

17. It would often happen that she fell asleep in front of the television whilst waiting for her husband to return, as he would come home late if the train arrived late at the station.

18. He was feeling sick. The thought that he was going to be ill once again rose before him like a threatening spirit. He ought to call for the doctor. He dialled his number, but no-one answered. What should he do? He sat down again in his armchair to await whatever had to happen. It was pointless to tell him that he was not ill — he knew the truth himself, only too well: for it was not the first time that he had known these symptoms.

19. The policeman turned towards the crowd.
    'What's going on here?' he asked.
    'It's the lorry', someone explained. 'This lorry here. It drove on to the pavement and almost ran over this poor gentleman.'
    'He's not a poor gentleman!' exclaimed the policeman. 'That's Jean Tuetout, the murderer. I've been looking for him for months. The lorry-driver's done

well — without realizing it, of course.'

20. What you think of others is your business, but there are times when it is wiser to say nothing and keep your thoughts to yourself. You can hardly blame people if they are angry with you because you tell them the truth about things which they have done and which they no longer want to remember.

A
137

1. ces livres-ci
2. cette table-là
3. en hiver
4. Ne faites pas ça.
5. leurs chevaux
6. Vous la mangiez.
7. Elle l'a mangée.
8. la veille de Noël
9. Où est mon livre?
10. Avez-vous fini?
11. Il n'a pas obéi.
12. Donnez-moi quelque chose.
13. Il vient quelquefois parce que tu le veux.
14. As-tu fait ton devoir?
15. Il a été ici en été.

B
137

1. Il a amené ses frères.
2. Quand est-ce que vous allez me rendre mes livres?
3. Mon mari m'a donné une nouvelle montre.
4. Il vous donnait les journaux au moment où la mère est entrée dans la maison avec ses enfants.
5. La voiture roule sur quatre roues au milieu de la rue.
6. Il ne faut pas donner l'argent à l'agent.
7. Ses chevaux ont tiré sa charrette.
8. Elle peigne les cheveux de sa fille pour la faire aussi belle que possible.
9. Il est arrivé dans la ville avec l'amie qu'il espère épouser.
10. La route est longue, mais elle est facile et tout à fait sans difficulté.

A
141

acheté	appartement	appelé
entrerai	universelle	proprement
queue	jouet	genou
geler	omelette	terre
rechercher	toutefois	tiennent

B
141

tellement	demain	sol(e)nnel	prud(e)mment
viennent	menacer	semence	renouveler
rentrer	f(e)mme	septembre	semelle
sensible	commence	semaine	

A
142

1. Le chien est un animal; et l'homme est aussi un animal.
2. Le col entre les montagnes est plus haut que le tunnel.
3. Elle n'est pas arrivée et elle n'a pas téléphoné.
4. Il nous en a parlé.
5. Vous avez fini?
6. Nous étions tous dans un coin de la salle.
7. Un grand oiseau descendait vers le plus petit des arbres.
8. C'était un petit enfant qui commençait à chanter.
9. Devant un hôtel un homme se tenait immobile, et attendait en silence.
10. Il ouvrit à trois heures, pas un moment trop tôt.

French-English vocabulary

Abbreviations: *adj*, adjective; *adv*, adverb; *v*, verb; *VL*, see Verb List;
qn, quelqu'un; *qch*, quelque chose; *s/o*, someone; *s/th*, something.

à, to, at, in, with, on, by, for
abandonner, to abandon, desert
d'abord, at first
abeille, f, bee
absolu, -e, absolute
aboyer, to bark
accepter, to accept
acceuil, m, reception
accident, m, accident
d'accord, agreed, in agreement
accompagner, to accompany; to take s/o
	(in a car, etc.)
s'accoutumer (à), to get used (to)
acheter, to buy
acquérir, to acquire
acteur, m, actor
actrice, f, actress
addition, f, bill
adieu, goodbye, farewell; faire ses adieux,
	say goodbye, take one's leave
adopter, to adopt
adresse, f, address; skill, dexterity
aéronaute, m, airman
aéroport, m, airport
affaire, f, affair; les affaires, business; be-
	longings
affiche, f, poster
afficher, to stick up (a poster, etc.)
affreux, -se, frightful, terrible
afin que, in order that, so that
agacer, to annoy, to disturb
âgé, aged
s'agenouiller, to kneel
agent, m, agent; agent de police, m, police-
	man
agir, to act, to do; il s'agit de, it is a ques-
	tion of, a matter of; de quoi s'agit-il?
	what is it about?
agréable, pleasant, agreeable
aider, to help
aiguille, f, needle; hand of clock
ailleurs, elsewhere
aimable, pleasant, kind
aimant, m, magnet
aimer, to love, to like; aimer mieux, to
	prefer
ainsi, so, thus
air: avoir l'air, to seem
aise, f, ease; mal à l'aise, ill at ease; mettre
	qn à son aise, put s/o at their ease
ajouter, to add
alcool, m, alcohol

Allemagne, f, Germany
allemand, -e, German
aller, to go; comment allez-vous? how are
	you?
s'allonger, to stretch out
allumer, to light, to turn on the light
allumette, f, match
alors, then
amener, to bring, to lead (person, animal)
ami, m, amie, f, friend
amuser, to amuse; s'amuser, to enjoy one-
	self; s'amuser bien, to have a good time
an, m; année, f, year
ancien, ancienne, old, former
anglais, English
angle, m, angle, corner
Angleterre, f, England
anniversaire, m, birthday, anniversary
annoncer, to announce
août, m, August
apercevoir, to notice, perceive
appareil, m, apparatus; camera (appareil
	photographique); telephone (appareil
	téléphonique)
apparence, f, appearance
appartement, m, flat
appeler, to call; s'appeler, to be called
applaudir, to clap
apporter, to bring (object)
apprendre, to learn
approcher, to approach; s'approcher (de
	qn, qch), approach (s/o, s/th)
après, after, afterwards; d'après, accord-
	ing to; après que, after
après-demain, the day after tomorrow
après-midi, m (or f), afternoon
araignée, f, spider
arbre, m, tree
arc-en-ciel, m, rainbow
argent, m, silver; money
arme, f, weapon; arme à feu, f, firearm
armoire, f, cupboard, wardrobe
arranger, to arrange
arrêter, to stop (s/o, s/th); s'arrêter, to
	come to a halt; s'arrêter de faire qch,
	to stop doing s/th
arrivée, f, arrival
arriver, to arrive; to happen
ascenseur, m, lift
assassin, m, murderer
s'asseoir, to sit down
assez, enough; fairly, rather

assiette, f, plate, dish
assis, seated
assister, to be present; to assist
assurer, to assure; s'assurer, to make sure
atelier, m, studio, work-room
attacher, to attach
attendre, to wait (for), await, expect
attirer, to attract
attraper, to trap, to catch
auberge, f, inn; auberge de la jeunesse, youth hostel
aucun, -e, any, anyone; ne . . . aucun, no one
au-dessous de, beneath
au-dessus de, above
aujourd'hui, m, today
auparavant, before, previously
aussi, also, as well; aussi . . . que, as . . . as
aussitôt, immediately, aussitôt que, as soon as
Australie, f, Australia
Australien, Australian
autant, as many, as much, so many, so much
auteur, m, author
auto, f, car
autobus, m, bus (in town)
autocar, m, long distance coach
automne, m, autumn
autoroute, f, motor-way
auto-stop: faire de l'auto-stop, to hitch-hike
autour, around, round about, autour de qch, around s/th
autre, other
autrui, others, another (person)
autrement, otherwise
autrefois, formerly
avancer, to advance; s'avancer, to come forward
avant, before (in time); avant-hier, m, the day before yesterday
avantage, m, advantage
avec, with; avec soin, carefully
avertir, to warn
aveugle, m, blind person; adj. blind; aveuglément, blindly
avion, m, aeroplane
avis, m, opinion, notice, advice; changer d'avis, to change one's mind; à mon avis, in my opinion
avoir, to have; avoir froid, chaud, peur, etc., to be (feel) cold, hot, afraid, etc.; avoir beau (dire), to (speak) in vain
avril, April

bagage, m, luggage (often in plural)
bagnole, f, old car, 'banger'
bague, f, ring
baigner, to bathe; se baigner, to have a bath
bain, m, bath

baisser, to lower; se baisser, to bend down
balayer, to sweep
balle, f, ball
ballon, m, balloon; football; ball
banc, m, bench
bande dessinée, f, comic strip
banlieu, f, suburbs
barbe, f, beard
barre, f, bar
bas, low; en bas, below, downstairs; à voix basse, in a low voice
bateau, m, boat, ship; bateau à voiles, sailing boat; bateau à vapeur, steamship
bâtiment, m, building
bâtir, to build; se faire bâtir, to have built (for oneself)
battre, to beat; se battre, to fight
bavarder, to gossip, to chat
beau, belle, beautiful, handsome; il fait beau, it (the weather) is fine; avoir beau (dire), to (speak) in vain
beaucoup, a lot, much, many
bébé, m, baby
besoin, m, need; avoir besoin de, to need; au besoin, if needs be
bétail, m, cattle
bête, f, animal, beast; adj. stupid
beurre, m, butter
bibliothèque, f, library, bookcase
bicyclette, f, bicycle
bien, well; très bien, very well, very good
bientôt, soon
bière, f, beer
biftek, m, steak
billet, m, ticket, note; billet de banque, bank-note
blâmer, to blame
blanc, blanche, white
blé, m, wheat, corn
blessé, wounded
blesser, to wound, to injure
blond, -e, fair, light (of hue); une blonde, a light ale
blue-jean, m, jeans
bœuf, m, bullock, ox
boire, to drink (VL)
bois, m, wood (material), a wood (trees); de bois, wooden
boîte, f, box, tin
bol, m, bowl
bon, bonne, good; de bonne heure, early
bonbon, m, sweet
bonheur, m, happiness; luck
bonjour, good day; good morning; good afternoon; hello
bonne, f, maid-servant
bonté, f, goodness, kindness
bord, m, edge; au bord de la mer, at the seaside
boucher, m, butcher
bouger, to stir, to move
bougie, f, candle; sparking-plug

bouillir, to boil
boulanger, m, baker
boule, f, ball, bowl
bouleverser, to overthrow, upset
bouquiniste, m, second-hand book dealer
bout, m, end, tip; à bout, exhausted; au bout, at the end
bouteille, f, bottle
bouton, m, button, pimple
brave, adj, (before noun) worthy; (after noun) brave
brique, f, brick
brosse, f, brush
bruit, m, noise
brûler, to burn; brûler un feu rouge, to jump the lights
bureau, m, office; writing-table; bureau de change, money-changing office
bus, m, bus
buvard: papier-buvard, m, blotting paper

cabane, f, hut, shed
cabinet de consultation, m, surgery
cacher, to hide
cadeau, m, gift, present
café, m, coffee; French bar where alcohol as well as coffee is served
cahier, m, school exercise book, note-book
caillou, m, pebble, small stone
camion, m, lorry; camionette, f, small lorry, van
campagne, f, countryside; à la campagne, in (or to) the country
canif, m, pen-knife
canot, m, canoe, small boat
carnet, m, note-book
carré, adj, square (shape)
carreaux, m.pl, squares (in a design or pattern)
carrefour, m, cross-roads
carte, f, card; map; menu
caserne, f, barracks
casser, to break
cause, f, cause, motive; à cause de, because of
causer, to chat; to cause
cave, f, cellar
caverne, f, cave
ceci, this
céder, to yield, to give way (VL)
ceinture, f, belt
cela, that
célébrer, to celebrate
celui-ci, celle-ci, the latter
celui-là, celle-là, the former
cep, cépage, m, vine-stock
cependant, adv, conj, yet, however, meanwhile
céréales, f.pl, cereals
cerf-volant, m, kite
certain, (after noun) certain, sure; (before noun) some one or other

cesser, to leave off, cease; cesser de faire qch, to stop doing s/th
chacun, chacune, each (one)
chaîne (stéréophonique), f, stereo record player
chaise, f, chair
chambre, f, room; chambre à coucher, bedroom
champ, m, field
champignon, m, mushroom
chance, f, luck
chandelle, f, candle
change, bureau de, m, money changing office
chanter, to sing
chapeau, m, hat
chaque, each
charger, to charge, to load; se charger de, to take on the responsibility for
charrette, f, cart
chasse, f, hunt, hunting; la chasse au tir, shooting (for sport)
chat, m, cat
château, m, château, castle, country mansion
chaud, -e, hot; il fait chaud, it (the weather) is hot
chauffage, m, heating
chauffeur, m, chauffeur, driver
chaumière, f, thatched cottage
chaussette, f, sock
chaussure, f, shoe
chemin, m, road, path, way; chemin de fer, railway line, railway system; chemin faisant, on the way
cheminée, f, chimney; mantlepiece
chemise, f, shirt
cher, chère, dear, beloved; expensive
chercher, to look for; envoyer chercher, to send for
cheval, m, horse; à cheval, on horseback
chevet, m, bedside
cheveux, m.pl, hair
chez, at the home/work place of
chien, m, dog
Chine, f, China
chips, m.pl, potato crisps
choisir, to choose
chose, f, thing; quelque chose, m, something
chou, m, cabbage
ciel, m, heaven, sky
cigare, f, cigar
cinéma, m, cinema
circulation, f, traffic
citoyen, citizen
clair, -e, clear, bright, light (of colour)
classe, f, class; school form
clé, clef, f, key; fermer à clé, to lock
client, -e, m, f, client, customer; patient
cloche, f, bell
club, m, club, society

cochon, m, pig

cœur, m, heart; avoir mal au cœur, to feel sick; à contre-cœur, unwillingly, grudgingly

coiffeuse, f, lady hairdresser; dressing-table

coin, m, corner

col, m, collar

colère, f, anger

colis, m, parcel

collectionner, to collect (as hobby)

coller, to stick

combien, how much, how many; combien de temps? for how long?

comme, as, like

commencement, m, beginning

commencer (à), to begin (VL)

comment, how, what, what like

commode, f, chest of drawers

compagnon, m, compagne, f, companion

compartiment, m, compartment

complet, m, suit of clothes; adj, complete, full

composer (un numéro), to dial (a number)

comprendre, to understand, to include

compter, to count

comte, m, count (title)

conducteur, m, driver

conduire, to conduct, to drive (a vehicle); se conduire, to behave

confiture, f, jam

confort, m, comfort

confortable, comfortable

connaissance, f, knowledge, acquaintance; faire la connaissance de qn, to meet s/o

connaître, to know, to be acquainted with (VL)

conquérir, to conquer

consigne, f, left-luggage office

constamment, constantly

constant, -e, constant

construire, to construct

conte, m, tale, story

content, -e, pleased (de, with); satisfied, happy

continent, m, continent

continuer, to continue

contraindre, to force

contre, against

contredire, to contradict

contrôler, to control

contrôleur, m, ticket-collector, controller

convaincre, to convince (VL)

copain, m, chum, pal

coq, m, cock bird

coque, f, shell; œuf à la coque, boiled egg

cordial, -e, cordial, friendly

corrompre, to corrupt

côte, f, rib; hill; coast

côté, m, side; de tous côtés, on all sides; de l'autre côté, on the other side; du côté de, on the side of, in the direction

of; à ses côtés, at his/her side; de côté, next door; mettre à côté, to put to one side

cou, m, neck

se coucher, to go to bed

couché, in bed; lying down

coudre, to sew

couler, to flow

couleur, f, colour; de quelle couleur est ...? what colour is ...?

coup, m, blow, stroke; coup de pied, kick

couper, to cut

cour, f, yard, court

courbé, m, crouched (sur, over); bent, curved

courir, to run (VL)

cours, m, course (of river), flow; exchange rate; lesson, course of lessons; un cours d'eau, a stream

course, f, race, errand; faire ses courses, to do one's shopping

court, -e, short

cousin, m, cousine, f, cousin

coussin, m, cushion

couteau, m, knife

coûter, to cost

couvert, m, cover; place laid for meal

couvert, -e, covered (de, with)

couverture, f, blanket, rug

couvrir, to cover

craindre, to fear

cravate, f, necktie, tie, scarf

crayon, m, pencil

créer, to create

crevaison, f, puncture

crevé, -e, punctured

cri, m, cry, shout

crier, to cry, shout

croire, to believe

cruel, -le, cruel

cueillir, to pick, gather

cuiller, cuillère, f, spoon

cuisine, f, kitchen

cuisinière, f, cook

cuisses de grenouille, f, frog's legs

curé, m, parish priest

curieux, -se, curious, inquisitive; odd

dame, f, lady

danger, m, danger

dangereux, -se, dangerous

danois, Danish

dans, in, into

danser, to dance

date, f, date (calendar)

davantage, more, even more; more so

débrouiller, to manage

décembre, December

décharger, to unload

déchirer, to tear

décider, to decide

découvrir, to discover, to uncover

décriver, to describe
décrotter, to clean, to remove mud from
dedans, in it, inside
danseur, m, danseuse, f, dancer
défendre, to forbid
défense, f, prohibition; défense de, it is forbidden to . . .
dégeler, to thaw
dégoûter, to disgust
dehors, outside
déjà, already, yet
déjeuner, m, lunch; petit déjeuner, breakfast; v, to have lunch
délabré, dilapidated, tumble-down
délaisser, to abandon
délégué, m, delegate
demain, tomorrow
demander, to ask
démarrer, to start moving, start off
demeurer, to reside, dwell
demi, half
dent, f, tooth
dentiste, m, dentist
dépêcher, to hurry; se dépêcher, to hurry up
dépenser, to spend
déposer, to deposit; to set down
depuis, since, for (a period of time)
déranger, to disturb, to upset
dernier, -ière, last
dernièrement, recently
dérobée, à la dérobée, by stealth, secretly
derrière, behind
dès, from, since; dès que, as soon as; from the moment that
désavantage, m, disadvantage
descendre, to descend, to go downstairs, to dismount, to alight
désert, m, desert
désirer, to want
désobéir, to disobey
dessin, m, drawing
dessiner, to draw
dessous, under (it)
dessus, above (it)
détail, m, detail
détruire, to destroy
deuil, porter le deuil de, to wear mourning for
deux, two; tous les deux, both
devant, in front (of it)
devenir, to become
deviner, to guess (VL)
devoir, to owe, have to, must (VL)
devoir, m, duty, exercise, task
diamant, m, diamond
différence, f, difference
dictionnaire, m, dictionary
dimanche, m, Sunday
dîner, m, dinner; v, to dine
dire, to say, to tell (VL)
directeur, m, director, headmaster

diriger, se, (vers), to go towards
discuter, to discuss
disparaître, to disappear
dizaine, about ten
document, m, document
doigt, m, finger
dommage, m, damage; quel dommage! what a pity!
donc, then, therefore, so
donner, to give; donner sur (of a window), to look out on to
dont, of whom, of which, whose
dormir, to sleep (VL)
dos, m, back
douane, f, custom-house; the customs
doubler, to overtake
doucement, quietly, softly, gently
douche, f, shower
doux, -ce, sweet, soft, mild, kind
douzaine, f, dozen
drap, m, cloth, sheet
dresser, to set up, to erect; se dresser, to rise up, stand up
droite, f, right; à droite, on the right; tout droit, straight ahead
drôle, comic, funny
duc, m, duke; duchesse, duchess
dur, -e, hard
durer, to last

eau, f, water
échapper, to escape
échapper belle, to have a narrow escape
échelle, f, ladder
éclair, m, lightening
éclairer, to light up, to enlighten
école, f, school; à l'école, at/to school
écossais, -aise, Scotch, Scottish
écouter, to listen (to)
écraser, to crush, run over
s'écrier, to exclaim
écrire, to write (VL)
écrivain, m, writer
effet, m, effect; en effet, in fact
effort, m, effort
égal, -e, equal; égal à égal, on equal terms
électrophone, m, record player
élever, to raise, to bring up
église, f, church
égout, m, drain, sewer
élève, m or f, pupil
embrasser, to kiss, embrace
s'émerveiller de, to marvel at
empêcher, to prevent
s'empirer, to grow worse
emploi, m, employment, job
employer, to use, employ (VL)
emprunter, to borrow
en, in, on
encore, still, yet, again
encre, f, ink

encrier, m, inkstand
endormi, asleep
s'endormir, to fall asleep
enfant, m or f, child
enfin, at last, in the end, finally
ennemi, m, enemy
ennuyer, to annoy; s'ennuyer, to be bored
ensuite, then, next
enseigne, f, sign
entendre, to hear; to understand; bien
   entendu, of course, agreed
entourer, to surround
entr'acte, m, interval
entre, between; entre nous, between you
   and me
entrée, f, entry, admission; entrance
entrer, to enter
envie, avoir envie de, to want to
environ, about
envoyer, to send (VL)
épargner, to save
épatant, -e, marvellous
époux, épouse, spouse
épouser, to marry
équipe, f, team, crew of racing boat
équitation, f, horsemanship
escalier, m, stairway, stairs
escargot, m, edible snail
escarpé, steep
Espagnol, m, Spaniard; espagnole, -e,
   Spanish
espérer, to hope
espion, m, spy
espoir, m, hope
essayer, to try
essence, f, petrol
essuyer, to wipe
et, and; et . . . et, both . . . and
étage, m, floor, storey
étang, m, pond
état, m, state
Etats-Unis, m, U.S.A.
été, m, summer
éteindre, to extinguish, put out the light
étendre, to extend, stretch
étoile, f, star
étonner, to astonish, surprise; s'étonner,
   to be surprised
étranger, -ère, foreign
étranger, m, foreigner, stranger; à l'etran-
   ger, abroad
être, to be (VL)
étude, f, study
étudiant, m, -e, f, student
étudier, to study
s'évanouir, to faint
éveiller, to wake up (s/o)
évidemment, evidently, clearly, of course
évident, evident, clear, obvious
éviter, to avoid
exact, -e, exact
examinateur, m, examiner

s'excuser, to apologize
exercice, m, exercise, practice
expliquer, to explain
extraordinaire, extraordinary

face, f, face; en face de, opposite; face à,
   facing
facile, easy
facilement, easily
façon, f, way, manner
facteur, m, postman
faible, feeble, weak
faillir, to fail, faillir faire qch, nearly to do
   s/th, just not do something
faim, f, hunger; avoir faim, to be hungry
faire, to do, to make (VL); faire semblant,
   to pretend; faire signe, to beckon,
   motion
faisan, m, pheasant
falloir (VL), to be necessary
famille, f, family
farine, f, flour
fatigué, tired
faubourg, m, suburb
faute, f, fault
fauteuil, m, armchair
faux, fausse, false
favori, favorite, favourite
fenêtre, f, window
ferme, f, farm
fermer, to close, shut; fermer à clé, to
   lock
fermier, m, farmer
fête, f, fête, feast, festival, celebration
feu, m, fire; un feu rouge, traffic light
feuille, f, leaf; page of book
février, m, February
fier, fière, proud
fil, m, thread; fil de fer, wire
fille, f, girl, daughter
fils, m, son
fin, f, end
finir, to finish
flaque, f, pool, puddle
fleur, f, flower
fois, f, time; deux fois, twice
foncé, dark (of colour)
fond, m, bottom, base; au fond, at the
   bottom; basically
forêt, f, forest
formidable, marvellous, outstanding
formule, f, kind, sort, form
fort, adv, very, very much
fort, -e, strong, loud
fortune, f, fortune, possessions
fou, fol, folle, mad, silly
foule, f, crowd
fourchette, f, fork
frais, fraîche, fresh
français, French; le français, French
   language
frapper, to hit

frère, m, brother
frites, f.pl, chips
froid, -e, cold
frontière, f, frontier
fruit, m, fruit
fruitier, m, fruiterer, greengrocer
fuir, to flee
fumée, f, smoke
fumer, to smoke
furieux, -euse, furious
fusil, m, rifle, gun

gagner, to win, to earn
gallois, -oise, Welsh
gamin, m, urchin, kid
gant, m, glove
garantie, f, guarantee
garçon, m, boy; bachelor; waiter
garder, to keep, take care of
gare, f, railway station
gâteau, m, cake
gauche, left; à gauche, on the left
geler, to freeze
gêner, to hinder, to annoy
général, m, general
généreux, -euse, generous
genou, m, knee
gens, m or f.pl, people
gentil, -lle, kind, nice
glace, f, ice; ice-cream; mirror
glissant, -e, slippery
gosse, m, lad, urchin
goûter, to taste
grand, -e, big, large, great; une grande
　personne, a grown-up; les grandes
　vacances, summer holidays; grand-
　père, m, grandfather
grappe, f, bunch; grappe de raisin, bunch
　of grapes
gras, grasse, fatty, fat (of animals)
gratter, to scratch, rub, scrape
grave, serious
grève, f, strike; en grève, on strike
grille, f, gate
grimper, to climb
gris, -e, grey
gros, grosse, fat, plump, large
groupe, m, group
guère: ne . . . guère, hardly, scarcely
guérir, to cure; se guérir, get better
guerre, f, war
guetter, to watch out for
guichet, m, ticket office
guide, m, guide
guitare, f, guitar
gymnaste, m or f, gymnast
gymnastique, f, gymnastics

habile, clever, skilful
s'habiller, to get dressed, to dress
habits, m.pl, clothes
habiter, to live in, to inhabit

habitude: d'habitude, usually
haie, f, hedge; fence
haut, -e, high; en haut, above, upstairs
hauteur, f, height
herbe, f, grass
hériter, to inherit
héritier, m, heir
héros, m, hero; heroïne, f, heroine
heure, f, hour; quelle heure est-il? what
　time is it?; de bonne heure, early
heureux, -se, happy
hier, yesterday
hisser, to lift up
histoire, f, story
hiver, m, winter
honnête, honest
honneur, m, honour
hôpital, m, hospital
horloge, f, clock
horreur, f, horror
hors, out; hors de soi, beside oneself
hôte, m, landlord, innkeeper; table d'hôte,
　set meal (at restaurant)
hôtel, m, hotel
hurler, to howl

ici, here
idée, f, idea
igloo, m, igloo
il y a, there is, there are
île, f, island
image, f, picture
immédiatement, at once, immediately
immobile, motionless
importe: n'importe, no matter; il importe
　de, it is important to
s'indigner, to become indignant
indonesien, -ne, Indonesian
infirmier, m, male nurse; infirmière, f, fe-
　male nurse
inquiet, -ète, anxious, worried
installer, to install
s'installer, to settle down (on a seat, etc.)
instant, m, instant
instituteur, -trice, primary school teacher
instrument, m, instrument; instrument de
　musique, musical instrument
insu: à l'insu de . . . , unknown to . . .
intelligent, intelligent, clever
intelligible, understandable
interdire, to forbid
intersection, f, crossroads
intéressant, interesting
s'intéresser à, to take an interest in
intérêt, m, interest
interrompre, to interrupt
interrupteur, m, switch
introduire, to introduce
intrus, m, intruder
Irelande, f, Ireland; irlandais, Irish
irrité, -e, annoyed, angry
ivre, drunk

ivrogne, m, drunkard

jade, f, jade
jamais, ever, never; ne . . . jamais, never
janvier, January
Japon, m, Japan; japonais, -e, Japanese
jardin, m, garden
jaune, yellow
jetée, f, pier, jetty
jeter, to throw; se jeter contre, to run
   into, crash into (VL)
jeudi, m, Thursday
jeune, young
joindre, to join
joli, -e, pretty
jouer, to play
jouet, m, plaything, toy
jour, m, day
journal, m, newspaper, diary
journée, f, day
juger, to judge
juillet, July
juin, June
jumeau, m, jumelle, f, twin
jument, f, mare
jus, m, juice
jusqu'à, as far as, up to

là, there
lac, m, lake
lâcher, to let go, release
laisser, to leave, to allow; laisser tomber,
   to drop
lambeau: en lambeaux, ragged
lampe, f, lamp
lancer, to throw, fling; se lancer, to rush,
   dash
langue, f, tongue, language
lapin, m, rabbit
large, wide; au large, out at sea
laver, to wash; se laver, to wash (oneself)
lecture, f, reading
léger, légère, light
légume, m, vegetable
lendemain, m, next day
lent, -e, slow; lentement, slowly
lettre, f, letter
lever, to raise; se lever, to get up (VL)
librairie, f, bookshop
libre, free
licorne, f, unicorn
lieu, m, spot, place; avoir lieu, to take
   place; au lieu de, instead of
ligne, f, line; pêcher à la ligne, to angle
limonade, f, lemonade
linge, m, linen
lire, to read (VL)
lit, m, bed
livre, m, book
livre, f, pound (weight or money)
loin, far, far off; au loin, in the distance;
   de loin, from afar

long, longue, long; le long de, along
longueur, f, length
longtemps, (for) a long time
lors, then; dès lors, since then
lorsque, when
lot, m, prize in lottery
loterie, f, lottery
louer, to let (for rent or hire)
loup, m, wolf; à pas de loup, stealthily
lumière, f, light
lune, f, moon
lunettes, f.pl, spectacles, glasses

maçon, m, mason
madame, madam, Mrs.
mai, May
maillot (de bain), m, bathing costume
main, f, hand
maintenant, now
mais, but
maison, f, house
maître, m, master, teacher, maîtresse, f,
   mistress
mal, badly; mal à la tête, headache; mal
   aux dents, toothache; faire mal, to
   hurt, to do wrong; avoir mal au cœur,
   to feel sick
malade, m, invalid; adj. ill
maladroit, -e, clumsy
malgré, in spite of
malheur, m, unhappiness; misfortune;
   malheureusement, unfortunately
maman, f, mummy
la Manche, f, the English Channel
manger, to eat
manquer, to want, to miss, to fail, to lack
marchand, m, tradesman, seller
marchandise, f, goods, wares
marché, m, market; bon marché, cheap
marcher, to walk; to work, go (of a machine, etc.)
mari, m, husband
marier, se marier, to marry
marin, m, sailor
marquer, to mark, show (time on a clock)
mars, March
match, m, match (game)
matelas, m, mattress
matière, f, matter; subject
matin, m, morning
mauvais, -e, bad
mécanicien, m, mechanic
méchant, (after noun) wicked, ill-
   tempered, ill-disposed; (before noun)
   naughty, worthless
médecin, m, doctor
médecine, f, science of medicine
médicament, m, medicine (remedy)
meilleur, -e, better
mêler, to mix
même, same, even; moi-même, myself
membre, m, member

menacer, to threaten (de, with)
ménage, m, housework, house-keeping
mendiant, m, beggar
mener, to lead (VL)
mentir, to (tell a) lie
menu, m, menu
menuisier, m, carpenter, joiner
mer, f, sea
mère, f, mother
mesure, f, measure, measurement; extent
métier, m, trade, profession
mètre, m, metre
métro, m, Metro, Paris underground railway
mettre, to put; se mettre à faire qch, to start doing s/th; se mettre en route, to set off (VL)
midi, m, midday, noon; le Midi, the South
milieu: au milieu, in the middle
mille, m, thousand; mile
millier, m, about a thousand; des milliers (de), thousands (of)
mine, f, look, appearance
minuit, m, midnight
minute, f, minute
miracle, m, miracle
miroir, m, mirror, looking-glass
mission, f, mission
modèle, m, model
moindre, less
moins, minus, less; to (in telling time); au moins, at least
moment, m, moment
monde, m, world; tout le monde, everybody; beaucoup de monde, a lot of people
monnaie, f, small change
monsieur, m, gentleman, sir, Mr.
montagne, f, mountain
monter, to go up, to go upstairs, to mount
montre, f, watch
montrer, to show
se moquer (de), to make fun (of), to laugh (at)
mort, f, death
mort, -e, dead
mot, m, word
mou, mol, molle, soft
mouchoir, m, handkerchief
mouillé, wet, soaked
mourir, to die; il est mort, he died, he is dead (VL)
mouton, m, sheep, mutton
Moyen Age, m, the Middle Ages
moyen, m, means, way
muet, muette, dumb; dumb person
muraille, f, large wall, rampart
musique, f, music
mystère, m, mystery

nage, f, swimming
nager, to swim

naissance, f, birth
naître, to be born (VL)
ne . . . pas, not
nécessaire, necessary
nappe, f, table-cloth
neige, f, snow; boule de neige, f, snowball
neuf, neuve, new
nez, m, nose
ni . . . ni, neither . . . nor
nièce, f, niece
niveau, m, level
nocturne, nocturnal
noir, black, dark
nommer, to name
nouveau, nouvel, nouvelle, new; de nouveau, again; à nouveau, anew; nouvelles, f.pl, news
nouvelle, f, short story
novembre, November
se noyer, to drown
nuage, m, cloud
nuit, f, night
nul, nulle, no, not any; ne . . . nulle part, not anywhere; nullement, by no means, in no way

obligatoire, compulsory
obliger, to oblige, to compel
occasion, f, chance, opportunity; bargain
occupant, m, occupier
s'occuper (à), to busy oneself (with)
octobre, October
œil, m, eye (pl. yeux)
œuf, m, egg; œuf à la coque, boiled egg
œuvre, f, work (by artist, writer, etc.)
officier, m, officer
offrir, to offer (VL)
oiseau, m, bird
omelette, f, omelet
on, one (pronoun), someone; they, you, people
oncle, m, uncle
ongle, m, nail (on finger or toe)
or, well now, now then
or, m, gold; d'or, golden, made of gold
ordonner, to order, command
ordre, m, order
orge, f, barley
orphelin, m, orphan
os, m, bone
oser, to dare
ou, or; ou . . . ou, either . . . or
où, where, when, in which
oublier, to forget
outil, m, tool, implement
ouvreuse, f, usherette
ouvrier, m, workman
ouvrir, to open (VL)

page, f, page (of book); m, page-boy
pain, m, bread; petit-pain, roll

paisiblement, peacefully
paix, f, peace
panier, m, basket
panne, f, breakdown (mechanical)
panser, to dress (a wound)
pantalon, m, trousers
papier, m, paper, piece of paper
Pâques, m, Easter
par, through, per, by, on
paraître, to appear, to come into sight;
    to seem (VL)
parallèle, parallel
parapluie, m, umbrella
parc, m, park
parce que, because
parchemin, m, parchment
pardessus, m, overcoat
pardon, excuse me
pareil, -eille, like, similar; à pareille heure,
    at such a time
parent, m, -e, f, relative; les parents,
    parents
parfait, -e, perfect
parler, to speak
part: f, quelque part, somewhere; pour
    ma part, for my part
participer, to take part
partir, to leave, depart, to set out (VL)
partout, everywhere
pas, m, pace, step; ne ... pas, not; pas du
    tout, not at all; pas encore, not yet
passage, m, crossing; passage clouté,
    pedestrian crossing
passeport, m, passport
passe-temps, m, pastime, hobby
passer, to pass; passer un examen, to sit
    for an exam, to take an exam; passer
    les vacances, to spend the holidays;
    passer voir, to look in on, call on
pauvre, poor
payer, to pay
pays, m, district; land; country
paysan, m, -ne, f, peasant
peau, f, skin
pécher, to sin
pêcher, to fish
pécheresse, f, sinful woman, sinner
pécheur, m, sinful man, sinner
pêcheur, m, -se, f, fisherman, -woman
peigner, to comb
peigne, m, comb
peindre, to paint (VL)
peine, difficulty; à peine, hardly; il vaut
    la peine, it is worthwhile
pelle, f, spade
pencher, se, to lean; penché, leaning
pendant, during; pendant que, while
pendule, f, clock (as used in house)
pensée, f, thought
penser, to think (de: of, à: about)
pente, f, slope
perdre, to lose

père, m, father
période, f, period, time
permettre, to allow (VL)
permis, m, permit; permis de conduire,
    driving licence
permission, f, permission
persister, to persist
personne, f, person; ne ... personne, no-
    one
petit, -e, little, small
pétrole, m, paraffin
peu, little; un peu, a little
peur, f, fear; avoir peur, to be afraid
peut-être, perhaps
phare, m, lighthouse
photographe, m, photographer
photographie, photo, f, photograph
phrase, f, phrase
pièce, f, room; piece, individual article
pied, m, foot; à pied, on foot
pierre, f, stone
piéton, m, pedestrian
pipe, f, pipe
pire, adj, worse
pis, adv, worse; tant pis! too bad!
piscine, f, swimming-pool
placard, m, cupboard
place, f, place, seat; square (in town)
placer, to place, put
plage, f, beach
plaine, f, plain
plaire, to please (VL); s'il vous plaît, please
plaisir, m, pleasure
plancher, m, floor
plante, f, plant; planter, to plant
plat, m, dish (container or contents)
plein, -e, full; faire le plein, to fill up; en
    plein air, in the open, out of doors
pleurer, to weep, cry
pleuvoir, to rain (VL)
plomb, m, lead (metal)
plonger, to dive
plupart, f, the majority, the greater part,
    most
plume, f, feather
plus, more; ne ... plus, no more, no
    longer
plusieurs, several
pneu, m, tyre
poche, f, pocket
pointe: heure de pointe, f, rush-hour
poire, f, pear; electric light switch
pois, m, pea; les petits pois, green peas
poisson, m, fish
poli, -e, polite; poliment, politely
police, f, police (force); agent de police,
    policeman
politesse, f, politeness
Pologne, f, Poland; polonais, Polish
pomme, f, apple
pommier, m, apple-tree
porc, m, pig; pork

portail, m, portal; large entrance doors
porte, f, door
portefeuille, m, wallet
porter, to carry; to wear
portrait, m, portrait
poser, to place, put
posséder, to possess
postal, -e, postal
poste, m, station (police); position, job;
   set (radio)
poste, f, postal system; **bureau de poste,**
   m, post office
pouce, m, thumb; **manger/boire sur le**
   pouce, take a hurried snack/drink
poulet, m, chicken
poupée, f, doll
pour, for; in order to
pourquoi, why
poursuivre, to pursue, chase
pourtant, yet, however
pousser, to push
poussin, m, chick
pouvoir, to be able, can (VL)
pouvoir, m, power
pratiquer, to take part in (a sport, etc.)
précieux, -se, precious, valuable
préférer, to prefer
premier, -ière, first
prendre, to take (VL)
préparer, to prepare, get ready
près, near (de: to)
présentation, f, introduction
presque, almost
prêt, -e, ready
prétendre, to claim
prêter, to lend
prévenir, to warn
prévoir, to foresee
prince, m, prince; **princesse,** f, princess
printemps, m, Spring (season)
priorité, f, priority
prix, m, price, prize
probable, probable; **probablement,**
   probably
problème, m, problem
prochain, -e, nearby, next; **un prochain,**
   a neighbour
proche, near
produire, to produce
professeur, m, teacher, professor
profond, -e, deep; **peu profond,** shallow;
   profondément, profoundly
profondeur, f, depth
promenade, f, walk, ride, trip, drive
se promener, to go for a walk, ride, drive,
   etc.
promettre, to promise
propos: à propos de, concerning, about
propre, clean; own; **proprement,** properly
propriétaire, m, f, proprietor
protester, to protest
prudent, -e, prudent, careful, wise

prudemment, prudently, wisely
public, -que, public
puis, then, next, after that
puisque, since, for the reason that

quai, m, platform
qualifié, qualified, experienced
quand, when
quant à . . . , as for . . .
quart, m, quarter
que, that, whom, which; **ce que,** what
   ne . . . que, only
quel, -le, which, what
quelconque, whatever
quelque, some; **quelque chose,** m, something
quelquefois, sometimes
quelque part, somewhere
quelqu'un, someone
queue, f, tail; queue
qui, who, whom, which, that
quincaillier, m, ironmonger
quinze, fifteen
quitter, to leave
quoi, what, which, that
quoique, although

rabattre, to pull down, lower
raconter, to tell (story)
radio, f, radio
rage, f, anger
rail, m, rail
raison, f, reason; **avoir raison,** to be
   right
rame, f, oar
rang, m, row
ranger, to arrange, put in order
rappeler, to recall, remember
rapport, m, relationship
rapporter, to take/bring back
rarement, rarely
rayon, m, shelf, bookshelf
réaction, f, reaction
recevoir, to receive
rechercher, to research, seek
réclame, f, advertisement
récolter, to harvest
recommencer, to begin again
reconnaître, to recognize
réfléchir, to reflect
refuge, m, refuge, shelter
se refugier, v, to take refuge
regarder, to look (at); **se regarder,** to look
   at each other
régiment, m, regiment
règle, f, rule; ruler
regretter, to regret
reine, f, queen
rejoindre, to reunite, rejoin
rejeter, to throw back
remarquer, to notice
rembourser, to reimburse, to pay back

remède, m, remedy, medicine
remercier, to thank
remettre, to put back, deliver
remplir, to fill
remporter, to carry back, to carry off, to win
rencontrer, to meet
rendre, to give back; to make; to yield; rendre visite à, to pay a call on; se rendre, to surrender
renommé, -e, famous
renouveler, to renew
renseignement, m, information
rentrer, to come/go home
reparaître, to reappear
réparer, to repair
repartir, to leave again
repas, m, meal
répliquer, to answer, reply
répondre, to answer, reply
réponse, f, answer
reposer; se reposer, to rest (oneself)
représenter, to represent
réprimande, f, reproof
respirer, to breathe
résolution, f, resolution, determination
ressembler (à), resemble, look like
ressortir, to go out again
rester, to remain
restes, m.pl, remains
résultat, m, result
retard: en retard, late
retenir, to retain, hold, detain
retourner, to return; se retourner, to turn around
réussir, to succeed; réussir à un examen, pass an exam
rêve, m, dream
rêver, to dream
réveil, m, alarm-clock
se réveiller, to wake up
revenant, m, ghost
revenir, to come back, return
reviser, to revise, review
revolver, m, revolver (pistol)
riche, rich
richesses, f.pl, riches
ridicule, ridiculous, silly
rien, ne . . . rien, nothing, not anything
rire, to laugh (VL)
risquer, to risk
rivière, f, river
robe, f, dress; robe de chambre, dressing-gown
rocher, m, rock
roi, m, king
roman, m, novel
rompre, to break
rond, -e, round
roue, f, wheel
rouler, to travel along (on wheels)
route, f, road, route; en route, on the way

rue, f, street
ruisseau, m, stream, gutter at side of street
Russie, f, Russia; russe, Russian

sable, m, sand
sac, m, bag
sage, wise, well-behaved
saisir, to seize
sale, dirty
salle, f, room, large public hall; salle à manger, dining-room; salle de bains, bathroom; salle des pas perdus, main hall of large railway-station; salle d'attente, waiting-room
salon, m, living-room
samedi, m, Saturday
sandwich, m, sandwich
sans, without
santé, f, health
sauter, to jump
sauver, to save; se sauver, to escape
savant, m, a learned person; savant, -e, learned
savoir, to know (as a fact); je sais nager, I can (know how to) swim (VL)
scolaire (adj), school
sec, sèche, dry
sécher, to dry
second, -e, second
secouer, to shake
secours, m, help; au secours! help!
secret, secrète, secret
self: restaurant self, m, self-service restaurant
semaine, f, week
sembler, to seem, appear
semelle, f, sole (of shoe)
sens, m, direction
sensible, sensitive
sentence, f, sentence (legal)
sentinelle, f, sentry
sentir, to feel, sense, smell (VL)
sept, seven
septembre, September
serrer, to squeeze
servante, f, woman servant
serveuse, f, waitress
serviette, f, brief-case; towel, napkin
servir, to serve; se servir de, to make use of; servir à, to be used for, as (VL)
seul, seule, only, sole
seulement, only
sévère, severe
si, if, whether; so; (contradictory) yes; si fait! yes indeed!
signal, m, signal
signe: faire signe, to beckon
silence, m, silence
silencieux, silent
simple, (before noun) lowly; (after noun) simple-minded
simplement, simply

situation, f, situation
slip, m, bathing trunks
société, f, society
sœur, f, sister
soif, f, thirst; avoir soif, to be thirsty
soigner, to take care of, to look after
soin, m, care; avec soin, carefully
soir, m, evening
soixante, sixty
sol, m, ground, soil
soldat, m, soldier
soldes, m.pl, sale; goods for sale
soleil, m, sun
solennel, -le, solemn
sombre, dark
sommeil, sleep; avoir sommeil, to be
    sleepy
sonner, to ring
sonore, sonorous, loud
sort, m, fate
sorte: de toutes sortes, of all kinds; quelle
    sorte de . . . ? what kind of . . . ?
sortie, f, exit, way out
sortir, to go out (VL)
soudain, sudden, suddenly
souffrir, to suffer
souhaiter, to wish for, want
soulier, m, shoe
soupe, f, soup
souper, m, supper
sourir, to smile (VL)
sourire, m, smile
souris, f, mouse
sous, under, beneath
souvenir, m, souvenir, memory
se souvenir (de), to remember, recall
souvent, often
spectateur, m, spectator
spectre, m. spectre, ghost, phantom
squelette, m, skeleton
stationnement, m, parking
statuette, f, statuette
stylo, m, fountain pen
stylo à bille, m, ball-point pen, biro
succès, m, success
sucre, m, sugar
Suède, f, Sweden; suédois, -e, Swedish
suffisant, sufficient
suisse, Swiss; Suisse, f, Switzerland
suivant, following
suivre, to follow (VL)
supposer, to suppose
sur, on; deux sur trois, 2 by 3
sûr, -e, sure, certain
sursaut: en sursaut, with a start
suspendu, -e, suspended, hanging
symbole, m, symbol
sympathique, likeable
syndicat d'initiative, tourist information
    office

table, f, table; table de nuit/de chevet, m,
    bedside table; table de toilette, f,
    dressing-table
tableau, m, picture, board; tableau noir,
    blackboard
tâche, f, task
tâcher, to try
taille, f, waist, height
se taire, to keep silent
tant, so much
tante, f, aunt
tapage, m, din
tapis, m, carpet
tard, late; plus tard, later
tasse, f, cup
tâtons: à tâtons, groping, feeling the way
taureau, m, bull
télégramme, m, telegram
téléphone, m, telephone
téléphoner, to telephone
télévision, f, television
tellement, so, so much
temps, m, time; weather
tenir, to hold
se tenir, to stand (VL)
tennis, m, tennis
tente, f, tent
se terminer, to come to an end
terrasse, f, terrace
terre, f, ground, earth
terrible, terrible
tête, f, head
thé, m, tea
tiers, m, third
timbre, m, (postage) stamp
tirage, m, draw (of lottery)
tirer, to pull, draw along; to shoot (wea-
    pon)
tiroir, m, drawer
toit, m, roof
tomate, f, tomato
tomber, to fall
tort, m, wrong; avoir tort, to be wrong
tôt, soon
toujours, always, still (in progress)
tour, m, turn, tour
tour, f, tower
touriste, m, f, tourist
tout, all, very; tout à coup, suddenly;
    tout à l'heure, presently; tout de suite,
    immediately; tout en, while; tout de
    même, all the same
tout le monde, everyone, everybody
toutefois, yet, however
train, m, train; en train de, in the act of
traiter, to treat
tranquille, quiet
transmettre, to pass on, transmit
transporter, to transport
travail, m, work
travailler, to work
traverser, to cross

trembler, to tremble
très, very
trésor, m, treasure
tressaillir, to shudder, shiver
trimestre, m, (school) term
triste, (after noun) sad; (before noun) wretched, despicable
se tromper, to make a mistake, be mistaken
trône, m, throne
trop, too, too many, too much
trottoir, m, pavement
trou, m, hole
troupe, f, troop
trouver, to find; se trouver, to be (situated, located)
turc, m, turque, f, Turkish; la Turquie, Turkey
tuer, to kill
tunnel, m, tunnel

université, f, university
universel, -le, universal
usé, worn, worn out
utile, useful
utiliser, to use

vacances, f.pl, holidays; les grandes vacances, summer holidays
vache, f, cow
vaincre, to vanquish (VL)
vaisselle, f, crockery; faire la vaisselle, do the washing up
valise, f, suitcase
valoir, to be worth, be worth while; il vaut mieux faire, it is better to (VL)
se vanter, to boast
vaste, vast, great
veille, f, the day before; la veille de Noël, Christmas Eve
vélo, m, bike
vendeur, m, shopkeeper, seller
vendre, to sell
vendredi, Friday
venitien, -ienne, Venetian
venir, to come (VL); venir de faire qch, to have just done s/th
vent, m, wind; il fait du vent, it is windy
ver, m, worm
verger, m, orchard
vérifier, to check
vérité, f, truth
verre, m, glass
vers, towards
version, f, translation
veste, f; veston, m, jacket
vêtement, m, garment, article of clothing
vêtir, to clothe; se vêtir, to put on clothes, to dress
veuve, f, widow
viande, f, meat

victoire, f, victory
vide, empty
vie, f, life
vieux, vieil, vieille, old; une vieille, an old woman
vilain, -e, ugly
village, m, village
ville, f, town; grande ville, big town, city
vin, m, wine
vingtaine, f, about twenty
virage, m, turn, bend (of a road)
visage, m, face
visite, f, visit; faire/rendre visite à, to pay a call on
visiter, to visit, call on; to look over (a building, etc.)
visiteur, m, visitor
vite, quick, quickly
vitesse, f, speed; à grande vitesse, fast, at high speed
vitre, f, window-pane
vitrine, f, shop window
vive! long live!
vivre, to live (be alive) (VL)
voici, here is
voilà, there is
voile, f, sail; faire de la voile, to go sailing
voir, to see (VL)
voiture, f, car, carriage; voiture-restaurant, dining-car on train
voix, f, voice; à voix basse, in a low voice; à haute voix, aloud, in a loud voice
volant, m, steering wheel
voler, to fly; to steal
voleur, m, thief; au voleur! stop thief!
vouloir, to wish, to want, to be willing; vouloir dire, to mean; en vouloir à, to be angry with (VL)
vouloir, m, will
voyage, m, travel, journey
voyager, to travel
voyageur, m, -euse, f, traveller
vrai, -e, true; vraiment, really
vue, f, view, sight

y, there, in that place
yeux, m.pl, eyes

zéro, m, nought

English-French vocabulary

Abbreviations: *v*, verb; *adj*, adjective; *adv*, adverb; *n*, noun; *qn*, quelqu'un; *qch*, quelque chose; *s/o*, someone; *s/th*, something; *VL*, see Verb List; *Ind*, for further information see Index.

able, to be able (to), pouvoir (VL); être capable (de faire qch); savoir (faire qch)

about (approximately), environ, à peu près, de; **about noon**, vers midi; (concerning) sur, au sujet de, à propos de

above, en haut, au-dessus

abroad, à l'étranger

absolute, absolu, -e

across, à travers; **to go across**, traverser

actor, un acteur; **actress**, une actrice

admire, v, admirer

admit, v, admettre

advance, v, s'avancer

aeroplane, un avion

afraid, adj, effrayé, -e; **to be afraid**, avoir peur

after, après; **afterwards**, plus tard; ensuite

afternoon, après-midi, m

again, encore, de nouveau

agency, une agence

ago, il y a (. . . ans, mois etc.)

agree, v, être d'accord

air, n, l'air, m; **by air**, par avion

airport, un aéroport

alarm-clock, un réveil

alcohol, alcool, m

alight, descendre

alive: to be alive, vivre

all, tout, toute, tous, toutes

allow, v, permettre (qch à qn)

almost, presque; **he almost fell**, il a failli tomber

alone, seul, seule; **to leave alone**, laisser

along, le long de

already, déjà

also, aussi

always, toujours

amusing, amusant, -e

and, et; **come and see**, venez voir

animal, un animal

annoy, agacer; **annoying**, agaçant

anorak, un anorak

answer, v, répondre (à); n, une réponse

anyone, quelqu'un(e)

anything, quelque chose; n'importe quoi

anyway, de toute façon

anywhere, n'importe où

appear, v, paraître; avoir l'air

apple, une pomme; **apple-tree**, un pommier

approach, v, (s')approcher (de)

arm, un bras

armchair, un fauteuil

arrest, v, arrêter

arrive, v, arriver

arrival, une arrivée

artist, un artiste; un peintre

as, comme; **as soon as**, aussitôt que; **as . . . as**, aussi . . . que; **as far as**, jusqu'à; **as for**, quant à

ask, v, demander (à qn de faire qch); **to ask for s/th (from s/o)**, demander qch (à qn)

asleep, endormi, -e; **to fall asleep**, s'endormir

at, à; chez

attack, v, attaquer

aunt, une tante

Australia, Australie, f

Autumn, automne, m

away: to go away, partir, s'en aller; **far away**, au loin

baby, un bébé

back: to come back, revenir; **to give back**, rendre

bad, mauvais, -e; **badly**, mal

bag, un sac

baker, un boulanger; **baker's shop**, une boulangerie

ball, une balle; **football**, un ballon

ball-point pen, un stylo à bille

basket, un panier

bath, un bain; **to have a bath**, se baigner, prendre un bain; **bathroom**, une salle de bains

be, être (VL); **to be situated**, se trouver; **to be . . . years old**, avoir . . . ans

beach, une plage

beard, une barbe

beat, v, battre (VL); vaincre (VL)

beautiful, beau, bel, belle

because, parce que; **because of**, à cause de

become, v, devenir (VL)

bed, un lit; **bedroom**, une chambre à coucher; **bedside table**, une table de nuit, table de chevet; **to go to bed**, se coucher

beer, la bière

before, (in time), avant; (position), devant

beggar, un mendiant

begin, v, commencer (VL)

beginning, le commencement; le début

behave, v, se conduire; **behave yourself!**
sois sage!, soyez sage(s)!

behind, derrière, par derrière

believe, v, croire (VL); penser

bell, une cloche

bend, v, se baisser

beside, à côté de; **besides,** d'ailleurs

best, adj, le meilleur, la meilleure; adv, le
mieux (Ind)

better, adj, meilleur(e); adv, mieux; **it is
better (to do s/th),** il vaut mieux (faire
qch) (Ind)

between, entre

bicycle, une bicyclette, un vélo

bicycle lock, un antivol

big, grand, -e; gros, grosse

birthday, un anniversaire

black, noir, -e

blush, v, rougir

boat, un bateau; **steamboat,** un bateau à
vapeur; **sailing boat,** un bateau à voiles

bone, un os; les ossements, m.pl

book, v, réserver

book, n, un livre; **old book,** un bouquin;
note-book, un carnet

bookshop, une librairie

born, adj, né, -e; **to be born,** naître (VL)

borrow, v, emprunter

boss, le patron, la patronne; le chef

both, tous les deux

bottle, une bouteille

bottom, fond, m; **at the bottom of,** au
fond de

box, une boîte; **letter-box,** une boîte aux
lettres; **box of matches,** une boîte
d'allumettes

bracelet, un bracelet

brave, courageux, -euse

bread, le pain

break, v, casser

breakfast, le petit déjeuner

bring, v, amener (qn); apporter (qch)

brother, un frère

brush, une brosse; v, brosser

build, v, bâtir; **to have (a house) built,** se
faire bâtir (une maison)

building, un bâtiment

bull, un bœuf; un taureau

bunch, une grappe; **bunch of grapes,** une
grappe de raisin

burglar, un cambrioleur

burst, v, crever

bus, un bus, un autobus

bus stop, un arrêt d'autobus

but, mais

butcher, un boucher

buy, acheter

by, par; in dimensions: 2 cm by 4 cm,
2 cm sur 4 cm

café, un café

cake, un gâteau

call, v, appeler (VL); **to be called,** s'appeler

can, (to be able), pouvoir (VL)

candidate, un candidat

candle, une bougie, une chandelle

car, une voiture, une auto

care, soin, m; **to care for s/o,** soigner qn

carefully, avec soin, avec attention

carry, v, porter; transporter

cat, un chat

catch, v, attraper

cathedral, une cathédrale

cellar, une cave

century, un siècle

certain, adj, certain(e); **certainly,** certainement, bien sûr

chair, une chaise

change, v, changer; n, la monnaie

cheap, bon marché

cheese, le fromage

chemist's, une pharmacie

cherry, une cerise

child, un(e) enfant

choose, v, choisir

Christmas, Noël, m; **Christmas Eve,** la
veille de Noël

church, une église

cinema, un cinéma

city, une grande ville; une cité

class, une classe

classroom, une salle de classe

clever, habile, intelligent

client, un client

climb, v, grimper

clock, une horloge; une pendule

close, près de

coach, un car, un autocar

coffee, le café

cold, le froid; **to feel cold,** avoir froid;
it (weather) is cold, il fait froid

coldly, froidement

collect, v, (as hobby), collectionner

collection, une collection

colour, une couleur; **what colour is?** de
quelle couleur est . . . ?

come, v, venir (VL); **come down,**
descendre; **come up,** monter; **come
back,** revenir; **come home,** rentrer;
come in, entrer

comfortable, confortable, agréable

compartment, un compartiment

completely, complètement, tout à fait

condemn, v, condamner

contain, v, contenir (VL)

continue, v, continuer (à faire qch)

contradict, v, contredire

convince, v, convaincre (VL)

cook, v, cuire, faire cuire; **cooking,** la
cuisine

corkscrew, un tire-bouchon

corner, un coin; un angle

cottage (thatched), une chaumière

count, v, compter; n, un comte

country, un pays; countryside, la campagne

course (of a meal), un plat; of course, naturellement, bien entendu

courtier, un homme de la cour

cover, v, couvrir

cow, une vache

cream, la crème

crime, un crime

cross, v, traverser

crossroads, un carrefour

crown, la couronne

cruel, cruel, -le

cry, v, pleurer; cry out, crier, s'écrier; n, un cri

cup, une tasse

curious, curieux, -se

cut, v, couper; cut off s/o's head, décapiter qn

danger, un danger

dangerous, dangereux, -euse

dare, v, oser

daughter, une fille

day, un jour, une journée; the day before yesterday, avant-hier; the day after tomorrow, après-demain; the day before, la veille

dead, mort, -e

dear, cher, chère

decide, v, decider; decide to do s/th, décider de faire qch, se décider à faire qch

deeply, profondément

delay, un délai

Denmark, le Danemark

dentist, un dentiste

desk, un pupitre; writing desk, un bureau

destination, une destination

destroy, v, détruire

diamond, un diamant

diary, un journal; un agenda

dictator, un dictateur

dictionary, un dictionnaire

die, v, mourir (VL)

different, différent, -e

difficult, difficile; without difficulty, sans difficulté

dine, v, dîner; dining-room, une salle à manger; dining-car (train), voiture-restaurant

dinner, le dîner

disappear, v, disparaître

disco(thèque), un discothèque

discover, v, découvrir, trouver

dish, un plat

disobey, v, désobeir (à)

disturb, v, agacer, déranger

dive, v, plonger

doctor, un médecin, un docteur

dog, un chien

donkey, un âne

door, une porte; car-door, une portière; door-keeper, un portier; to ring the door bell, sonner à la porte

doubtless, sans doute

down: v, go/come down, descendre (Ind)

downstairs, en bas

draw (lottery), un tirage; draw, v, dessiner

drawer (in chest, cupboard, etc.), un tiroir

dream, v, rêver; n, un rêve

dress: v, to dress oneself, s'habiller; dress a wound, panser

dress, une robe

drink, v, boire (VL); n, boisson

drive, v, conduire (VL)

driver, un conducteur, un chauffeur

driving-lesson, une leçon de conduite

driving-licence, un permis de conduire

drunk, adj, ivre

duke, un duc; duchess, une duchesse

during, pendant

each, adj, chaque; each one (pronoun), chacun(e); each other, l'un l'autre

early, de bonne heure

Easter, Pâques, m

easy, facile; easily, facilement

eat, v, manger

egg, un œuf

elementary, élémentaire

emotion, émotion

employ, v, employer (VL)

employment, un emploi

empty, v, vider; adj, vide

end, v, finir, terminer; n, la fin

endure, v, supporter

enemy, un ennemi

England, l'Angleterre, f

English, anglais, -e; Englishman, un Anglais

enormous, énorme

enough, assez; big enough, assez grand; to be enough, être suffisant, suffir

enter, v, entrer

entrance, une entrée

envelope, une enveloppe

errand, une course; run an errand, faire une course

even, même

every, adj, tout, toute; everybody, tout le monde; everything, tout; every day, tous les jours

everywhere, partout

examination, un examen; to sit for an exam, passer un examen; to pass an exam, réussir à un examen

examiner, un examinateur

example, un exemple; for example, par exemple

except, sauf

exceptional, exceptionel, -elle

exchange, v, échanger; exchange office,

bureau de change, m
exclaim, v, s'écrier
excuse, une excuse
excuse, v, excuser; excuse oneself, s'excuser; Excuse me! Pardon!
exercise, n, exercice, m; school exercise, un devoir; exercise-book, un cahier
expensive, cher, chère; couteux, -euse
explain, v, expliquer
explosion, une explosion
extremely, extrêmement
eye, un œil, pl. des yeux

fairly, assez
fall, v, tomber
false, faux, fausse
family, une famille
famous, connu, -e; renommé, -e; célèbre
farm, une ferme; farmer, un fermier
fast, adj, rapide; adv. vite
fat (person), gros, -se; (animals, meat), gras, -se
father, un père; father-in-law, beau-père
fear, v, craindre
feast, festival, une fête
feed, v, nourir
feel, v, sentir (VL; Ind)
fetch, v, aller chercher
few: a few, quelques; few, peu de (Ind)
field, un champ
fight, v, se battre
file, un dossier
film, un film
find, v, trouver; to find out, découvrir
fine: it is fine (weather), il fait beau; that's fine! chic alors!
finish, v, finir (VL), terminer
firearm, une arme à feu
first, adj, premier, première; firstly, first of all, d'abord
fish, n, un poisson; v, pêcher
fisherman, pêcheur
floor, un plancher; (storey) un étage
flour, la farine
flower, une fleur
fly, v, voler
follow, v, suivre
food, la nourriture
foolish, ridicule; fou, fol, folle
foot, un pied; on foot, à pied
football, le football
footpath, un sentier
for, pour; (during) pendant; depuis; (because) car (Ind)
forbid, v, défendre (qch à qn); it is forbidden to (smoke), défense de (fumer)
foreign, adj, étranger, étrangère
forget, v, oublier
freeze, v, geler; it is freezing (weather), il gèle
French, adj, français, -e; a Frenchman, un

Français; French (language), le français
fresh, frais, fraîche
fried, frit, -e
friend, un ami, une amie
frightened, effrayé; to be frightened, avoir peur
from, de; depuis (Ind)
front: in front, en face; in front of, devant
fruit, un fruit
full, plein, -e; complet, -ète; at full speed, à toute vitesse
fun: to have fun, s'amuser; to make fun of, se moquer de
funny, amusant, -e; drôle
furious, furieux, -euse

garden, un jardin
general, un général; adj, général, -e
gentleman, un monsieur
Germany, Allemagne, f; German, adj, allemand(e)
get, v, obtenir; go and get, aller chercher
get down, descendre
get up, se lever
gift, un cadeau
gilded, doré, -e
girl, une jeune fille
give, donner; give back, rendre
glass, un verre; looking-glass, une glace, un miroir
glasses, (spectacles), lunettes, f.pl
go, v, aller (VL); go away, s'en aller, partir; go out, sortir (VL); go down, descendre; go up, monter; go back, retourner; go on, continuer
God, Dieu, m
gold, or, m
good, bon, bonne; good-bye! adieu! au revoir!; good morning, good afternoon, good day, bonjour; good evening, bon soir; good night, bonne nuit; good! bon! bien! very good, très bien; to have a good time, s'amuser bien
granddaughter, une petite-fille
grandfather, un grand-père
grandmother, une grand-mère
grandson, un petit-fils
grape, un raisin
grass, herbe, f
great, grand, -e
Greece, la Grèce
green, vert, -e
ground, terre, f; terrain, m; on the ground, par terre
ground floor, la rez-de-chaussée
group, un groupe
grumble, v, grommeler
guess, v, deviner
guest, un visiteur
guide, un guide
guillotine, la guillotine; v, guillotiner

gun, un fusil; un canon

habit, une habitude
half, un demi; une moitié (Ind)
hall, un vestibule; **large entrance hall**, une
    salle d'entrée; **public hall**, une salle
hand, une main
handkerchief, un mouchoir
handsome, beau, bel, belle
happen, v, arriver
happiness, le bonheur
happy, content, -e; heureux, -euse
hard, dur, -e; difficile; **to work hard**,
    travailler dur/fort
hardly, ne . . . guère
have, avoir (VL); **have to** (= must), devoir
head, une tête
headache, un mal de tête
heart, un cœur
help, n, aide, f; v, aider (qn à faire qch)
here, ici, là; **here you are!** vous voici!
    vous voilà!
hide, v, cacher
high, haut, -e
holidays, vacances, f.pl; **summer holidays**,
    les grandes vacances; **on holiday**, en
    vacances; **to spend one's holidays**,
    passer les vacances
home: **at home**, à la maison; **at my home**,
    chez moi, etc.; **to come home**, rentrer
homework, les devoirs, m.pl
hope, v, espérer
horrible, horrible
horse, un cheval; **to ride a horse**, monter
    à cheval
hospital, un hôpital
hot, chaud, -e; **to feel hot**, avoir chaud;
    it (weather) is hot, il fait chaud
hour, une heure
house, une maison; **at our house**, chez
    nous
how, comment; **how many, how much**,
    combien?; **however**, cependant; **how
    are things?**, ça va?; **how are you?**,
    comment allez-vous? (Ind)
hunger, la faim
hungry, adj, affamé, -e; **to be hungry**,
    avoir faim
hurry, v, se dépêcher; **hurry up!**, dépêche-
    toi!
hurt, v, faire mal (à)
husband, un mari
hut, une cabane

ice, la glace
ice-cream, une glace
idea, une idée
if, si (Ind)
ill, malade
illusion, une illusion
important, important, -e
in, dans, en, à (Ind); **in it**, dedans

information, un renseignement
ink, encre, f
inside, n, intérieur, m; **inside s/th**, dans
    qch
instead (of), au lieu (de)
instruct, v, instruire
intelligent, intelligent, -e
interest: **to be interested in**, s'interesser à
interesting, intéressant, -e
into, dans, en (Ind)
invalid, un(e) malade
invite, v, inviter

jewel, un bijou
job, un emploi, un travail
join, v, joindre (VL)
journey, un voyage
judge, n, un juge; v, juger
jump, v, sauter
just, adj, juste; **to have just done s/th**,
    venir de faire qch; adv, précisément,
    exactement, justement

keep, v, garder; tenir (une promesse)
key, une clef, une clé
kill, v, tuer
kilometre, un kilomètre
kind, n, espèce, f, genre, m; adj, gentil, -le
king, un roi
kitchen, une cuisine
knife, un couteau; **pocket-knife**, un canif
know, v, (as a fact, by heart) savoir (VL);
    (to be acquainted with a person/place)
    connaître (VL) (Ind)

lad, un jeune homme, un garçon
ladder, une échelle; **to climb a ladder**,
    grimper à une échelle
lady, une dame; **ladies and gentlemen**,
    messieurs-dames
landing, un palier
language, une langue
last, v, durer; adj, dernier, dernière; **last
    night**, cette nuit; **at last**, enfin
late, tard; **it is late**, il se fait tard; **he is
    late**, il est en retard; **to go to bed late**,
    se coucher tard
later, plus tard
latter, celui-ci, celle-ci
laugh, v, rire (VL); **laugh at**, se moquer
    de
lead, v, amener, conduire (VL)
leaf, une feuille
learn, v, apprendre (VL); **to learn to do
    s/th**, apprendre à faire qch
least, le moins; **at least**, au moins
leave, v, partir (VL); **to leave a place**,
    quitter; **to leave s/th behind**, laisser
    qch
lend, v, prêter
letter, une lettre; **letter-box**, une boîte
    aux lettres

lie, v, mentir (VL); lie down, se coucher

lift, n, un ascenseur

light, n, la lumière; adj, léger, légère; (= light coloured) clair, -e; v, to light, to turn on the light, allumer

lighthouse, un phare

like, v, aimer; adj, pareil, -le, égal, -e; like this, comme ceci; what is (s/th) like?, comment est (qch)?

lion, un lion

listen (to s/o, to s/th), écouter (qn, qch)

little, petit, -e; adv, peu; a little, un peu (Ind)

litre, un litre

live, (= be alive) vivre; (= dwell) demeurer; to live in, at, habiter; long live . . . ! vive . . . !

lock, n, une serrure; (for bicycle) un anti-vol; v, fermer à clef

long, long, longue; for a long time, long-temps, pendant longtemps; no longer, ne . . . plus; long live! vive . . . !

look, v, (at) regarder; look (sad, etc.), avoir l'air (triste); look after, soigner, s'occuper de; look out! attention!; look for, seek (s/th), chercher (qch); look over (a building, etc.), visiter; look in at/on, passer à/chez

lose, v, perdre

lot, a lot, beaucoup (de) (Ind)

love, v, aimer; n, l'amour, m

low, bas, -se; in a low voice, à voix basse

luck, la chance

luckily, heureusement

lunch, n, le déjeuner; to have lunch, v, déjeuner

lying (down), couché; stretched out, allongé, -e

mad, fou, fol, folle

magnificent, magnifique

maid-servant, une bonne

majority, la plupart

make, v, faire (VL); make use of, se servir de; to make up one's mind, se décider

man, un homme; mankind, le genre humain

man-servant, un serviteur

manage, v, (= to direct, control) diriger; (= to make do) se débrouiller; to manage to do s/th, réussir à faire qch

mantlepiece, une cheminée

many, beaucoup (de); as many . . . as, autant . . . que

map, une carte

marche, v, marcher

market, un marché

marriage, un mariage

marry, v, épouser qn, se marier avec qn

master, un maître, un professeur

matter, la matière; what's the matter? qu'est-ce qu'il y a?

meal, un repas

mean, v, vouloir dire

medicine, (= remedy) médicament, m; (= science) la médecine

meet, v, rencontrer

mend, v, réparer

midday, midi, m

middle, un milieu; in the middle of, au milieu de

midnight, minuit, m

milk, le lait

mind: do you mind (doing s/th), voudriez-vous (faire qch); to make up one's mind, se décider (à)

minus, moins

minute, une minute

mistake, une erreur, une faute

modern, moderne

moment, un moment

money, argent, m; (= small change) la monnaie

month, un mois

moped, un vélo, une moto

more, plus, plus (de qch); yet more, davantage; no more, ne . . . plus

morning, un matin, une matinée; of/in the morning, du/au matin

most, le plus; most of . . . , la plupart de . . .

mother, une mère

motion, le mouvement

motor (engine), un moteur; motorbike, une moto

motorway, une autoroute

mountain, une montagne

move, v, mouvoir, bouger; moving stair-case, un escalier roulant

much, beaucoup (de); so much the worse, tant pis

museum, un musée

musician, un musicien

must, devoir (VL), falloir (VL), one must . . . , on doit . . . , il faut (+ infin)

name, un nom; what is your name? comment vous appelez-vous?

nation, une nation

naturally, naturellement

naughty, méchant, -e

near, près (de); nearly, presque

necessary, adj, nécessaire; it is necessary (to do s/th), il faut (faire qch)

necklace, un collier

need, v, avoir besoin de

neighbour, le voisin; neighbourhood, le voisinage

neither . . . nor, ne . . . ni . . . ni

never, ne . . . jamais

new, neuf, neuve; nouveau, nouvel, nou-velle; New Year's Day, le jour de l'an

newspaper, un journal

next, prochain; next day, le lendemain;

next door, à côté
nice, agréable; gentil, -le; sympathique;
  aimable
night, une nuit; **last night**, cette nuit;
  nightmare, un cauchemar
nobody, (ne . . .) personne
noise, un bruit; **noisy**, bruyant, -e; **noisily**,
  avec beaucoup de bruit
note: bank-note, un billet; **notebook**, un
  carnet; **to make a note of**, noter (qch)
nothing, ne . . . rien; **for nothing**, pour
  rien
notice, v, remarquer; apercevoir, faire
  attention (à qch)
novel, un roman
nowhere, nulle part

obey, v, obéir (à)
off: far off, au loin; **to take off**, (hat,
  clothes), ôter
offer, v, offrir (VL); n, un offre
office, un bureau
often, souvent
old, vieux, vieil, vieille; ancien, ancienne;
  old man, un vieillard; **old woman**, une
  vieille; **ten years old**, âgé de dix ans;
  how old is he? quel âge a-t-il?
older (oldest), elder (eldest), (l')aîné, -e
on, sur, à, en; **on a fine day**, par un beau
  jour; **to go on**, continuer; **onwards**, en
  avant; **on foot**, à pied; **on it**, dessus, là-
  dessus
once, une fois; **at once**, immédiatement,
  aussitôt
one (number) un, une; (= someone, they,
  you, etc.), on
oneself, soi-même; se (reflexive)
only, seulement; ne . . . que; adj, seul(e)
open, v, ouvrir (VL)
opinion, une opinion; **in my opinion**, à
  mon avis
or, ou
orchard, un verger
order, v, commander; ordonner; **in order
  to**, pour + infinitive
other, autre; **otherwise**, autrement
out: outside, dehors; **go out**, sortir; **put
  out (light)**, éteindre; **out of doors**, en
  plein air
over, par-dessus, au-dessus de; **it is over**, il
  est fini, terminé; **over there**, par là, là-
  bas; **overtake**, v, doubler, rattraper
owe, v, devoir (VL)

pain, un douleur; **to have a pain**, avoir mal
  (à la tête, etc.)
painfully,   peniblement
paint, v, peindre (VL)
paper, le papier; **newspaper**, un journal
parcel, un paquet, un colis
parents, les parents
park, un parc; **to park a car**, stationner;

car-park, un parking
part, v, séparer; n, une portion, un mor-
  ceau
party, une soirée
pass, v, passer; **pass an exam**, réussir à un
  examen
passenger, un passager, un voyageur
passport, un passeport
passer-by, un passant
past, adj, passé; **past 2 o'clock**, après deux
  heures; **ten past two**, deux heures dix
patronize (as a customer), v, favoriser
pay, v, payer (qch à qn); **pay attention**,
  faire attention
pea, un petit pois
peace, la paix
peach, une pêche
pear, une poire
peasant, un paysan, une paysanne
pen, un stylo
pencil, un crayon
people, les gens
per, par; **per cent**, pour cent; **per lb**, la
  livre
perhaps, peut-être
permit, v, permettre (à) (VL)
petrol, essence, f
pick up (s/o), v, chercher (qn)
picture, un tableau, une image
place, v, placer
plane, un avion
plant, v, planter; n, une plante
plate, une assiette
play, n, une pièce; v, jouer; **play a game**,
  jouer à . . . ; **play a musical instrument**,
  jouer de . . .
playground, une cour de récréation
pleasant, agréable
please, v, plaire (à qn) (VL); **please**, s'il vous
  plaît; **be pleased**, être content, -e
put back, remettre
pocket, une poche
poem, un poème
police, la police; **policeman**, un agent de
  police
pool, une flaque
poor, pauvre
portrait, un portrait
possession, la possession
possible, possible
post, (= **mail**) la poste; (= **job**) un emploi;
  post a letter, mettre une lettre à la
  poste
poster, une affiche
postman, un facteur
pound (weight or money), une livre
pour, v, (rain) pleuvoir à verse
poverty, la misère
power, le pouvoir
practical, pratique
pram, une voiture d'enfant
prefer, v, préférer

prepare, v, préparer
present, un cadeau
preserve, v, préserver; sauver (de)
pretend, v, faire semblant (de)
pretty, joli(e)
prevent, v, empêcher (de)
priest, un prêtre
prince, un prince; princess, une princesse
prize, un prix
probably, probablement
produce, v, produire
profoundly, profondément
promise, n, une promesse; v, promettre
proud, fier, fière; orgueilleux, -se
public, public, publique
pull, v, tirer
pupil, un(e) élève
purse, un porte-monnaie
push, v, pousser
put, v, mettre (VL); poser; placer (VL);
    put on, mettre; put back, remettre

quarter, un quart; a quarter past, . . . et
    quart; a quarter to, . . . moins le quart
queen, une reine
question, v, poser une question; interroger
quick, vîte; quickly, vite, rapidement
quiet, tranquille; quietly, doucement; be
    quiet, v, se taire
quite, tout à fait; assez

race: the human race, le genre humain
rain, v, pleuvoir (VL) n, la pluie
rainbow, un arc-en-ciel
raise, v, élever (VL); soulever
rather, plutôt; assez
read, v, lire (VL)
reading, la lecture
really, vraiment
reason, une raison, une cause
receive, recevoir
receptionist, (in hotel) un(e) employé, -e
refuse, v, refuser (de faire qch)
reign, v, régner
rejoin, v, (= answer back) répliquer;
    (= reunite) rejoindre
remain, v, rester
repair, v, réparer
repay, v, rembourser
replace, v, remplacer
reply, v, répondre (à qn, à une question)
represent, v, représenter
republic, une république
rest, n, le reste; les autres; the rest of us,
    nous autres
rest, v, se reposer
restaurant, un restaurant
restore, v, rétablir, restaurer
return, v, revenir, retourner; return home,
    rentrer; by return (post), par retour
revolution, une révolution
revolutionary, révolutionnaire

rich, riche
ride, v, (a bike) se promener à vélo; (a
    horse) monter à cheval; go for a ride in
    a car, se promener en voiture
ridiculous, ridicule
rifle, un fusil
right: on the right, à droite; right side, le
    côté droit; right (= true), vrai, -e; right
    (= fair), juste; be right, v, avoir raison
ring, v, sonner; n, un anneau, une bague
rise, se lever
river, un fleuve
rob, v, voler (qch à qn)
robin, un rouge-gorge
roast, rôti, -e
roll, v, rouler
roll, un petit pain
room, une pièce; bedroom, une chambre
    à coucher; bathroom, une salle de bains;
    plenty of room, beaucoup de place
ruler, une règle
run, v, courir (VL); run away, se sauver en
    courant, s'en fuire

sad, triste
sail, v, naviguer, faire de la voile; n, une
    voile
sailing-ship, un bateau à voiles
same, même; all the same, tout de même;
    quand même
satchel, une serviette
satisfy, v, satisfaire
save, v, sauver; (money) épargner
saw, v, scier; n, une scie
say, v, dire (VL)
scarcely, à peine; ne . . . guère
school, une école; to/at school, à l'école;
    adj, scolaire
scissors, ciseaux, m.pl
scold, v, gronder
scratch, v, gratter
sculpture, une sculpture
sea, la mer
seat, une place
see, v, voir (VL)
seem, v, sembler; paraître (VL); avoir l'air
self, -même
self-service restaurant, un restaurant self
sell, vendre (VL); seller, vendeur, -euse
send, envoyer (VL); send for, envoyer
    chercher
servant, (male) un serviteur; (female) une
    servante
set off, v, partir; set up, v, établir
shake, v, secouer
shed, un hangar, une cabane
ship, un bateau, un navire
shirt, une chemise
shoot, v, tirer
shop, une boutique; un magasin
shopping: to do the shopping, faire les
    courses

short, court, -e
shoulder, une épaule
show, v, montrer
shower, une douche
shut, fermer; shut in, enfermer
side, côté; on the other side, de l'autre
   côté; at his side, à ses côtés
sight, une vue
signal, un signal; v, signaler
silently, en silence
silly, ridicule
silver, n, argent, m; adj, en argent
since, depuis; (= because), puisque
sing, v, chanter
single, seul, -e
sister, une sœur
sit, v, s'asseoir (VL), (= to be seated)
   être assis, -e
sitting-room, un salon
sleep, v, dormir (VL); to go to sleep,
   s'endormir; to be sleepy, avoir sommeil;
   n, le sommeil
slow, lent(e); slow train, un train omnibus
slowly, lentement
small, petit, -e
smile, v, sourire
smoke, v, fumer; n, la fumée; no smoking,
   défense de fumer
snail, un escargot
snow, v, neiger
so, si, ainsi, comme ça; so many, so much,
   tant de
soaked, trempé
sock, une chaussette
society, une société
sofa, un canapé
soft, mou, mol, molle; doux, douce
sole, adj, seul, seule
solid, solide
some, du, de la, des; en; quelques
someone, quelqu'un
something, quelque chose
sometimes, quelquefois
somewhere, quelque part
son, un fils
soon, bientôt; as soon as, aussitôt que;
   sooner or later, tôt ou tard
soup, la soupe, le potage
sparkle, v, briller
speak, parler
spectacular, spectaculaire
spider, une araignée
spill, v, renverser
spite: in spite of, malgré
spoon, une cuillère
sport, le sport
spot (= stain, mark) une tâche; (= place)
   un endroit
spring, le printemps
square, adj, carré, -e
squirrel, un écureuil
staircase, un escalier

stamp, (postage) un timbre
stand, v, se tenir
start, v, commencer; se mettre à; wake
   with a start, se réveiller en sursaut
steak, un bifteck
steal, v, voler (qch à qn)
steam, la vapeur; steamer, un bateau à
   vapeur
steep, escarpé, -e
stereo, adj, stéréo(phonique)
stick, v, coller; n, un bâton
still (= yet), toujours, encore
stop, v, arrêter qn, qch; s'arrêter; stop!
   halte!
stores, vivres, m.pl
storey, un étage
story, une histoire
strange, étrange, curieux, -se
straw, la paille
stream, un ruisseau
street, une rue
study, v, étudier; n, étude, un cabinet de
   travail
suburbs, la banlieue
succeed, v, réussir
suddenly, soudain
sugar, le sucre
summer, l'été, m
sun, le soleil; it is sunny, il fait du soleil
surprise, v, surprendre; n, une surprise
swim, v, nager; swimming costume, un
   maillot de bain; swimming-pool, une
   piscine
symbol, un symbole

table, une table; table-cloth, une nappe
take, prendre (VL); to take s/th away,
   emporter qch; to take s/o (away),
   emmener; to take away, enlever; to
   take s/o (in a car), accompagner qn;
   to take off (a garment, hat, etc.), ôter;
   to take out s/th, sortir qch; to take
   part in (a sport, exercise), pratiquer
tall, (of persons), grand, -e; (of buildings,
   trees, etc.), haut, -e
tape-recorder, un magnétophone
tea, le thé
teach, v, enseigner; teacher, professeur;
   instituteur
team, une équipe
tear, déchirer
telephone, v, téléphoner (à qn); n, un
   téléphone
television, la télévision
tell, v, dire, raconter
than, que, de
thank, v, remercier (de)
thatched cottage, une chaumière
then, ensuite, puis, alors, donc
there, là; there is, there are, il y a
therefore, donc, ainsi
thief, un voleur

thing, une chose; **things** (= belongings),
les affaires, f.pl
think, v, penser (**about**, à; **of**, de)
thirst, la soif; v, avoir soif
through, par, à travers
throw, v, jeter (VL)
thus, ainsi
thunder clap, un coup de tonnerre
ticket, un billet
ticket-office, un guichet
tie, une cravate
tiger, un tigre, une tigresse
till, **until**, jusqu'à (ce que . . .)
time, le temps; **pass the time**, passer le
temps; **from time to time**, de temps
en temps; **what time is it?** quelle heure
est-il?; **next time**, la prochaine fois;
how many times? combien de fois?;
another time, une autre fois
tired, fatigué, -e
to, à, vers, en, jusqu'à (Ind)
today, aujourd'hui
together, ensemble
tomato, une tomate
tomorrow, demain
tongue, une langue
too, trop; (= also) aussi; **too bad**, tant pis
top, le haut
touch, v, toucher
tour, un tour
tourist, un(e) touriste
towards (**motion**), vers; (**feeling**), envers
tower, une tour
town, une ville
train, n, un train; v, s'entraîner
tramp, un vagabond
translation, une traduction
travel, v, voyager
travel agent's, une agence de voyages
tree, un arbre
tribunal, un tribunal
troop, une troupe
trousers, un pantalon
trumpet, une trompette
trunk, un tronc; (**box**), une malle
truth, la vérité
try, v, essayer (de faire qch)
turn, un tour
twin, un jumeau, une jumelle

ugly, laid, -e
umbrella, un parapluie
uncle, un oncle
under, sous, au-dessous de
understand, v, comprendre (VL)
underwear, le linge
undress, v, se déshabiller
unfortunately, malheureusement
university, une université
unknown (**to s/o**), à l'insu (de qn)
up: **to go up**, monter; **throw up** (**into the
air**), jeter en l'air; **up and down**, de

haut en bas; **up there**, là-haut; **upside
down**, sens dessus dessous
use, v, se servir de; employer (VL)
usual, habituel, -le; **usually**, d'habitude

vain: **in vain**, en vain
valley, une vallée
valuables, les objets de valeur, m.pl
vase, un vase
Venice, Venise; **Venetian**, vénitien,
-ienne
very, très, fort, bien
view, une vue
village, un village
visit, v, rendre visite à qn; visiter qch

wait (**for**), v, attendre (qn/qch)
waiter, un garçon; **waitress**, une serveuse
waiting-room, une salle d'attente
wake, v: **to wake up**, se réveiller, s'éveiller;
to wake s/o, réveiller qn
walk, marcher, aller à pied; se promener,
faire une promenade
wall, un mur; une muraille
wallet, un portefeuille
want, v, désirer, vouloir (VL); avoir envie
(de)
war, une guerre
warm, chaud, -e
wash, v, se laver, laver (qn/qch)
washing up: **to do the washing up**, faire la
vaisselle
watch, v, regarder, veiller sur qn; n, une
montre
water, eau, f
wave, faire signe
week, une semaine; **a week from today**,
aujourd'hui en huit
welcome, v, bien recevoir
when, quand, lorsque, où
where, où
while, pendant que
whisper, v, chuchoter
whistle, v, siffler
whole, entier; (= all the) tout le . . .
whose, dont, à qui, de qui
why, pourquoi
wide, large
widow, une veuve
wife, une femme
win, gagner
wind: **to wind up** (**a watch**), remonter
(une montre)
window, une fenêtre
wine, le vin; **wine glass**, un verre à vin
winner, un gagnant, une gagnante; le
premier, la première
winter, l'hiver, m
wipe, essuyer
wire, un fil de fer
wireless set, un poste de radio
wish, vouloir (VL)

with, avec, de, à (Ind)
within, dans, en; à l'intérieur, dedans
without, sans (Ind)
woman, une femme
wonderful, merveilleux, -euse
wood, le bois; adj, en/de bois
word, un mot
work, le travail
work, v, travailler; (of machine) marcher;
   (of tool, etc.) fonctionner; work hard,
   travailler dur/fort
worker, un travailleur, une travailleuse;
   workman, un ouvrier
world, la terre; le monde
worse, adj, pire; adv, pis; so much the
   worse! tant pis!
worth: to be worth, valoir (VL); it is not
   worth while, il ne vaut pas la peine
wound, blesser
write, v, écrire (VL)
writer, un écrivain

year, un an, une année
yesterday, hier
yet, encore
yield, v, céder (VL)
young, jeune; young folk, les jeunes gens;
   the youngest, le cadet, la cadette

Index